Visual Power, Representation and Migration Law

Visual Power, Representation and Migration Law
Framing Migrants

Dorota Anna Gozdecka

EDINBURGH
University Press

Edinburgh University Press is one of the leading university presses in the UK. We publish academic books and journals in our selected subject areas across the humanities and social sciences, combining cutting-edge scholarship with high editorial and production values to produce academic works of lasting importance. For more information visit our website: edinburghuniversitypress.com

© Dorota Gozdecka, 2024, 2025

Grateful acknowledgement is made to the sources listed in the List of Illustrations for permission to reproduce material previously published elsewhere. Every effort has been made to trace the copyright holders, but if any have been inadvertently overlooked, the publisher will be pleased to make the necessary arrangements at the first opportunity.

Edinburgh University Press Ltd
13 Infirmary Street
Edinburgh EH1 1LT

First published in hardback by Edinburgh University Press 2024

Typeset in 11/13pt Adobe Garamond Pro by
Cheshire Typesetting Ltd, Cuddington, Cheshire

A CIP record for this book is available from the British Library

ISBN 978 1 4744 5998 3 (hardback)
ISBN 978 1 4744 5999 0 (paperback)
ISBN 978 1 4744 6000 2 (webready PDF)
ISBN 978 1 4744 6001 9 (epub)

The right of Dorota Gozdecka to be identified as the author of this work has been asserted in accordance with the Copyright, Designs and Patents Act 1988, and the Copyright and Related Rights Regulations 2003 (SI No. 2498).

Contents

List of Figures	viii
Acknowledgements	ix
Introduction	1

PART I LAW AND THE ETHICS OF LOOKING

1 The Migrant in Our Gaze — 11
- Introduction — 11
- Ethics Interrupted at the Border — 12
- The Distinction Between Citizen, Migrant and Refugee — 16
- Gazing at the Migrant — 20
- Spectacle of the Border and Figures of the Migrant — 23
- Five Archetypal Figures of the Migrant — 25
- Conclusions — 29

2 Looking, Feeling and Judging the Law — 32
- Introduction — 32
- Law and the Art of Visual Persuasion — 33
- The Image of Power and the Image of Law — 37
- Law, Justice and Legitimacy — 39
- Law, Visibility and Legal Persons — 43
- Archetypes and the Figures of Citizen and Migrant — 45
- Conclusions — 47

PART II FIGURES OF THE MIGRANT

3 The Janus-Faced Refugee: The Interplay Between the 'Genuine' and the 'Bogus' Asylum Seeker — 53
- Introduction — 53
- The 'Genuine' and the 'Bogus' and Proving 'Genuineness' — 54
- Victimhood, Suffering and the Host Gaze — 57
- The Frames of 'Bogusness' in Comics — 59

vi   VISUAL POWER, REPRESENTATION AND MIGRATION LAW

    The 'Authentic' Suffering of the Genuine — 65
    Legal Responses to Bogusness and the Rising Legal Threshold of
      Genuineness — 67
    Conclusions — 69

4 The Spectre of the Invisible Illegal — 73
    Introduction — 73
    Why Illegality Often Remains Invisible — 74
    The 'Illegal' Migrant as a Haunting Spectre — 76
    The Hauntological Invisibility of the Migrant — 78
    British, Australian and American Spectropolitical Imagery of the
      Migrant — 79
    Out of Sight and Outside the Law — 84
    Conclusions — 85

5 The Figure of the Absolute Other — 89
    Introduction — 89
    Exclusion Within and Inheriting 'Migrant' Status — 90
    Complex Forms of Racism and Visual Othering — 92
    Swiss Visual Campaigns on Banning Minarets and Migration — 94
    Subsequent Legal Changes — 98
    Who 'Owns' the Right to Regulate Access to Rights? — 99
    Conclusions — 102

6 The Migrant as an Inhuman Mass — 106
    Introduction — 106
    The Flood and *Homo Oeconomicus* — 107
    Non-human People: Viruses and Bodies Without Organs — 109
    The Figure of the Mass in Visual Discourse — 111
    Brexit and the EU–Turkey Agreement: Keeping the 'Mass' at
      Bay — 116
    Conclusions — 120

7 The Figure of the Innocent — 124
    Introduction — 124
    The Image of a Child and Ethics: The Puzzle of Children's
      Autonomy — 125
    The Threshold of Innocence and Migrant Children — 127
    Aylan Kurdi's Image: The Ultimate Innocent and the Challenge
      to Refugee Reception Laws — 130
    Challenging the Cruelty of Existing Legal Systems — 132

    Other Images of Migrant Children   134
    Conclusions   136

PART III THE COMPLICITY OF THE PICTURE
8 The Challenge of Navigating the Ethics of Law in the Pictorial Era   143
    Introduction   143
    Can We Challenge the Broader Archetypes of Foreignness?   144
    Do Pictures Really Influence Viewers?   145
    Borders as Spaces Penalising Ethics   147
    Conclusions   151

Conclusion   156

Bibliography   159
Index   179

Figures

3.1	NO WAY graphic novel, Australian Department of Immigration and Border Protection, 2014	61
3.2	NO WAY graphic novel, Australian Department of Immigration and Border Protection, 2014	62
3.3	NO WAY graphic novel, Australian Department of Immigration and Border Protection, 2014	63
4.1	US Customs and Border Protection gallery, along US borders, 2016	81
4.2	NO WAY poster, Australian Department of Immigration and Border Protection, 2014	82
5.1	'More Security' poster campaign, the Swiss People's Party (SVP), Alamy	97
6.1	'Breaking Point' poster campaign, UKIP, 2016, Alamy	111
6.2	Syrian refugee influx reporting, 2018, Alamy	113
7.1	Aylan Kurdi on a banner during a protest in Athens, original photograph, Nilüfer Demir, 2015, Alamy	130
7.2	Photo provided by US Customs and Border Protection to reporter on tour of Ursula detention facility in McAllen, Texas, 2018, Alamy	135

Acknowledgements

This book took shape over many years during discussions and talks with multiple colleagues in several areas of research. I would like to extend my gratitude to everyone who has asked questions and pointed out the inconsistencies in the project. I sincerely hope that I have accommodated your remarks and answered your questions. I would particularly like to extend my thanks to Professor Desmond Manderson, who has been an outstanding colleague and mentor during my years at the ANU Centre for Law, Arts and the Humanities. Your work has always been an inspiration, and I am grateful beyond words for the many opportunities to share and present the research included in this book. I would also like to thank my wonderful ANU Law School colleagues, Professor Margaret Thornton and Doctor Anne Macduff, who have always been supportive and keen to discuss problems of exclusion and otherness that I have been focused on exploring throughout my academic career. I would like to extend special thanks to Professor Pia Letto-Vanamo for providing me with the opportunity to work in the highly research-supportive environment at the University of Helsinki. These thanks extend also to Professor Risto Kunelius, Director of the Helsinki Institute for Social Sciences and Humanities and the former Director of Helsinki Inequality Initiative (INEQ). The inspiring INEQ environment and its excellent research team have been a perfect place to conduct this research. To my many dear friends scattered across two continents and several countries, a big 'thank you' for keeping me motivated. This book would not have been written without you. And to Christopher Goddard for the wonderful editorial help.

I dedicate this book to my mom, Wanda.

Introduction

In the past two decades migration has become a central topic of news coverage, political debate and electoral campaigning across the globe. Interest in regulating migration and details of migration law have become central not only in traditionally migration-receiving countries but also in those once perceived as migration-producing. As a result of increasing political tensions over controlling borders, multiple countries across the globe have experienced rapid changes in regulation of who and under what circumstances can enter their territories, reside in them and enjoy the full benefits of belonging. In the aftermath of these rapidly accelerating changes, those leaving the territory of their own state and moving to the territory of another state have often experienced increasingly comprehensive forms of control over their lives. Beginning from the moment of their appearance at the border, and sometimes even beforehand, the lives of migrants have become strictly regulated across continents and legal contexts.

While migration has always been considered an area where state sovereignty is relatively unrestricted, recent years have expanded the notion of sovereignty and challenged the way that international standards are interpreted and applied in the area of migration and refugee law. For instance, Australia's offshore processing of asylum seekers – known as the 'Pacific Solution' – initially drew heavy criticism in terms of its legality and compliance with international standards as established under the Refugee Convention of 1951. Despite mounting legal critiques and serious reservations expressed by international human rights bodies, soon afterwards, in response to the so-called Syrian refugee crisis of 2015, a similar approach was proposed in the EU–Turkey deal, which aimed at reducing the number of people claiming asylum in the European Union. While refugee law has become one of the focal points of political campaigns, suspicion of migration more generally has touched nearly all forms of both legal and irregular migration. Sentiments expressed globally by local populations have aimed at controlling even further the already heavily controlled lives of migrants. Support for anti-migration parties has been expressed in elections and impacted on the results of direct referenda. The Swiss referendum on restricting the building of minarets and the famous Brexit referendum have been fuelled largely by anti-migration sentiments. Across Europe, America and Australia, many populist anti-migration parties and politicians have been successful in securing a mandate and have influenced the direction of legal changes in the area of migration. Some of these political changes have been expressed in such unprecedented legal policies as former US President Donald Trump's travel ban, or changes to Hungarian migration and asylum law – the latter considered to be in violation of EU law. Popular support for anti-migration policies has grown significantly in recent years, leading many to ask what drives these attitudes (e.g. Rydgren 2008; Heizmann 2016; Golec de Zavala et al. 2017) and how far law can accommodate them (Butz and Kehrberg 2019). Those familiar with the US Supreme Court decision in *Trump v. Hawaii* maintaining Trump's travel ban (Johnson 2020) or the Australian High Court decision sanctioning the indefinite detention of asylum seekers in *Al-Kateb v. Goodwin* (Curtin 2005) may have been wondering why law has become increasingly comfortable with accepting the ever-widening paradigms for exclusion of those arriving. The continuously expanding use of criminal law methods in control of migration, theorised by Juliet Stumpf (2006) as 'crimmigration', or the sweeping expansion of security discourse in migration law (Huysmans 2006) have been drawing criticism from legal experts for decades. Yet criticism has brought little change as anti-migration rhetoric has succeeded in convincing many voters (Schmuck and Matthes 2015). These voters appear to support increasingly shocking, brutal and restrictive methods of controlling the lives of those arriving and find even the most unprecedented legal changes justified and legitimate.

This book is an attempt to contribute to the ongoing work of those academics who try to explain the growing anti-migration phenomenon. The research undertaken here positions law within a broader spectrum of discourses on belonging and exclusion. By approaching law as an area deeply immersed in discourse and its surrounding reality, I intend to show that law is heavily impacted by societal perceptions, regardless of its purported neutrality and objectivity. Even if law in its final form is accessible only to those intimately trained in its art, at the same time law is constantly dependent on perceptions of its legitimacy, validity and justifiability. To be seen as legitimate, law needs both to follow the requirements of procedural legitimacy and to be perceived as 'legitimate' and 'just'. This volume intends to show how perceptions of legitimacy and fairness of legal rules are influenced by the aesthetics of surrounding visual representation.

Decades ago, in her seminal work on the male gaze, Laura Mulvey (1975) showed why representation matters in film and how gender representation is often seen through the prism of the male gaze. Scholars following this analysis have argued that representation matters not just on screen, but also in real life, impacting, for instance, on gender equality and the position of women in multiple societies (Bareket et al. 2019; Mignanelli 2019). In this book I develop studies of the gaze and intend to show how the theory of the gaze operates in our encounters with migrants. I take Mulvey's notion of the 'male gaze' and develop it further, proposing the notion of the 'host gaze' – a specific lens through which a migrant is viewed by the host society even prior to their arrival in the host territory. While the host may know little about the actual migrant arriving at the border, the migrant is often already presented to the host via specific images accessible to the host through a certain frame, gaze point and selected field of appearance. These representations of migrants (including refugees), seen through the lens of the host gaze, carry with them a world of assumptions actively influencing the dynamics of welcome and hospitality.

Throughout this book I approach hospitality through a Derridean lens. I therefore understand hospitality as an aporetic ethical challenge hinged on the opposition between hospitality and hostility (Derrida 2000; Derrida and Dufourmantelle 2000). The host standing at the threshold of their house – or, in the case of migration, at the border – always determines how narrow or broad the threshold is and whether an arriving guest is seen as deserving of hospitality. This prerogative on the part of the host to exclude allows our notion of hospitality also to perpetually harbour its very opposite – hostility. A host who decides to narrow the threshold or determines a guest to be 'unworthy' of hospitality typically responds with hostility by closing the door, or, in case of migration, closing the option of legal border crossing. Following Jacques Derrida (Derrida 2000; Derrida and Dufourmantelle 2000) and Maria Fotou (2016), I use this notion of 'hostipitality' (an aporetic fusion of 'hospitality' and 'hostility') as the foundation for explaining the troubled ethics of welcome operating at borders. I argue that the troubled logic of hostipitality underpins the encounter between host and guest during each and every crossing of the border. While the host is represented at the border by its officials and its laws, the guest arrives as an individual who is assessed through ever-stricter criteria every time they leave the territory of their own state. As I argue in this volume, the nature of this encounter is often predetermined prior to the guest's arrival. I show how the laws welcoming the guest at the border and changes within those laws are constantly influenced by how the host views and imagines the guest.

This imagination is reinforced by a set of pre-existing archetypal representations of migrants, which, following Thomas Nail (2015), I call 'figures of a migrant'. These figures can be encountered in multiple forms, both in materials aimed at deterring migrants from arriving as well as in those that often encourage support for migrants. They can be used by authorities, political parties, NGOs, the media and other state or non-state actors. What makes these figures archetypal is that they embody multiple pre-existing assumptions concerning the agency or intentions of those arriving. While these assumptions may not be based in the actual reality of those seeking asylum or applying for migration status, they often include a cluster of the host's anxieties about the 'other'. This book focuses on five archetypal figures shaping the relationship between host and guest in contemporary migration laws. It is worth noting that the figures distinguished here can, in some representations, overlap and are by no means an exclusive listing of how migrants are seen and how they could be seen. The five figures distinguished here, however, shape the perceptions of 'us' and 'them' and are likely to be found in most societies dealing with regulation of migration. They are not necessarily empirical figures, but are, rather, rhetorical figures that recur in images and discourses of who alleged migrants are and how they 'should' be welcomed or rejected. This book attempts to show why these figures rarely embody an objective representation. It illustrates that instead, more often than not, migrant images are mere phantasms presented through the prism of the host gaze. As such, they influence and impact the perception of how much hospitality ought to be extended to those arriving and under what circumstances.

This book is thus neither an empirical analysis of thousands of different images, nor a sociological piece measuring different attitudes. While research in those areas has been informative and inspirational for this volume, the work presented here fundamentally differs. Analysis of the gaze and its implications for the operations of hospitality presented here are a work on the ethics of representation. I hope that this volume provides a philosophical study of the relationship between dominant aesthetic frames and their impact on perceptions of the legitimacy of migration laws. I intend to show how 'being seen' translates into being welcome or unwelcome; and how being classified as unwelcome leads to a narrowing of the threshold of hospitality. I also hope to illustrate that when hospitality turns into hostility, there are no limits on how restrictive, cruel or dehumanising law can become.

I understand legitimacy as a process that only occasionally translates into direct referenda or other formal ways of seeking approval of new laws. These extraordinary processes are examined here as the culmination of far deeper but less visible workings of the ideological apparatus of the state. Building on Louis Althusser's (2014) notion of ideological state apparatus, I show how visual reality is implicated in the silent process of everyday legitimation of authority, law, and legal categories and distinctions that we rely on as legal subjects. These legitimacy processes are often invisible, simply because they appear to be 'natural' and necessary, so that the legal solutions – and sometimes divisions – they bring are seen as necessary. As illustrated here, for instance, the division between 'us' and 'them' is often so normalised that it is hardly seen as a source of exclusion, growing cruelty and the increasing punitiveness of migration systems. As I argue, though, once the ethical distance between host and guest is established with the help of visual and verbal discourse, the legal response is focused on maintaining that distance and protecting the host. My approach, situated within the broader discipline of law and aesthetics, thus differs from sociological methods of measuring attitudes and analysing them through statistical evidence. Instead, what is illustrated here is that some forms of looking will produce particular ways of being seen. In turn, these ways of being seen will result in the normalisation of certain ethical approaches, which are then legitimated socially and upheld legally. In other words, the more pervasive a certain way of 'looking' is, the more 'natural' the approach to those looked at will appear. Subsequently, even the most controversial legal solutions will be perceived simply as ways of 'solving problems' depicted in surrounding representations. I hope that this analysis will contribute to the growing understanding of why some – often ethically problematic – ways of discussing migration are capable of gaining support from local populations, who would doubtless be shocked or appalled should similar approaches be applied to governing their own lives.

To illustrate the relationship between the host and the figure of a migrant in our current visual reality, I begin my analysis with the Janus-faced figure of the 'bogus' refugee and its counterpart, the 'genuine' asylum seeker. I show how displaying autonomy and agency are seen as hindrances to the perception of 'genuineness'. In Chapter 1, the focus is on the figure of the invisible 'illegal'. I show how the breadth and somewhat ephemeral nature of 'illegality' in migration law caters to the spectropolitical play with the notion of a ghostly and unspecified threat to the community. Following the figure of an invisible 'illegal', I examine the figure of an absolute other, which relies on emphasising the distance between the host community and those arriving as something inherent and 'natural'. The notion of inalienable difference, while often built on essentialisation and racialisation, nonetheless allows for control over the rights of those with migrant heritage. The next figure distinguished in this volume is the figure of the migrant as an anonymous mass. I argue that this figure broadens the already vast distance between host and guest to the point where no ethical encounter is possible any longer. When the ethical gap between host and guest becomes so vast, the host community is capable of legitimising a legal overhaul of acceptable legal standards, even at great cost. In the final analysis of figures of the migrant, I focus on the figure of an innocent who acts as an ethical counterbalance in the increasingly inhospitable visual landscape of migration. Yet, as this chapter illustrates, even the figure of an innocent faces a higher threshold of proof in the so-called hierarchy of innocence.

I have selected images used by public authorities and bodies, political parties and the media to show how the figure of the migrant is often represented visually. While multiple other images could be found and multiple counter-images could also be pointed out, the images circulated by these actors have a capacity to reach large numbers of viewers and are aimed at informing a possibly wider audience. They also often (although not always) carry an air of 'neutrality', particularly when they feature in public information campaigns. While I am naturally aware that social media could likewise be used as a rich source of illustrations, analysing this rapidly expanding landscape would require a different type of methodology which would have to account for their statistical significance and impact. Circulation of images on social media is less controlled and rarely directly linked to public bodies such as governments or political parties. I believe that a great need exists for further research on the impact of social media on anti-migrant attitudes but am at the same time firmly convinced that due to the archetypal nature of the figures distinguished here, many – if not the majority of – depictions of migrants circulating on Facebook, X (formerly Twitter) or Instagram could be classified as fitting one of the archetypes distinguished here or a blend thereof.

When analysing visual depictions of the archetypes distinguished here, I focus on the gaze point, the frame and the field of appearance to show how these elements capture multiple pre-existing presumptions present in wider migration discourse. I then analyse how each of these representations – and the presumptions they embed – affects the host's ethical response and shapes the boundaries of hospitality. To show the impact on law and its legitimacy, I link each figure with specific legal responses and legal changes showing how the ethical response generated by the images legitimates new or harsher forms of legal solution. Depending on the depth of the ethical gap between host and guest, the legal response oscillates between deterrence, limitations or even severe controls over the rights of migrants. In the case of vast unbreachable distance, the legal response can aim at preventing migrants from arriving altogether. As shown here, the depth of this distance is often established even before the arrival of a migrant at the border.

While this study could no doubt be conducted through a different prism and with the help of direct interviews or other methods of measuring public opinion, work of that kind has been growing in communication theory and socio-political context (Arendt 2010; Boomgaarden and Vliegenthart 2009; Dalsklev and Kunst 2015; Esses et al. 2008, 2017). By venturing on a route less travelled and by undertaking a study in the philosophy of legal aesthetics, I intend to go beyond illustrating how many people support particular migration solutions and why. Instead, I hope to show that the predominance of certain visual representations of those arriving lead to forming specific ways of imagining people as legal subjects. Once the way of looking at the subjects is fixed, the legal imagination develops as an extension of visual and ethical imagination and works to maintain the existing status quo. If such a position is based on the paradigm of exclusion, then exclusion will appear 'legitimate' because the ethical gap between host and guest is perceived to be not only 'normal' but indeed desirable. The extent of support by individuals for particular harsh policies is thus relevant in determining the extent of exclusions that can justifiably be applied, but will not explain why such exclusions happen in the first place. I hope to show that being seen as a part of the community versus being seen as an inalienable 'other' will always predetermine how law approaches the migrant. The gradation of the exclusion exercised through law will be based on just how 'alien' or 'dangerous' the particular figure of the migrant is deemed to be at any specific time. The wider the ethical gap between host and guest, the further the exclusions can go and harsher legal steps can receive public legitimacy, regardless of how ethically problematic they may be.

References

Althusser, Louis. *On the Reproduction of Capitalism: Ideology and Ideological State Apparatuses*. Verso, 2014.

Arendt, Florian. 'Cultivation effects of a newspaper on reality estimates and explicit and implicit attitudes.' *Journal of Media Psychology: Theories, Methods, and Applications* 22, no. 4 (2010): 147–59.

Bareket, Orly, Nurit Shnabel, Dekel Abeles, Sarah Gervais and Shlomit Yuval-Greenberg. 'Evidence for an association between men's spontaneous objectifying gazing behavior and their endorsement of objectifying attitudes toward women.' *Sex Roles* 81, no. 3 (2019): 245–56.

Boomgaarden, Hajo G., and Rens Vliegenthart. 'How news content influences anti-immigration attitudes: Germany, 1993–2005.' *European Journal of Political Research* 48, no. 4 (2009): 516–42.

Butz, Adam M., and Jason E. Kehrberg. 'Anti-immigrant sentiment and the adoption of state immigration policy.' *Policy Studies Journal* 47, no. 3 (2019): 605–23.

Curtin, Juliet. 'Never say never: Al-Kateb v. Godwin.' *Sydney Law Review* 27 (2005): 355–70.

Dalsklev, Madeleine, and Jonas Rønningsdalen Kunst. 'The effect of disgust-eliciting media portrayals on outgroup dehumanization and support of deportation in a Norwegian sample.' *International Journal of Intercultural Relations* 47 (2015): 28–40.

Derrida, Jacques. 'Hostipitality.' *Angelaki: Journal of Theoretical Humanities* 5, no. 3 (2000): 3–18.

Derrida, Jacques, and Anne Dufourmantelle. *Of Hospitality*. Stanford University Press, 2000.
Esses, Victoria M., Leah K. Hamilton and Danielle Gaucher. 'The global refugee crisis: Empirical evidence and policy implications for improving public attitudes and facilitating refugee resettlement.' *Social Issues and Policy Review* 11, no. 1 (2017): 78–123.
Esses, Victoria M., Scott Veenvliet, Gordon Hodson and Ljiljana Mihic. 'Justice, morality, and the dehumanization of refugees.' *Social Justice Research* 21, no. 1 (2008): 4–25.
Fotou, Maria. 'Ethics of hospitality: Envisaging the stranger in the contemporary world.' PhD dissertation. London School of Economics and Political Science (LSE), 2016.
Golec de Zavala, Agnieszka, Rita Guerra and Cláudia Simão. 'The relationship between the Brexit vote and individual predictors of prejudice: Collective narcissism, right wing authoritarianism, social dominance orientation.' *Frontiers in Psychology* 8 (2017): art. 2023.
Heizmann, Boris. 'Symbolic boundaries, incorporation policies, and anti-immigrant attitudes: What drives exclusionary policy preferences?' *Ethnic and Racial Studies* 39, no. 10 (2016): 1791–811.
Huysmans, Jef. *The Politics of Insecurity: Fear, Migration and Asylum in the EU*. Routledge, 2006.
Johnson, Richard. 'The institutions didn't stop Trump: They empowered him.' *Political Insight* 11, no. 3 (2020): 4–7.
Mignanelli, Nicholas. 'Equal protection and the male gaze: Another approach to New Hampshire v. Lilley.' *Journal of Gender, Race & Justice* 22 (2019): 265–90.
Mulvey, Laura. 'Visual pleasure and narrative cinema.' *Screen* 16, no. 3 (1975): 6–18.
Nail, Thomas. *The Figure of the Migrant*. Stanford University Press, 2015.
Rydgren, Jens. 'Immigration sceptics, xenophobes or racists? Radical right-wing voting in six West European countries.' *European Journal of Political Research* 47, no. 6 (2008): 737–65.
Schmuck, Desirée, and Jörg Matthes. 'How anti-immigrant right-wing populist advertisements affect young voters: Symbolic threats, economic threats and the moderating role of education.' *Journal of Ethnic and Migration Studies* 41, no. 10 (2015): 1577–99.
Stumpf, Juliet. 'The crimmigration crisis: Immigrants, crime, and sovereign power.' *American University Law Review* 56, no. 2 (2006): 367–419.
Trump v. Hawaii, No. 17-965, 585 U.S. ___ (2018).

PART I
LAW AND THE ETHICS OF LOOKING

1

The Migrant in Our Gaze

Introduction

As a result of increased discourse about migration, hardly a day passes without news about migrants, migration policy plans or newly introduced migration laws. While the COVID-19 pandemic temporarily slowed migration and temporarily held borders closed, the Ukrainian conflict quickly reversed this tendency, resulting in intensified discourse on the boundaries of welcome owed to the latest group of people escaping strife. At the same time, a wave of new accidents has already dominated the media, from those occurring in the Mediterranean Sea to news of a truck – recently discovered in San Antonio – where migrants tragically lost their lives. Yet, despite the term 'migrant' or 'immigrant' assailing the ears almost daily, there is little certainty as to who the 'migrant' is, how they cross the border and what their relationship with the law is. Despite seeing migrants in photographs, news reports or on government posters, we have a rather narrow image of the 'migrant' – a figure encompassing a wide array of people crossing borders for diverse reasons. A migrant remains primarily a synonym for the figure of an outsider waiting at the gates of the community to be found worthy of inclusion and let into the community. This somewhat narrow image goes against the lived reality of people crossing borders whose different aspects of life are regulated by different legal provisions depending on their purpose, intention to stay or family status. Indeed, those who fit the narrow category of a 'migrant' include a broad range of people crossing borders, from the specialised worker overseas on a posting, through a seasonal worker, someone joining their family, all the way to an individual fleeing persecution or escaping circumstances such as war, famine or climate change. People crossing borders differ vastly and may arrive via specified legal routes granting them 'legal' status or may be crossing borders irregularly, often resulting in their classification as 'illegal'. The term 'migrant' is indeed so broad, yet at the same time so pervasive, that we often speak of 'first', 'second' or 'third' generation 'migrants' or 'naturalised citizens' who are almost always distinguished from those born with the citizenship of a given country (Anderson 2013, p. 111). Confusion around the term 'migrant' results in conflation of different legal categories into the problematic figure of an outsider who is always left to the judgement and the shifting attitudes of host country citizens.

This chapter examines the origins of the distinction between the citizen and the migrant and delves into the problems of the ethics of looking. It examines how gazing differs from looking and how it perpetuates the distinction between the citizen and the denizen. It focuses on how the figure of the 'migrant' needs to rely on the boundaries of hospitality of host states and how these boundaries can be influenced by visual discourse. It investigates the notion of hospitality underpinning contemporary migration laws and shows how the ethics of looking constantly influence a visual discourse that oscillates between acceptance and rejection. It explains how the nature of hospitality is influenced by archetypal 'figures of a migrant'.

Ethics Interrupted at the Border

While migration has existed since the beginning of human civilisation, the relatively recent birth of the nation state (Anderson 2006; Hobsbawm 2012) has brought with it the emergence of legal citizenship, borders and today's complex migration regimes. Having its origins in the notion of being a royal subject (Anderson 2013, pp. 29–41), citizenship has slowly replaced the category of the subject of a monarch and affixed to the notion of belonging to the 'imagined community' of a nation state. Whether acquired by birth within the boundaries of a given nation state (*ius soli*) or by being born to parents who hold its citizenship (*ius sanguini*), the centrality of citizenship took over any other identification defining the relationship between a person and a land. It rejected other traditional and indigenous ways of identification (Palmater 2011; Canessa 2012). The emergence of citizenship divided people into citizens and denizens, with only citizens enjoying the full rights of belonging (De Genova 2015). Rights more generally, despite being proclaimed as being awarded to everyone regardless of their citizenship status (UDHR), have in fact – as Hannah Arendt (1973) famously observed in 1951 – been mainly the privileges of citizens. This profound distinction between citizen and denizen brought with it the contemporary figure of the migrant – a person wishing to enter and reside in the territory of a nation state they do not hold citizenship of. A migrant, originally a figure who could eventually acquire citizenship and become part of another nation's community, has slowly become viewed with suspicion and thus subjected to an increasing amount of legal regulation. The migrant has become the absolute other of the nation state. In Nicholas De Genova's words:

as we have seen, the inexorable requirement that citizenship produces and sustains an avalanche of exclusions has haunted citizenship with the grievances of its 'others,' and mired its democratic conceits in the brute realities of our modern forms of despotism and exploitation. The otherness of citizenship, however, is not reducible to a mere inventory of its others. The otherness of citizenship resides in its intrinsic alignment with state power, whereby the sovereignty of the state is predicated upon the cannibalization of our own powers and freedoms – the powers and freedoms of life itself. (De Genova 2015, p. 201)

The power of the nation state to regulate and control this 'otherness' of denizens has resulted in the emergence of multiple legal categories of migrants, all of which have been classified according either to the method of crossing the border or to the purpose of arrival. Naturally, some regulation of arrivals existed prior to the appearance of visas and was established already at the turn of eighteenth and nineteenth centuries, for instance in the regulation of entry into and out from the new colonies (Anderson 2013, pp. 35–7). Similarly, within earlier control regimes the entry of migrants could at times be severely controlled via reception centres such as those on Ellis Island in the United States, where migrants were subject to multiple – sometimes invasive – controls (Yew 1980). But this citizen–denizen distinction became universal only with the emergence of the nation state. Today we see it as 'natural' and unchangeable.

As an archetypal other whose life is strictly regulated by the power of the state, the life of a migrant has increasingly often been regulated and at times restricted in terms of access to rights, equality and often even dignity. Instead, a migrant has become subjected to more frequent considerations of the limits of legally sanctioned violence and its applicability. Being an 'other' is always testing in our contemporary legal systems, which operate with categories that often challenge or disable the workings of ethics. I have previously argued that an ethical encounter with the other can reinvigorate the emancipatory potential of rights (Gozdecka 2015, 2018). Basing my theory on Levinasian 'responsibility' (Levinas 1979) and combining it with Deleuzian 'becoming' (Deleuze and Guattari 1987), I have sought to provide a model in which responsibility for multiple becomings of multiple others allows for endless reinterpretation of the emancipatory potential of rights in the presence of multiple others. When it comes to migrants, however, the problem with the ethics of rights lies in the very existence of the a priori established difference between citizen and denizen. The fundamental distinction between the citizen and the citizen's 'other' makes the ethical encounter with those crossing borders not only more difficult, but also immediately interrupted.

The border, as a site of the power of the sovereign state, establishes a threshold that the other must cross before the host country, its citizens, its legal system or its system of rights can assume any ethical responsibility at all for their rights.

As to the migrant, the ethical encounter with the other faces multiple disruptions as soon as the other appears at the border of the host state. The border strips a migrant of any vestiges of equality and puts them in the vulnerable position of a guest. Not only their rights but their body and possessions can be controlled, limited and in extreme circumstances taken away at the border. A migrant is not just the other that slips off the scales of justice (Gozdecka 2015), but instead is the one who cannot be approached ethically until after successfully crossing the threshold of the community. The border as the 'wild zone of power' (Buck-Morss 2000) allows for ultimate control of any subject crossing it. Not only does the border disrupt ethical responsibility, but – as recent developments illustrated in the last chapter of this book have shown – the border often legally penalises citizens who approach migrants with the sense of ethical human-to-human obligation. Such punitive workings of the border regime, void of ethical considerations, have resulted in prosecution cases against citizens of host states who have undertaken attempts to provide lifesaving help for migrants or to rescue them. These prosecutions have occurred in many jurisdictions across the globe with multiple cases emerging simultaneously. Those analysed in the final chapter of this volume focus on the teacher prosecuted for providing water to migrants at the US–Mexico border (Cade 2020) and an Italian captain prosecuted for rescuing migrants at sea (Gordon and Larsen 2022), but are not the only prosecutions in recent years. The use of law in curtailing ethical actions is possible because the border is a zone of power capable of simply disrupting and at times extinguishing the workings of ethics. The border is a zone where absolute power can enforce inequality between host and guest and penalise attempts to disrupt this hierarchical relationship.

The figure of the migrant is a figure waiting at the gates of a nation state. A welcome migrant is typically chosen and carefully selected from the remaining crowd and is conditionally let in as a guest. While the selected few may be welcome, the rest of the crowd are rejected on different grounds. Migrant reception centres, detention centres and sometimes offices of border officials typically serve as the places where such selection and evaluation takes place. Historically these included places such as Ellis Island where those arriving to the US were evaluated, or Bonegilla Reception Centre where those arriving to post-World War II Australia were 'trained' for their new lives in the host community. While those centres no longer exist, similar evaluation practices carry on to a different extent, allowing for careful scrutinising of those who are to be let in and those who are to be left outside. While the crude practices of places such as Bonegilla, where the migrants were supposed to become more like their anglophone hosts, are no longer used, contemporary gates of the community still often rely on the perception of the difference between the migrant and the welcoming host.

Philosophically, this paradoxical and conditional nature of the border was captured by Jacques Derrida in his writings on hospitality (Derrida and Dufourmantelle 2000) and his subsequent development of the notion of 'hostipitality' (Derrida 2000). In his consideration of the border and the reaction between host and guest, Derrida observes that our notion of hospitality, entrenched in the Kantian conceptions underpinning our contemporary legal and political systems, is always conditional (ibid., p. 3). Unconditional hospitality, which would allow for the workings of ethics and true facing of the stranger, is not possible in our legal systems, defined as they are by the notion of sovereignty, citizenship and the border. Instead, conditional hospitality as a philosophical principle underpinning our notion of the nation state and its guests is always dependent on the host's judgement of those arriving at the border. The border, akin to the threshold of a house, can determine whether an arriving person is a welcome or unwelcome guest. The border as the zone of arbitrary judgement of the host state can be the site of hospitality or hostility:

> Already hospitality is opposed to what is nothing other than opposition itself, namely, hostility [*Feindseligkeit*]. The welcomed guest [*hôte*] is a stranger treated as a friend or ally, as opposed to the stranger treated as an enemy (friend/enemy, hospitality/hostility). The pair we will continue to speak of, hospitality/hostility, is in place. (Derrida 2000, p. 4)

Hospitality at our borders, as Derrida reminds us, is thus always aporetic – it hides within itself a degree of hostility towards those deemed unwelcome. To capture this aporetic nature of our approach to guests, in his further considerations Derrida coined the notion of 'hostipitality', indicating that an ethical encounter with the guest is always entrenched in the authority of the host to welcome, accept, invite or – equally simply – reject a stranger (Derrida 2000, p. 6). The hostipitality of the border is akin to the master or mistress of the household welcoming or rejecting a guest at their threshold (ibid., p. 10). The encounter at the threshold is thus a prelude to the ethics of welcoming a stranger to one's home. If the guest is allowed through the threshold, hospitality requires the host to approach the guest in an ethical and welcoming manner. However, if the guest is rejected, no responsibility is borne by the host – indeed, the guest never even has the chance to face the host. The threshold is of course a metaphor for the workings of the border.

The border reduces and fragments ethics, making ethics conditional on the power of the host to classify the arriving guest:

> Hospitality is owed to the other as stranger. But if one determines the other as stranger, one is already introducing the circles of conditionality that are family, nation, state, and citizenship. Perhaps there is an other who is still more foreign than the one whose foreignness cannot be restricted to foreignness in relation to language, family, or citizenship. (Derrida 2000, p. 8)

This judgement involves a variety of criteria through which the host can assess the guest. In legal terms, this distinction is drawn at the border by using a legal assessment of meeting or failing to meet the criteria for legal arrival. Yet, as Derrida points out, the threshold cuts deeper than the boundaries of the state and the law. The threshold of hospitality is often determined and influenced by multiple extra-legal criteria for belonging, including language and other extra-legal criteria, such as appearance, religious traditions or other cultural practices. These criteria determining the threshold of belonging exist and operate on a daily basis within the territory of the host state. At times, these criteria of judging the guest find their way into new policies of welcoming or rejecting the guest at the border. These policies in turn determine the breadth of the threshold of welcome. These internal criteria of belonging exist within multiple discourses, including visual discourses, which influence the perception of being welcome or unwelcome by the host community.

The Distinction Between Citizen, Migrant and Refugee

Upon crossing the border, migrants become further classified according to the complex host state migration regulation. The true complexity of migration regulation only began evolving after World War I, when regulation of migration took a new turn with the arrival of the passport and subsequently the visa (Torpey 2001), a form of legal permit certifying that a person is allowed to lawfully enter and reside in the territory of another nation state. As a token presented at the border, the passport became a document entitling one to cross borders legally under conditions specified by the host state. It irrevocably linked the migrant with the nation state of their origin and separated them from their individual identity in favour of a group identity. Saul Steinberg captured this relationship in his work *The Passport*. The page of a mock passport he designed (Steinberg 1954) emphasises the power of the state over the holder of the passport. The symbolism of authority, in the form of state emblems, stamps and official notes, towers over the symbolic figure of a fingerprint man standing for the holder of the passport. It reduces the humanity of the passport holder solely to their citizenship (Bankier 2020) and allows for segregation and marginalisation on the grounds of nationality.

With the emergence of passports and visas, increasingly complex – and sometimes impermeable to non-experts – migration law regulations and visa policies have developed across the globe, further classifying migrants into multiple distinct legal categories. This segregation allowed for increased control and management of mobility (Salter 2006). World War II brought with it another distinct category attached to those crossing borders, namely the legal notion of a refugee. The figure of the refugee, a person who often crosses borders without a visa or valid documentation to claim asylum from persecution, was defined in the 1951 Refugee Convention as someone who, because of

> a well-founded fear of being persecuted for reasons of race, religion, nationality, membership of a particular social group or political opinion are outside the country of their nationality and unable or, owing to such fear, unwilling to avail themselves of the protection of that country. (Refugee Convention, Article 1(A)2)

Post-war recovery efforts and the gradual evolution of the European Communities into what is currently known as the European Union even further diversified the figure of the migrant. The Treaties founding the Communities, and subsequently the Union, gave life to a specialised migration law system featuring the right of EU citizens to seek employment and reside in another member state of the Union (Article 3(2) of the Treaty on European Union (TEU); Article 21 of the Treaty on the Functioning of the European Union (TFEU)). In addition to these localised systems of managing migration, multiple countries have enacted complex laws featuring special, often-changing rules, for example:

- seasonal workers who cross with visas allowing short-term work
- students who come to obtain qualifications, or
- those migrating to join their families already residing in the territory.

Of course, this very brief list cannot attempt to cover the wide and complex network of legal regulation governing the lives of migrants in different countries today. The list merely shows the complexity and diversity of the classification of migration and migrants, and how complex and dependent on different legal regimes is current regulation of so-called legal migration. Those whose arrival is regulated by this complex web of different laws – often emerging on the domestic, regional and international legislative and judicial scene – are often juxtaposed with migrants who arrive irregularly. Thanks to the increased focus on classification and governance of the lives of migrants, people crossing borders in an irregular manner, without proper visas and documentation, have gradually come to be considered as 'illegal' (Dauvergne

2008; De Genova 2014). The emergence of the 'illegal' migrant, someone who arrives outside existing legal channels, has resulted in increased suspicion of all migrants, starting with refugees, who – thanks to the typically irregular nature of their movement across borders – became the first suspects in the discourse of 'illegality' and 'bogusness'. Beginning from the early 1990s, which was marked by increased migration from the Global South (Scheel and Squire 2014), the gradual appearance of an 'illegal' migrant, not only in discourse but also in legislation, has resulted in employing criminal law methods to control migration. This trend, also known as 'crimmigration', a term used first by Juliet Stumpf (2006), has turned the border into an increasingly perilous space, where the migrant – regardless of their reasons for arriving at the border – can be denied entry for even the slightest suspicion of 'illegality'. With the rise of crimmigration, suspicion of illegality has translated not only into a denial of entry, but also into a possibility of being placed in immigration detention until confirmation of the legal or illegal migrant status of a denizen. In the case of countries like Australia, this has often meant the possibility of being deprived of freedom indefinitely and without legal recourse, for instance in some circumstances surrounding statelessness (*Al-Kateb v. Goodwin*). The perilous space of the nation state border has become the scene of ultimate exclusion thanks to constant reinforcement of the distinction between citizens and their others, who can never fully escape the suspicion of illegality (De Genova 2013). The suspicion of illegality as a broad and – as shown later – somewhat ephemeral category casts its shadow on any migrant, whether they be a visa overstayer, a *sans-papiers*, a victim of trafficking or a refugee planning their arrival in a particular manner. This breadth of suspicion towards denizens and their potential to be considered 'illegal' has led to a discursive confusion between the complex legal categories of denizens. Almost as if working in the opposite direction to the growth of a complex web of visas, permit categories and other specifics of migration laws, the suspicion of illegality is increasingly simplified and widening, indiscriminately touching anyone crossing borders for any reason. This suspicion has led to the blurring of legal categories and interchangeable use of terms related to different legal migration categories. This has been true particularly in the case of the 'migrant' and the 'refugee' (Goodman and Speer 2007), regardless of the fact that these two figures signify quite distinct legal categories of non-citizens whose arrival is regulated by distinct legal documents and processes. Discursively, however, the confusion among categories operating in discussions of migration has been obscuring the complexity of migration law ever since the figure of an 'illegal' migrant appeared in political discussion on denizens.

This suspicion of illegality was captured by contemporary artist Pilar Castillo in her work depicting another mock passport but this time issued in contemporary times and specifically to the figure of a migrant (see Castillo 2019 for the entirety of the work). Under the names, the migrant is simply referred to as a 'foreigner' or 'immigrant'. Their nationality is defined as 'alien', the place of birth as 'suspect' and the date of expiration as 'undocumented'. Use of all these words on a single page signifies the dehumanising relationship between the host state and the migrant as well as an overarching suspicion of 'illegality'. The migrant is always a suspect and always simply an alien who does not share common humanity. The migrant needs to be evaluated and is always left at the mercy of the host state. Castillo's work also captures the confusion among categories. All these trigger words, such as 'foreigner', 'immigrant', 'alien', feature daily in discourse on migration and are often connected with the perception of illegality. This discursive confusion further widens the ethical gap between the host and arrivals at the border. The migrant is always anonymous, is never a person, but instead a threatening figure triggering a cluster of anxieties in the host. It does not matter how the migrant arrives, they need to be scrutinised first before being let in, to keep away those who are 'too alien' and 'suspect' – particularly the 'undocumented'.

In the next chapter, this book examines further images and their relationship with host anxieties that inform and drive changes in migration law. It shows how confusion among categories works visually and perpetuates stereotypical images of migrants. Because of the overarching suspicion of illegality and the overwhelming confusion among categories present in the visual discourse, I choose to refer to denizens crossing borders as simply 'migrants' or 'people crossing borders' regardless of the complexity of their legal status, unless their status is relevant for regulation of a specific body of migration law. In those cases, the legally relevant terminology is employed and contrasted with the discursive figure of a migrant. This choice may appear awkward in a book examining impact on law, but as I will show in the following chapters, images rarely operate with specific legal categories. Instead, they appeal to emotions by using symbols and figures emphasising 'illegality', 'bogusness', 'overwhelming numbers' or general suspicion of the migrant. While these emotional figures may emerge as a response to a discourse related to a specific type of denizens, such as refugees or EU citizens, their discursive impact is far broader and eventually spreads to touch all non-citizens, regardless of how their migrant status could be characterised legally. While this vagueness may create resistance from my fellow lawyers, I hope to show why the simple label 'migrant' is relevant for an understanding of the impact of visual discourse on various areas of migration law and the complex web of legal classification. Confusion among categories is in fact a distinctive feature of the discourse on the rights of denizens, whether refugees, irregular migrants or others who do not hold a citizenship of the country they arrived in or have been residing in.

Gazing at the Migrant

As illustrated above, the border regime cultivates power, allowing the host to welcome or reject the guest according to criteria established by the host. The judgement on 'worthiness' to enter, live and belong in our communities, while typically formalised as a law, is also informed by other, extra-legal factors. These include discourse and the visual elements that dictate the encounter between host and guest. This wide array of factors determines whether the guest is welcome and ultimately what rights the guest enjoys. Before offering hospitality, the host usually has ample opportunity to gaze – rather than look – at an expected guest. Images circulating in the realm of visual discourse precede the guest's arrival, allowing the host to gaze at them and form a judgement on their worthiness. This judgement, based on legal and extra-legal grounds, subsequently translates into the level of hospitality that the host is willing to extend before any actual encounter with a concrete person crossing the border. This pre-encounter visual experience is facilitated through multiple representations of migrants circulating in discursive visual space, often resulting in judgements consistent with the presumptions, prejudices and fears embodied in those representations.

This exercise is also an exercise in gazing, rather than looking – two visual practices that are not necessarily synonymous. While looking can be an ethical experience, gazing is typically an exercise of power. In his analysis of the Panopticon, Michel Foucault famously observed that the relationship between those who look and those who are looked at can be a site of power controlled by the one who is looking. For Foucault, once the power of the gaze is established, the individuals who engage in the process of looking and being looked at cease to be crucial for the existence of visual power (1975, p. 205). Power begins to operate on its own through the very mechanisms and tools that allow gazing. The mere possibility of being gazed at is the very site where visual power hides and allows for entrenching of inequality between the observer and the observed. A prisoner in a panoptic prison serving as the model showing the power of surveillance effectively disempowers the observed but empowers the observer. As a site of power, it results in prisoners always watching their moves regardless of who occupies the position of observer. For Foucault the mere possibility of being gazed at disciplines subjects of surveillance and makes them control themselves and behave in an expected manner (Elmer 2012, p. 23). This means of course that the one who controls the position from which one can gaze at someone else holds and controls surveilling power. The potent power of the gaze differs substantially from ethical conceptions of the look. The Levinasian conception, for instance, assumes a look is not in itself a site of power. Quite the contrary, Emmanuel Levinas assumes that looking at the other and encountering the other's face gives birth to mutual infinite responsibility of one for the other and is thus an ethical experience. But the Levinasian look and the Foucauldian gaze differ substantially. While looking allows the observed to look back and engage in an ethical encounter, gazing or staring, by contrast, remains a unidirectional activity in which the one gazed at is often unable to see the one who is looking or sometimes even realise that they are being looked at. Unable to return the gaze, the observed has no power over the frame or the gaze point through which the onlooker is staring at them. Nick Crossley, in reference to Jean-Paul Sartre, describes the experience of being looked at in the following words: 'The effect of the look is described by Sartre in terms of alienation. To experience "the look" is to experience oneself as no longer belonging to oneself but as belonging, as an object, in the project of the other' (1993, p. 408).

Being an object in someone else's gaze, or being looked at is thus thoroughly disempowering and serves the purposes or the power of the observer. This of course was clearly demonstrated by feminist theorists analysing the male gaze as well as scholars of postcolonialism in their analyses of the orientalising gaze. Laura Mulvey illustrated the disempowerment of being the observed in her analysis of the male gaze. Her seminal article 'Visual Pleasure and Narrative Cinema' (Mulvey 1975) explicated how cinema applies a male gaze in which women remain objects in a male spectrophilic experience. This experience is centred on the male experience of pleasure and the male control of the frame. The male gaze defines the role that women play and the way they are portrayed. The unidirectional nature of the gaze gives the observer control of the frame, the aesthetic field, and the gaze point to – in the case of Mulvey's analysis – the male. The same dynamic occurs in the practice of the orientalising gaze and the postcolonial gaze. Ever since Edward Said observed that colonisers develop a power relationship between the observer and the observed which manifests as orientalisation, the theory of the postcolonial gaze has powerfully illustrated that the orientalising gaze establishes a subject-versus-object relationship between coloniser and colonised. The postcolonial gaze defines the norm through the eyes of the coloniser, and characterises those who do not fit the norms established by the coloniser as the 'savage' and the orientalised other (Said 1978). Ever since Said captured this distinction, the decolonisation project has attempted to reverse this gaze and review the imperial power entrenched within it (Döring 1997, p. 4). The theory of the gaze has eventually developed into examination of the racialised gaze (Alcoff 2005) and shown that visible racial identities, just like other practices of gazing, are controlled through those holding and manipulating visual power. The theory of the gaze shows just how potent is the power between the observer and the observed.

This volume contributes to these accounts by illustrating that analogical gazing practices are employed in visualising migration. This power is exercised through multiple elements of the visual experience distinguished by theorists of spectatorship. In my analysis I will focus on the frame, the gaze point, and the field of appearance as the main factors defining and ultimately controlling the relationship between the observer and the observed. The frame is perhaps the key element that cuts out a fragment of visual reality and presents it as 'the' reality (Tagg 2009, pp. 1–6). The frame limits the visual experience by focusing attention on one selectively chosen fragment of an otherwise broad visual field: the gaze point. The gaze point determines the focus within the selected field of the frame. It determines the direction from which the look is coming and the perspective through which the visual reality within the frame is experienced. As determinant of the perspective, the gaze point is capable of manipulating the ethical distance between the observer and the observed. In addition to the frame and the gaze point, the aesthetic of the field of appearance imparts messages through metaphors, metonyms, colours and other aesthetic elements which can manipulate the affective response to an image. Through a multitude of visual elements, it can strengthen pre-existing judgements and reinforce existing discourses. In the following chapters these elements will be used as tools for assessing the presence of essentialising frames, disempowering gaze points, and the nature of the visual power behind the picture. I will show that the host gaze – much like the male gaze, the postcolonial gaze or the racialising gaze – depicts migrants as objects in relation to the host. As an object, the migrant is not equal to the observer but instead put in a position where their existence, place in the community, and access to the community can be manipulated in accordance with host expectations of the ideal migrant. This happens precisely because the host holds the power to dictate how the elements of spectatorship are used in relation to the migrant. The predominant imagery of migration that we encounter is presented through the frame, the gaze point, and the aesthetic tools familiar to the host but often alien to the migrant themselves. Through use of these elements, the host gaze reinforces and strengthens the power to extend or withdraw hospitality depending on whether the migrant fits within the narrow frames of worthiness shaped by the host's image of the ideal migrant. As this book shows, the host gaze underpinning recurring representations of migrants is a powerful tool which shapes the politics and laws regulating migration as well as migrant access to the community and rights.

Spectacle of the Border and Figures of the Migrant

The host gaze dictates the appearance of the migrant and establishes the reality in which citizens imagine the arrival of the guest. Faced with this pre-existing image of their life and circumstances, the migrant can rarely challenge pre-existing frames or speak to their validity. These narratives, familiar to the host, often create or reinforce the ethical gap between citizens and denizens. The power of the host gaze will operate in similar ways to the Foucauldian gaze and exist regardless of the presence of the observer. Those looking at a specific image can even disagree with it. Any such disagreement notwithstanding, the visual power embedded in the images presented through the host gaze will already have assumed the usually unequal relationship between the migrant and the citizen and present it as 'the reality' of migration and belonging. The visual field familiar to the host will typically encapsulate the host's anxieties and presumptions of who a migrant is and what their background, circumstances and concerns are. Whether the people depicted in those visual figures actually exist or whether the host society actually looks at the press or official governmental publications dictating the host-centric frames eventually becomes irrelevant. The power of the gaze will operate as an omnipresent form of visual discourse which reinforces the inequality in power relations between the host and the arriving guest. Presenting itself as the visual reality, the power of the gaze will operate regardless of how many people are looking at actual physical images or how many individual people agree with them. The power of the gaze will form a point of reference which will subsequently influence other discourses, including the political and legal. Within these discourses we can distinguish recurring themes and recurring figures which operate as the starting point for further discussions and collective decisions regulating migrant arrival, reception and belonging.

This volume refers to the selected depictions of migrants seen through the prism of the host gaze as the figures of a migrant – a term borrowed from Thomas Nail (2015). These figures are a visual phantasm helping the host society imagine the lives of migrants and reinforce the host–guest relationship. They help reaffirm the host's role in the exercise of hostipitality at the border and re-emphasise the power to control its threshold through policy and law. The figure of the migrant, while it may occasionally reflect an actual event or an actual migrant, often exists without any relation to the lived realities of the lives of migrants. This is possible because, as Nail phrases it:

> A figure is not a fixed identity or specific person but a mobile social position. One becomes a figure when one occupies this position. One may occupy this position to different degrees, at different times, and in different

> circumstances. But there is nothing essential about a person that makes the person this figure. The figure of the migrant, for example, is like a social persona that bears many masks (the nomad, barbarian, and the like) depending on the relative social conditions of expulsion. (Nail 2015, p. 16)

A figure as a part of discursive and visual reality is merely an element used in the exercise of power relations. In host-centric visual power, the figure of a migrant, rather than a factual migrant, begins to dictate the ethical and legal relations between host and guest. As a figure familiar to the host, the migrant exists in the imagination of the host prior to any actual encounter with a person who is crossing borders. In other words, the host meets the figure of a migrant even before anyone arrives at the actual border or enters the actual community thanks to the circulating visual depictions which those arriving may not be aware of or may never even see. In W. J. T. Mitchell's words:

> Images 'go before' the immigrant in the sense that before the immigrant arrives, his or her image comes first in the form of stereotypes, search templates, tables of classification, and patterns of recognition. At the moment of first encounter, the immigrant arrives as an image-text whose documents go before him or her at the moment of crossing the border (Mitchell 2011, p. 127)

As this volume will illustrate, these images encountered by the host population – despite being perceived as reality – are in fact rarely a 'neutral' representation. Quite the contrary, more often than not they carry assumptions embedded in the host gaze. As such, they include 'a subtle web of discourse through which realism is enmeshed in a complex fabric of notions, representations, images, attitudes, gestures and modes of action which function as everyday know-how, norms within and through which people live their relation to the world' (Tagg 1988, p. 100). An image of the guest, dictated by the host gaze, is thus not a 'simple' representation that allows the host to encounter the anticipated arrival, but often a representation which already carries a burden of social knowledge and prejudices available to the host prior to the encounter. This knowledge often manipulates the visual field and reinforces existing stereotypes or produces new social knowledge (ibid., p. 98) about those arriving. As shown throughout this book, the images through which the host approaches the guest frequently single out migrants and asylum seekers and appeal to values and emotions of the host societies (Papademetriou and Heuser 2009). The presumptions behind available imagery perpetuate beliefs about 'natural' cultural differences (Abali 2009) or perceptions of migrant illegality (Saran 2009). Certain ideas implanted with the help of these images encourage thinking, feeling and deciding in a particular way (Entman 2007, p. 164) and rely on preconceived notions according to which migrant lives are 'grievable', as Judith Butler would conceptualise it (2009, p. 4), or worthy of hospitality, as this volume argues. These host-centric visualities become part of a wider migration rhetoric (Entman 2007, p. 164) leading to the conviction that certain subjects cannot be immediately, or indeed sometimes ever, included in the existing community. This conviction then leads to exclusionary practices and laws directed towards migrants and those perceived as culturally 'foreign', reinforces the gaze as a form of power, and is capable of affecting the understanding of the legal and political world (Reese 2011, p. 3).

Once the host gaze operates as one of the forms of power, it affects the encounter at the border, influencing the host's judgement in terms of how individual experiences are measured and applied against existing law and policy. As a result, the border becomes 'a spectacle of enforcement' (De Genova 2013). In this spectacle, the figures of the migrant are made strikingly visible in the host's spectacle of power to welcome and exclude. What follows is that the border becomes a scene where actual people are judged through the presumptions attached to figures that arrived before them. This in turn allows the host to apply a wide range of exclusions and narrow the threshold of who is and who is not welcome. As De Genova summarises it, 'Border Spectacle, therefore, sets the scene – a scene of ostensible exclusion, in which the purported naturalness and putative necessity of exclusion may be demonstrated and verified, validated and legitimated, redundantly' (2013, p. 1181). Thus the figures existing in the imagery of the host gaze work firstly as a form of visual reality, secondly as discursive tools impacting the shape of laws, and thirdly as measuring tools helping to reinforce the workings of the border. They play a pivotal role in the border spectacle of welcome, worthiness and rejection.

Five Archetypal Figures of the Migrant

Since the host gaze operates as a form of power, it reverberates through an infinite number of migrant images. Despite their variety, I argue that most of them can be classified as repeating figures in the visual discourse on migration. I focus on five figures, which I consider primary and archetypal to multiple representations of migrants. We encounter these figures through official governmental materials, political campaigns, societal discourse or simply media reports. These figures often exist on their own or in combination with other figures and can at times traverse between two or more figures. Their primary function is to help the host define their relationship with the arriving migrant and as a result control the threshold of hospitality. These archetypal figures exert an influence on the balancing act between the hospitable and hostile sides of the aporia of hospitality. They become the archetypes that envision the ethical relationship between the host and those crossing borders and subsequently reinforce legal discourse and approaches to migration regulations. They often display highly emotive qualities, having the ability to sway judgement on what is desirable in the legal regulation of migration and what political stance is favoured in terms of deciding on who and under what circumstances can enter the territory of a nation state. At the same time, these figures are rarely neutral and often carry with them a dense web of pre-existing prejudices and presumptions regarding migration. Despite displaying regional qualities in places where they appear, their analogical clones exist across legal contexts and across boundaries. Their archetypal nature allows them to be modified and reflect the dominant discourses and trends identified in migration discourse in a given place. While migration law and refugee law literature dealing with critical discourse often understands these figures in verbal rather than visual ways, this book intends to illustrate that the discursive, legal and visual realms are intimately connected, indeed sometimes inseparable. The intertwining of verbal, visual and legal discourse gives these figures prominence in terms of their impact on migration regulation. In my analysis I distinguish five archetypal figures existing in visual and verbal migration discourse.

The first figure with which I begin my analysis is the Janus-faced figure of the 'genuine' refugee, as contrasted with the 'bogus' asylum seeker. As frequently analysed in refugee law literature (Kmak 2015; Zagor 2015), this figure underpins the contemporary understanding of who a refugee is and goes to the very core of how refugee law is understood and applied. The notion of the 'genuine' refugee extends hospitality only to those most deprived in a similar way that charity is extended only to those most deserving. Being in constant interplay with the figure of the 'bogus' asylum seeker, the figure of the 'genuine' refugee determines the breadth of the threshold of hospitality in refugee law. As my analysis will show, this threshold is frequently narrowed in the fear of welcoming a 'bogus' asylum seeker instead of a 'genuine' refugee. Those who qualify for genuineness are often those most grievable, who 'deserve' our charitable response, rather than those simply falling under the legal definition of a refugee embedded in the Refugee Convention. At times, those who meet the criteria can still be classified as 'bogus' if they fail to perform their 'genuineness' according to the set expectations of deservingness. My analysis of these two figures complements existing refugee law literature with a visual analysis of the images of these figures and examines how the dichotomy described in refugee law literature is portrayed visually. I examine the existing frame – look and gaze – against analyses of autonomy and refugeehood and show how existing visual imagery perpetuates assumptions about who is and who is not a refugee. Furthermore, I argue that the presence of these two figures fuels the above-mentioned confusion among categories in migration discourse. It is thanks to the figure of the 'bogus' asylum seeker that further figures, such as the 'illegal' migrant, have been born. Thus, these figures, while originating in refugee law, have expanded beyond it and have had a continuous impact on broader migration law, leading to the ever-expanding category of 'illegality' prominently featuring in migration discourses across the globe.

The second archetypal figure in contemporary migration discourse is the figure of the 'illegal' migrant. As a direct extension of the 'bogus' asylum seeker, this figure can exist in multiple contexts and relate to refugees, irregular migrants, *sans-papiers* and more. It is the key figure exemplifying the confusion among different categories of people crossing borders. The breadth of 'illegality' implied by this figure is possible because, as I argue, illegality is intimately related to invisibility (Gozdecka 2020). This symbiotic visual relationship between invisibility and illegality allows for being implicitly 'depicted' without actually being seen. This in turn allows for being mired in the broad spectacle of 'illegality'. As an invisible spectre always able to materialise at the border and threaten the host, the figure of the 'illegal' migrant allows for infinite legal manipulation of the conditions of entry. This figure and its somewhat sinister visual nature can lead to the ultimate exclusion of some migrants from the workings of the legal system. The breadth of 'illegality' in turn can lead to use of the harshest crimmigrant methods of control, which will be seen as legitimate, regardless of whether those associated with this figure have committed any crime. When analysing the figure of the 'illegal' migrant, I highlight how contemporary legal and social discourses allow for the existence of ever-tighter and more punitive forms of control of migration flows.

The third archetypal migrant figure distinguished in this volume is the figure of a migrant as an 'absolute other'. This figure is closely linked with the following figure of a migrant as an 'anonymous mass'. The absolute other extends the workings of the border to regulate the lives of migrants already within the territory. To justify continuing exclusion at the border and even after crossing the border, this notion relies on accentuating the differences between the host community and those who migrate. As shown in this chapter, this figure allows for inheriting migrant status and is reflected in discourses on 'second generation' or even 'third generation' migrants. Focusing on difference rather than belonging, the figure of an absolute other utilises often racialised imagery emphasising that which is considered alien by the host community. Representations of migrants as an absolute other often result in dehumanising those targeted and subsequently expanding, maintaining and justifying a range of legal exclusions from the community. The chapter analysing this figure shows how absolute otherness creates an impossible-to-close ethical gap between the host community and those arriving and how this gap can persist through generations. As the chapter argues, this firmly established gap allows for suspending or even entirely abandoning the workings of ethics even for those who have arrived legally and have been contributing to the community for an extended period of time.

The fourth figure analysed here is the figure of the migrant as an 'anonymous mass'. This figure is closely related to an 'absolute other' while also sharing some discursive qualities with the figure of an illegal migrant. In contrast to those figures, however, the figure of a mass is represented as an indistinguishable torrent, which is visually the exact opposite of invisibility or racist essentialisation. The purpose of this visual representation is to overwhelm the viewer and completely disassociate the migrant from their humanity. The figure of a mass is often described using metaphors such as 'flood' or 'sea' and allows for concealment of diversity, legal circumstances of migrants or their contribution to the community. Being described by non-human nouns, migrants represented through the image of the mass become a form of non-human assemblage which is nonetheless seen as exercising a form of threatening agency. Once disassociated from humanity, this figure allows for complete dismantling of ethics and effectively prevents any workings of hospitality. Pairing of the migrant with multiple non-human dangers, such as viral or mechanical threats, this archetype allows for justifying extreme forms of legal control which prevent the migrant from ever reaching the border. As shown in this chapter, the affective power of this threat is capable of creating new legal paradigms to the point of challenging existing legal consensus. This is because the threatening power of the mass can obscure all nuances of the legal realm. As illustrated here by the example of Brexit, it can also result in justifying and legitimising new forms of legal solution, often detrimental not just to the migrant but also to the host.

In contrast to the four preceding figures, the fifth selected archetype is the figure of the innocent, which exists as a counterbalance to the four main archetypes underpinning diverse forms of exclusion. This chapter focuses on the power of innocence in terms of closing the ethical gap between host and guest. It also argues that due to the prominence of the other figures, it is extremely hard for migrants to pass as 'innocents'. Such innocence is typically limited to images of migrant children who, occasionally and only in the right circumstances, are able to challenge arbitrary measures aimed at controlling migration. This chapter shows that empathy, stirred by depictions of suffering migrant children, often prompts viewers to respond ethically in a visual landscape saturated with suffering and 'compassion fatigue'. Despite the presence of the figure of an 'innocent', however, migrant children, as this chapter shows, normally face a much higher threshold in what has been called 'the hierarchy of innocence' than children of the host community.

Conclusions

The gap between host and guest appears to be a space for constant negotiation of whether the guest can be invited and welcomed inside the community. The aporetic nature of hostipitality allows for the breadth of the threshold to be determined through the prism of the host gaze. The judgement on how hospitable the host can be to the guest is continuously influenced by multiple factors including discourse and imagery. In times when images travel rapidly and almost always arrive before the actual guest, the use of a specific frame, gaze and visual field can be decisive in terms of the message they impart and the subsequent political and legal discourse that emerges as a consequence. When these images become archetypal representations, they are difficult to shake and challenge. In the following chapter I examine how archetypal visual figures can impact not only the extent of the host community's welcome, but also that community's perception of what is and what is not legitimate in terms of the legal realm. The next chapter delves into the relationship between the gaze and the legal imagery of the law.

References

Abali, Oya S. 'German public opinion on immigration and integration.' In *Migration, Public Opinion and Politics: The Transatlantic Council on Migration*, ed. Bertelsmann Stiftung and Migration Policy Institute. Bertelsmann Stiftung, 2009.
Alcoff, Linda Martín. *Visible Identities: Race, Gender, and the Self*. Oxford University Press, 2005.
Anderson, Benedict. *Imagined Communities: Reflections on the Origin and Spread of Nationalism*. Verso, 2006.
Anderson, Bridget. *Us and Them?: The Dangerous Politics of Immigration Control*. Oxford University Press, 2013.
Arendt, Hannah. *The Origins of Totalitarianism*. Harvest, 1973.
Bankier, Miriam E. 'Passe Pas: Rethinking the Passport.' BA thesis. Scripps College, 2020.
Buck-Morss, Susan. *Dreamworld and Catastrophe: The Passing of Mass Utopia in East and West*. MIT Press, 2000.
Butler, Judith. *Frames of War: When Is Life Grievable?* Verso, 2009.
Cade, Jason A. 'All the border's a stage: Humanitarian aid as expressive dissent.' In *Law and the Citizen*, ed. Austin Sarat. Emerald Publishing, 2020.
Canessa, Andrew. 'New indigenous citizenship in Bolivia: Challenging the liberal model of the state and its subjects.' *Latin American and Caribbean Ethnic Studies* 7, no. 2 (2012): 201–21.

Castillo, Pilar. *Passport*. Artwork, 2019, available at: <http://castlepillar.com/passport.html>, last accessed 21 September 2023.

Convention Relating to the Status of Refugees (Refugee Convention), 28 July 1951, United Nations, Treaty Series, vol. 189. UN General Assembly.

Crossley, Nick. 'The politics of the gaze: Between Foucault and Merleau-Ponty.' *Human Studies* 16, no. 4 (1993): 399–419.

Dauvergne, Catherine. *Making People Illegal: What Globalization Means for Migration and Law*. Cambridge University Press, 2008.

De Genova, Nicholas. 'Spectacles of migrant "illegality": The scene of exclusion, the obscene of inclusion.' *Ethnic and Racial Studies* 36, no. 7 (2013): 1180–98.

De Genova, Nicholas. 'Immigration reform and the production of migrant illegality.' In *Constructing Immigrant 'Illegality': Critiques, Experiences, and Responses*, ed. Cecilia Menjívar and Daniel Kanstroom, pp. 37–62. Cambridge University Press, 2014.

De Genova, Nicholas. 'Denizens all: The otherness of citizenship.' In *Citizenship and Its Others*, ed. Bridget Anderson and Vanessa Hughes, pp. 191–202. Palgrave Macmillan, 2015.

Deleuze, Gilles, and Félix Guattari. *A Thousand Plateaus: Capitalism and Schizophrenia*. Trans. Brian Massumi. University of Minnesota Press, 1987.

Derrida, Jacques. 'Hostipitality.' *Angelaki: Journal of Theoretical Humanities* 5, no. 3 (2000): 3–18.

Derrida, Jacques, and Anne Dufourmantelle. *Of Hospitality*. Stanford University Press, 2000.

Döring, Tobias. 'Turning the colonial gaze: Re-visions of terror in Dabydeen's Turner.' *Third Text* 11, no. 38 (1997): 3–14.

Elmer, Greg. 'Panopticon–discipline–control.' In *Routledge Handbook of Surveillance Studies*, ed. Kirstie Ball, Kevin D. Haggerty and David Lyon, pp. 21–9. Routledge, 2012.

Entman, Robert M. 'Framing bias: Media in the distribution of power.' *Journal of Communication* 57, no. 1 (2007): 163–73.

Foucault, Michel. *Discipline and Punish*. Trans. Alan Sheridan. Gallimard, 1975.

Goodman, Simon, and Susan A. Speer. 'Category use in the construction of asylum seekers.' *Critical Discourse Studies* 4, no. 2 (2007): 165–85.

Gordon, Eleanor, and Henrik Kjellmo Larsen. '"Sea of blood": The intended and unintended effects of the criminalisation of humanitarian volunteers rescuing migrants in distress at sea.' *Disasters* 46, no. 1 (2022): 3–26.

Gozdecka, Dorota A. *Rights, Religious Pluralism and the Recognition of Difference: Off the Scales of Justice*. Routledge, 2015.

Gozdecka, Dorota. 'Spectropolitics and invisibility of the migrant: On images that make people "illegal".' *Index Journal* 2 (2020): 195–212.

Hobsbawm, Eric J. *Nations and Nationalism Since 1780: Programme, Myth, Reality*. Cambridge University Press, 2012.

Kmak, Magdalena. 'Between citizen and bogus asylum seeker: Management of migration in the EU through the technology of morality.' *Social Identities* 21, no. 4 (2015): 395–409.

Levinas, Emmanuel. *Totality and Infinity: An Essay on Exteriority*. Trans. Alphonso Lingis. Springer Science & Business Media, 1979.

Mitchell, W. J. T. 'Migration, law, and the image: Beyond the veil of ignorance.' In *The Migrant's Time: Rethinking Art History and Diaspora*, ed. Saloni Mathur, pp. 59–77. Sterling and Francine Clark Art Institute/Yale University Press, 2011.
Mulvey, Laura. 'Visual pleasure and narrative cinema.' *Screen* 16, no. 3 (1975): 6–18.
Nail, Thomas. *The Figure of the Migrant*. Stanford University Press, 2015.
Palmater, Pamela D. *Beyond Blood: Rethinking Indigenous Identity*. UBC Press, 2011.
Papademetriou, Demetrios G., and Annette Heuser. 'Council statement: Migration, public opinion and politics.' In *Migration, Public Opinion and Politics: The Transatlantic Council on Migration*, ed. Bertelsmann Stiftung and Migration Policy Institute. Bertelsmann Stiftung, 2009.
Reese, Stephen D. 'Prologue – framing public life: A bridging model for media research.' In *Framing Public Life: Perspectives on Media and Our Understanding of the Social World*, ed. Stephen D. Reese, Oscar H. Gandy, Jr. and August E. Grant, pp. 7–31. Routledge, 2011.
Said, Edward. *Orientalism: Western Concepts of the Orient*. Pantheon, 1978.
Salter, Mark B. 'The global visa regime and the political technologies of the international self: Borders, bodies, biopolitics.' *Alternatives* 31, no. 2 (2006): 167–89.
Saran, Ayesha. 'A commentary on public attitudes on immigration: The United Kingdom in international context.' In *Migration, Public Opinion and Politics: The Transatlantic Council on Migration*, ed. Bertelsmann Stiftung and Migration Policy Institute. Bertelsmann Stiftung, 2009.
Scheel, Stephan, and Vicki Squire. 'Forced migrants as illegal migrants.' In *The Oxford Handbook of Refugee and Forced Migration Studies*, ed. Elena Fiddian-Qasmiyeh, Gil Loescher, Katy Long and Nando Sigona, pp. 188–99. Oxford University Press, 2014.
Steinberg, Saul. *The Passport*. Harper, 1954.
Stumpf, Juliet. 'The crimmigration crisis: Immigrants, crime, and sovereign power.' *American University Law Review* 56, no. 2 (2006): 367–419.
Tagg, John. *The Burden of Representation: Essays on Photographies and Histories*. University of Minnesota Press, 1988.
Tagg, John. *The Disciplinary Frame: Photographic Truths and the Capture of Meaning*. University of Minnesota Press, 2009.
Torpey, John. 'The Great War and the birth of the modern passport system.' In *Documenting Individual Identity: The Development of State Practices in the Modern World*, ed. Jane Caplan and John Torpey, pp. 256–70. Princeton University Press, 2001.
Treaty on European Union (TEU), European Union, Consolidated version of 13 December 2007, 2008/C 115/01.
Treaty on the Functioning of the European Union (TFEU), European Union, Consolidated version of 13 December 2007, 2008/C 115/01.
Universal Declaration of Human Rights (UDHR), UN General Assembly, 10 December 1948, 217 A (III).
Yew, Elizabeth. 'Medical inspection of immigrants at Ellis Island, 1891–1924.' *Bulletin of the New York Academy of Medicine* 56, no. 5 (1980): 488–510.
Zagor, Matthew. 'The struggle of autonomy and authenticity: Framing the savage refugee.' *Social Identities* 21, no. 4 (2015): 373–94.

2

Looking, Feeling and Judging the Law

Introduction

Many would argue that nothing is further apart than the subjective experience of an image and the objective experience of the law, unswayed by emotions. Costas Douzinas and Lynda Nead remind us that the jurisprudence of modernity has put an apparent distance between the concerns of the law and the concerns of art and literature (1999, p. 3). If we look at the law simply through the lens of positive law, or so-called black-letter law, nothing hints at the importance of an image and the relevance of the visual realm in assessing how law operates, creates legal categories or forms legal judgments. The mere existence of visual frames, certain forms of gaze or modes of appearance may indeed seem irrelevant for the daily experience of the law and its regulation. But, as Douzinas and Nead insist, this imagined distance between the legal and the visual is simply a form of pretence through which law attempts to close itself off from other discourses and practices in order to keep itself 'pure' from the outside influence of the non-legal (ibid., p. 4). Just as numerous other law and aesthetics scholars have insisted, this volume, too, emphasises that the distance between law and the surrounding visual realm is illusory. As we shall see, an understanding of images that shape and influence political and legal discourse in diverse legal areas is crucial for an understanding of the visual affect implicated in creating and maintaining the social bond (ibid., p. 9).

Migration law will of course be no exception in this regard. As already hinted at in the previous chapter, this volume argues that the visual figures of migrants underpinning migration discourse are relevant for the maintenance of power relations between host and guest, often even before the migrant arrives at the border. Visual figures of the migrant bring with them multiple assumptions and fears that impact on the understanding of justice and fairness in migration law. The affect and assumptions these figures create will play a role in how people see, interpret and understand what is just and what ought to be legal. In agreement with Linda Mulcahy, I understand the visual as a part of a broader legal culture which, as Mulcahy reminds us, impacts people's encounters with the law:

> Engagement with the visual involves a consideration of the ways in which images prepare people for a particular type of encounter with law and how art becomes an aspect of legal culture which is anchored in daily practice or facilitates learned habits of interpretation that go without saying. (Mulcahy 2017, p. 122)

In turn, these habits of interpretation form our assumptions about what kind of law is legitimate and what kind of law ought to underpin the social bond. Peter Goodrich famously observed that it is through symbols and images of social place that we as legal subjects recognise and form our affective attachments to law (1997, p. 1038). As a result, as subjects of legal authority we are far more often bound to law through images and what Goodrich calls 'phantasms of a shared substance' than by the actual dictates of positive law (ibid.). In other words, thanks to the omnipresence of certain images, we often have a clear judgement on what law 'should be like', but only few will have the full picture of what law is actually like. This judgement on what law 'should be like' will be crucial in legitimating laws that regulate the boundaries between being welcome and unwelcome and between belonging and exclusion.

This chapter examines how we feel and judge the law through our links to the available visual imagery and why the presence of images – particularly those that can be considered archetypal – is crucial for understanding how law operates, changes and evolves. While images are certainly not the main sources of influence on law and its reception, they play a crucial role in forming a wider understanding of justice and fairness and the practical consequences of rules and decisions. This chapter will illustrate why images are crucial in law's legitimation and how they influence our understanding of legal subjects. Using the rich theory of law and aesthetics, I intend to show that law is in fact inseparable from its surrounding reality and that imagery is one of the factors that make us 'feel' and judge the law.

Law and the Art of Visual Persuasion

Even those most sceptical of the connection between law and visual imagery admit the existence of an undeniable intersection between the law and the visual in what has been distinguished as visual political propaganda. Typically, however, the underlying assumption is that propaganda is not a regular visual activity but rather an exception occurring in the visual realm (Behrman 2019; Manderson 2017, 2018b). Propaganda is seen as an intentional activity that is often malicious in intent and in some instances, such as war propaganda, banned under international law (Larson 1966; Kearney

2007). It is often seen as a historical aberration used by totalitarian regimes such as the Nazis (Welch 2004) or the Soviet Union (Hirsch 2008), which has, however, recently resurfaced in Russian communication concerning the war in the Ukraine. Yet, as shown by Colin Moore (2010) in his historical analysis of the intimate relationship between art and the social and political realms, visual propaganda has most likely been involved in persuasion since the very beginnings of human civilisation. From monuments celebrating the victors and humiliating the foe, through portraits of kings to religious art, images have been used far and wide to create and change societal perceptions. The word 'propaganda' joined the lexicon rather late. It first appeared in 1622 in documents of the Catholic Church and was incorporated into the English language only in the nineteenth century (ibid., p. 7). Despite this late emergence as a concept, propaganda is far from consisting exclusively of information that is biased and misleading or used strictly for political persuasion (ibid., p. 8). Indeed, as Moore illustrates, 'propaganda is a reciprocal activity, a continuous dialogue between the giver and receiver, long recognised by historians as a faithful and sensitive index to the changes that occur in society' (ibid., p. 8).

Different forms of propaganda thus typically accompany processes of social change, while images that aim to persuade are spread far wider and are present in every society, at all times. While the word 'propaganda' will remain contentious (Ross 2002) and some images may not be classified as such, nevertheless electoral visual campaigns (Seidman 2008) and many images used by public authorities (Jowett and O'Donnell 2018) will often at the very least be reminiscent of propaganda. Alike to propaganda, their primary function as imagery is to influence preferences and slowly shift or change societal perceptions. Whether classified as propaganda or not, many images achieve this goal quietly by repeatedly reinforcing visual messages. While multiple theories abound as to how propaganda works (ibid.), the end goal of political imagery is to eventually shift societal perceptions to one or the other side through presenting what appears to be overwhelming visual evidence.

Due to its links with politics, the art of persuasion is intimately intertwined with the workings of power and could in fact be viewed as intrinsic to it rather than exceptional. While the example of propaganda can persuade even the most hardened sceptic that the law and the image can be powerful allies, we do not need to resort solely to the power of propaganda to evidence the long-lasting alliance between the visual and the legal. Even if we choose to drop the focus on propaganda altogether, the links between the visual and the legal appear to have been present for centuries. Goodrich has illustrated that the visual realm has always been involved in governance of power and subsequently law as an extension of that power. The visual has had an impact not only on how law is viewed, but also on how legal persons are perceived. Goodrich emphasises that the alliance between law and image influences legal reality through 'lines of visibility [...] [which] define "us and them", person and non-person, glory and defeat, majesty and monstrosity in their various forms' (2012, p. 55). In other words, as Goodrich further elaborates, individuals and their relationship with the sovereign and community have never been given but have instead been created and conceived amongst others through the use of images (ibid., pp. 55–6). Indeed, so much so that Goodrich, relying on Michel Foucault and Louis Althusser, conceives of the existence of an 'optical apparatus' (ibid., p. 56). Apparatus or *dispositif* in the Foucauldian understanding is a

> heterogeneous ensemble consisting of discourses, institutions, architectural forms, regulatory decisions, laws, administrative measures, scientific statements, philosophical, moral and philanthropic propositions [...]. The apparatus itself is the system of relations that can be established between these elements. (Foucault 1977, p. 194)

While for Foucault relationships of power are omnipresent and the apparatus is a consequence of those relationships, for Althusser the apparatus is more sinister and serves the very purpose of performance and maintenance of power. Power, argues Althusser, is maintained through ideological state apparatuses (ISAs), functioning alongside repressive state apparatuses. Ideologies reinforced by ISAs are so deeply embedded in our psyche that we cannot normally notice them because they are reinforced and introduced from early stages of societal development. For Althusser (1970), anything from family, through culture to law is part of an ISA. This apparatus is primarily based on indoctrination through culture, images and other societal institutions, but can be reinforced through normative systems such as religion or law. Relying on Althusser's apparatus, and further writings on the *dispositif*, Goodrich examines the notion of an 'optical apparatus', which he sees as

> a visuality that precedes and exceeds language. Intrinsic to the visuality of power is the necessity that it operates where diplomacy, conversation and presence are not possible. Division, therefore, is first ostensive, panoptic and, in early modern historical argot chorographic (according to location), a matter of generic visibility and similarity that defines and defends the habitus of groups, the buildings, the trophies, the monuments and their inscriptions. (Goodrich 2012, p. 55)

Thus, while propaganda may be the most ostensible manifestation of the optical apparatus, the manifestation that becomes clearly visible and distinguishable, the optical apparatus normally operates subtly and in smooth correlation to other parts of the ideological apparatus, for example the workings of societal institutions. The optical apparatus is so omnipresent and so intimately embedded in the workings of power that it not only remains unnoticeable, but appears to be 'natural'. This is possible, I argue, because the optical apparatus forms part of the societal scaffolding that maintains existing structures. This apparatus is a part of what Slavoj Žižek (1989) would call 'ideology', in this case the ideology of images. In 'The ideology of the aesthetic', Terry Eagleton famously pointed out that structures of power must become structures of feeling and the tool of that mediation is aesthetics (1988, p. 330). Persuasion through the optical apparatus or the ideology of aesthetics works subtly through visual representations of power (Marin 1988), performance of legal judgment (Etxabe 2013) and imagery of who is understood to be a legal person (Goodrich 2012, p. 55). If we take Althusser's broad understanding of the ISA, the connections between visual and non-visual are deep, omnipresent and impossible to challenge. They change and evolve slowly, together with changes in societal discourse more generally. Eagleton observes that the aesthetic realm is crucial in shaping the relationship between values and social practice (1988, p. 332). And as Desmond Manderson further notices, this relationship extends to the process of shaping the societal values that underpin our understanding of justice:

> There are two ways in which the aesthetic process relates to our ideas of justice and can help to inform it. First, the aesthetic dimension is part of our best understanding of the nature of justice in our society. This is the aesthetic nature of justice. Second, the aesthetic is, in itself, a liberatory process [. . .] Appreciating aesthetics is part of the work of making a better society. This is the just nature of aesthetics. (Manderson 2000, pp. 195–6)

Law and visual persuasion are thus connected through the processes of visually shaping the understanding of sovereign power and in further impacting on the 'feeling' of the sense of justice and legal legitimacy in regard to different societal institutions and legal persons. This relationship between the aesthetic and the legal is mutually reinforcing, as it firstly establishes ideas of legitimate power and subsequently reinforces the position of that power by impacting values and societal feeling of what law and justice should 'be like'. The optical apparatus thus works alongside the legal apparatus in the form of a constant, unbreakable and mutually reinforcing circle, which – as shown further – also shapes the perception of how the migrant fits into their host community.

The Image of Power and the Image of Law

The intimate relationship between the visual realm and sovereign power is unmistakable when we consider the mythologies surrounding power, nationhood, justice and the law (Manderson 2015). Myth – as Manderson reminds us – comprises a collection of images and scenes that help accommodate individuals within social structures (ibid., p. 212). Legal 'mythology', which allows legal subjects to form their relationship with legal power, is perpetuated through images of authority, conveyed in royal portraits (Marin 1988), legal emblems (Goodrich 2014) or numerous and diverse images of justice (Curtis and Resnik 1986). Taking a look at the form of power embedded in royal portraiture, Irene Winter (2009) emphasises that royal images have always oscillated between factual portraiture and the person portrayed being 'coded' for leadership (ibid., p. 262) in their visual representation. Since antiquity, a 'lordly' appearance would typically be exaggerated by specific symbols related to power, regardless of the actual resemblance of portraiture:

> The ruler's appearance [. . .] declared to have been molded by the gods in order to make him recognizable as one fit to rule, suggests that his 'ideal' qualities were paramount, not the realia consistent with modern notions of portraiture. In the representation, in addition to those signature elements marking the physiognomy, there would also have been signs external to the person: headgear, clothing, accoutrements. These markers would, to the ancients, have been so inseparable from identity that recognition of the office, if not the office holder, was immediate. (Winter 2009, p. 266)

The same has of course been true of power since antiquity. Louis Marin (1988) famously analysed a portrait of Louis XIV to show the link between the image of the king and the image of power itself. Marin argues that power is intimately related to its symbolic representation. He argues that power not only materialises through its representation, but that it is the representation itself which gives it power. In Emmanuelle Tall's words, 'where there is no sign, nor material underpinning, there is no power underpinning, there is no power' (Tall 2014, p. 247). Power thus not only lives and breathes through its visual representation, but is also given life through the values and messages coded in the images and symbolism maintaining it.

Since sovereign power is intimately related to law and law-giving, the constitutive function of visual symbols of power stretches to the legal realm. Law as an expression of the sovereign not only exists in its verbal and written expression, but is also partly created and partly reinforced through its visual symbolism. Goodrich reminds us that legal art is full of vocabulary related to looking. He insists that the necessity of looking, of being able to see the law and apprehend its symbols, is intrinsic to the legal profession and what he calls 'the lawyer's art' (2014, p. 49). He observes further that law itself relies on vocabulary related to its own visuality. We, for instance, 'observe' the law, 'recognize' its validity and 'appear' before it (ibid.). Thus, for Goodrich power is conveyed through visible signs and legal structures relying on the visual for the legitimacy, convention and norm of public performance of law (ibid.).

This means that legal power continuously reinforces itself through visible signs and rituals. It is coded into the designs of courthouses and their decorations (Martyn 2012), legal emblems (Goodrich 2014) or the way in which judges are portrayed (Richardson 2018). Law's presence and gravitas exists as much in words as it does in its visuality that continuously emphasises its importance and special position in society. Hidden behind these often-intimidating legal symbols lurks arcane knowledge of the law, accessible only to privileged legal practitioners who have acquired the secret and somewhat esoteric skill of reading, understanding and practising the law (Goodrich 2014, p. 55). Reliance on symbolism and visibility is therefore paramount to the existence of the law. In the visual realm, accessible to everyone, law plays out its own spectacle (Leiboff 2019) in which its apparent power is on display to behold and respect. Behind this spectacle, however, its true meaning remains hidden and accessible only to those trained to access the specialised and arcane knowledge of the law. Thus, images related to the law have as their subject 'ritual and ceremony, of praise and celebration, of honor and sanctification as inscribed in the architecture of the social and in the figures of administrative and political as well as legal presence' (Goodrich 2014, p. 63).

If it were not for this visual ritualism, law would be likely to lose its air of gravitas. For the law to retain its power over legal subjects, those subjects need to have some form of understanding of the nature of legal power. At the very least, legal subjects need to acknowledge that law can legitimately resolve conflicts, regulate legal relationships and punish wrongdoers. Since the letter of the law will not be accessible to all or intimately understood by all, the symbolic power of the law legitimises what otherwise remains esoteric for non-lawyers. As legal subjects, whether we understand the intricacies of the law or not, we all have an image of the importance and seriousness of law. We understand its authority, partly because its symbolism and rituals constantly reiterate its importance. The rituals of the courtroom, the symbolism of legal proceedings, and other visual and symbolic expressions of the legal realm allow us to understand that nobody remains above the law and that its power stretches over all of us. This happens regardless of whether we are trained to peek behind the visual ritual to read, understand and practise the law, or whether all that we can observe is the power conveyed through legal rituals and proceedings. While the details of legal symbolism may change with time, rituals and visuality will help us internalise the importance of legal authority. In Leif Dahlberg's words:

> our concrete and conceptual images of law and authority are both internal and external, and are mediated both through physical media – including courtroom design and courthouse architecture – and through the living and active memory of human actors. The images of law and authority are not static but are changing with evolving conceptions of law and justice. (Dahlberg 2012, p. 5)

This role of the visual, while crucial for reinforcing the societal values that shape law's authority, at the same time often remains unnoticeable precisely because it has been so deeply internalised through our daily encounters with the visual symbolism of legal authority. This symbolism, in contrast to the past, where legal authority was emphasised through art and architecture, is nowadays reiterated in every aspect of the visual media including film, television, photography and social media. While watching these images and films, whether for learning or entertainment, we encounter legal symbolism and ritualism in stories played out and displayed on big and small screens. These stories tell us how law impacts our reality and often include messages both on what law is and what law ought to be like. Stories of injustice attempt to highlight law's inadequacy, while others attempt to emphasise law's authority. This daily spectacle is internalised so deeply that most spectators remain unaware that the power of the law is accentuated even through those benign and seemingly non-legal encounters.

Law, Justice and Legitimacy

Internalisation of the weight and importance of legal power through images is only one aspect through which the realm of the law and the realm of the image intersect. As already hinted above, they also converge through images communicating ideas about law, justice and legitimate authority. While law and justice have a complex relationship, the fundamental idea entrenched deep in the collective psyche of our societies is that law is meant to do 'justice' and that jurisprudence can clarify what justice means (Douzinas and Gearey 2005, pp. 3–4). There are of course fundamental difficulties with defining what exactly is 'just' and how law should capture justice in its text and practice. While nobody truly knows what 'justice' encapsulates and even the most powerful legal minds struggle with whether justice lies in just procedures, just institutions or something else entirely novel, everyone – whether scholar or not – will have their own idea of 'justice'. This idea may be influenced by multiple factors, such as personal circumstances and background or surrounding reality. While some have suggested that just law can be created in separation from those ideals and created from behind a 'veil of ignorance' where personal preferences remain irrelevant (Rawls 1999), multiple scholars have shown that such an ideal model remains just that – an ideal. Regardless of how utopian defining justice is, its very existence as a concept is intimately linked with values.

As an idea so deeply pervading our legal imagery, Justice has of course also been a subject of multiple depictions capturing its complex nature and conflicting conceptions. As Dennis Curtis and Judith Resnik observe in their analysis of visual depictions of Justice, the image of Justice has a remarkable longevity: 'For more than 2000 years, people have looked at images of Justice, drawn meanings from them, and written about them. More than simply an artifact of Western culture, Justice stands as a quasi-religious, quasi-political icon' (1986, p. 1729). As they notice further, depictions of Justice show its changing understanding over the centuries and serve several purposes. These include some instructive and didactic purposes of educating the public about justice as well as warnings to judges of the consequences of unjust rulings (ibid., p. 1743). In other words, images of Justice communicate powerful ideas about what law ought to do in the name of Justice and how law legitimates Justice. Despite being originally one of many virtues often depicted in the Renaissance, Justice evolved into its own icon with its own public mythology allowing its spectators to imagine what a 'just' ruling or 'serving justice' means. Throughout its many iterations Justice eventually became the familiar blindfolded Lady Justice we often encounter today in public buildings hosting legal authorities or offices of judicial power. Her blindfold, symbolising impartiality and being unswayed by emotion (ibid., p. 1727), has been a subject of controversy amongst scholars insisting that early depictions illustrated her with her eyes open (Manderson 2018a, pp. 35–41; Jay 2013) and that such a posture in fact may in some circumstances offer a better and more informed judgment that redresses wrongs before her very eyes (Jay 2013, pp. 78–9). The reverse has of course found its way into the popular understanding that Justice stands behind the blindfold so as to prevent her from seeing privilege and treating the powerful better than the powerless (ibid., p. 68; for a detailed discussion of the allegorical figure of Lady Justice, see Hayaert 2023).

Notwithstanding disagreement as to which depiction would in fact embody a better and fairer conception of Justice, her image clearly communicates several ideas related to how we see the role of law and legal authority. These ideas primarily include clarity, objectivity and the power to pass legitimate judgments. All of these qualities come together in a related ideal used to assess the legitimacy of the legal system, courts and judges – namely the rule of law. The rule of law in the Western legal canon has become a litmus test for the legitimacy of sovereign power. While the idea of Justice normally embodies the idea of the rule of law, the truth is that sovereign power has always attempted to associate itself with Justice in order to validate its power and legitimate the violence of its legal system. In Curtis and Resnik's words, paraphrasing Edith Roper and Clara Leiser's research on depictions of courts in Nazi Germany, 'all sovereigns claim (notwithstanding evidence to the contrary) that their violence goes forth in the name of Justice' (1986, p. 1734). Images can powerfully aid this claim by the sovereign. Legally, however, the notion of the rule of law, whether in its narrowest procedural understanding or in its deeper and more comprehensive meaning, will be used to assess the legitimacy of authority.

The rule of law will be a criterion distinguishing legitimate authority from one illegitimately imposed and democratic authority from authoritarian. While the intricacies of the rule of law will be complex and subject to a variety of interpretations, it would be a mistake to assume that images cannot influence our perception of how we see the rule of law and assess the legitimacy of authority. In his analysis of Governor Arthur's Proclamation, Manderson (2011) has shown us how the notion of the rule of law can be manipulated with the help of images. The image addressed to the Aboriginal inhabitants of Tasmania – back then Van Diemen's Land – showed equal treatment of white and black inhabitants as means to legitimate Governor Arthur's authority. While this was not in fact true, the image communicated the idea that the legitimate authority treats all inhabitants equally. While this was, in that case, used solely for political purposes, Manderson reminds us that 'the "rule of law" is not merely a legal term. It is a social fact, and our sources must extend beyond the arid pages of textbooks into the social world, art, literature, children's books, movies, and newspapers' (2011, pp. 288–9). This is possible because people's idea of justice and the rule of law is a somewhat fuzzy conglomerate of diverse influences affecting legal subjects. Most people will perceive something as 'just' if it corresponds to their notion of fairness. How fairness is perceived, though, can be affected by a multitude of factors, including social background, race (Miller et al. 1986) or gender (Feather 1996). Similarly, images, discourses and popular cultural depictions of the justice system (Sherwin 2000) have an impact on what comes to be seen as just and perceived as fair. Thus we all have an image of justice, just law, legitimate authority and the rule of law that is constantly influenced by societal discourse comprising, on the one hand, political discourse and, on the other, visual, artistic and other forms of discourse that shape the idea of what it means to be treated fairly and what type of authority and law is legitimate. Goodrich reminds us that it is through symbols and images that we recognise and form our attachments to law (1997, p. 1038). Similarly, Manderson notes that justice in itself has aesthetic qualities, like the idea of balance or the very idea of 'doing justice' (Manderson 2000, p. 196). These notions have an aesthetic value that will impact the imagery of what we imagine as fair (ibid., p. 197). The aesthetic values we share as a society will impact on our societal values and on the theories of law we adopt. These theories and visions of justice will depend on the aesthetic values and the images through which we feel and judge the world:

> Where is the aesthetic in law? The answer is, everywhere. Law is a cultural medium of expressive form, through which senses and symbols are combined, communicated, and interpreted. In the multiple levels of that expression are to be found the aesthetic dimensions of law and justice. (Manderson 2000, p. 201)

While law changes slowly and evolves as a result of legislative and judicial processes, its complex body is subject to legitimacy processes, including being seen as legitimate by those affected by it. If the law is perceived as 'unjust', it can be challenged through either democratic processes, acts of resistance or civil disobedience towards the authority that is seen as illegitimate (Singer 1974). As a force responding to societal change, law slowly adjusts to the social context and ever-changing ideas of what is just and fair. If we understand law as broadly affected by diverse influences on the idea of justice, it becomes clearer that visual imagery is a potential influence on how people see, feel and judge the law. Richard Sherwin calls the visual register in which the ideas of a legitimate social contract circulate around us the 'visual economy'. With the increasing importance of images circulating promptly thanks to the instant availability of social media, we can even speak of 'visiocracy' (Sherwin 2018) – a system where the imagery circulating in the visual register helps us commit to the current terms of the social contract. Within our 'visiocracies' different visual economies can operate and influence how we legitimate law. The visual economy needs to reflect the values and aesthetic registers through which reality is conveyed to us (ibid., p. 332). If it does not, we risk 'not feeling' the law's validity:

> Experiencing law's validity as a matter of its compliance with the right set of rules or principles without any sense of its felt significance, which is to say, without an adequate account of what binds us to law's authority in the first place, leads us to Kafka's law: a law that is valid but lacks significance. (Sherwin 2018, p. 335)

If we accept Sherwin's assertion that we all exist in a 'visiocracy', the difference between images of Justice from pre-modern times and the early modern era and the current visual register becomes apparent. While the authorities will always attempt to use Justice and its images as one of many tools of legitimation, in our contemporary era saturated with images, we will experience an intense competition between different visual ideals of what is fair and what is just. In other words, different images of justice and fairness will compete for the feelings of the audience. If they succeed, a new visual economy will emerge, and a new idea of Justice will, at least for a while, take hold. This visual competition for the affective response of the audience can focus on any aspect of the visual register associated with law. In a 'visiocracy', different images will compete for what law should 'look like', how diverse legal subjects are depicted, what issues constitute justice, and what legitimate authorities should 'look like'. Once any of these ideas becomes commonly 'felt', law's response to it becomes seen either as legitimate or as failed. This influence stretches to different areas affected by law where different perceptions may operate. While some areas can be seen as justly regulated, others may be seen as unfair, badly regulated or as in need of changes and adjustments.

Law, Visibility and Legal Persons

Notions of visual legitimacy and fairness are not solely limited to the realm of legitimating public authority and its law-giving capacity. Visual reality is so strongly embedded in our daily lives that it also shapes the ideas of model legal subjects including their role and appearance. For centuries the ideal legal subject was captured in the figure of a straight, white male who embodied the ideas of legal personhood and the ability to vote, own property, and participate in public and political life. While this ideal has been slowly challenged, the visual register of the social order has continued to influence perceptions of social roles including gender roles or racial roles (Munshi 2018). In his analysis of the optical apparatus, Goodrich (2012) puts key emphasis on how this apparatus shapes the role of legal persons. He sees visual power as intrinsic to creating visibility and division between different subjects (ibid., p. 55). The notion of legal personhood is for him a form of 'theatrical category, the actor's mask, the stage presence' (ibid., p. 56). Different individuals with their personal characteristics become 'legal persons' because, as he argues further, the optical apparatus brings them to the realm of social visibility and makes them 'appear' (ibid.). Goodrich refers to the theatrical device that lifted the actor onto the stage to make them appear as a metaphor for how the optical apparatus makes us visible to the legal system and how it legitimates us as 'valid' legal subjects (ibid.). To be a legal person, Goodrich insists, 'is to be seen, to appear on stage, in the atrium or the forum, in public or private, as part of the political or economic scene' (ibid., p. 57). If, as Goodrich argues, legal personality is a visible manifestation that accompanies our individual being, it has a power of assigning us perceived legal roles, including the right to be included or excluded:

> These lines of visibility and enunciation graphically define 'us and them,' person and non-person, glory and defeat, majesty and monstrosity in their various forms. The iconicity of person and relation, the identity of sovereign and community, are not given but created, conceived in images and it is precisely that creation of images, that modality of appearances, manifestation and transmission, that is the root meaning of apparatus and the primary function of theological disposition. (Goodrich 2012, p. 56)

As Ariella Azoulay adds in her observations concerning photography, the way we appear in what she calls a 'civil contract of photography', but which could also be called a 'civil contract of the visual realm', is intimately connected to the power embedded in the act of gazing (2008, p. 95). In terms of photography, she illustrates how the power of the observer over the one being photographed controls the existence of subjects. She emphasises that the power involved in gazing that accompanies the act of photographing often perpetuates social relations of power and stages the weak, the disadvantaged, and marginal populations such as ethnic minorities as marginalised objects (ibid., p. 109). As a consequence, these groups, including migrants, serve as 'guinea pigs' in utilisation of visual power by the modern state (ibid.). This civil contract embedded in the creation of the visual manifestations that accompany us each day carries within it societal assumptions, prejudices and discourses. These in turn impact on whether we are seen as belonging, worthy of rights, in a position to challenge injustice or able to hold a position of power. Frames that are applied often exclude some of us from view and overemphasise the role of others.

In *The Burden of Representation*, John Tagg powerfully shows that photography, albeit seemingly 'neutral' and 'objective', in fact operates as a certain form of apparatus. Tagg illustrates that the use of photography in, for instance, surveillance or recording evidence, was a form of struggle between different representations which produced photographic meanings and created an entirely new form of disciplinary power over legal subjects. Exercising power through the image is possible because of the existence of the frame, which determines the breadth of the field of appearance. In *The Disciplinary Frame: Photographic Truths and the Capture of Meaning*, Tagg further develops the idea of the frame and its role in creating visibility and invisibility. He argues that photography seems to be 'objective' because the frame is rarely acknowledged and appears invisible, but the work it does goes to the very heart of the power to include and exclude:

> Yet the frame also troubles the very division it brings into existence. Like the supplement, the frame is an adjunct that is neither inherent nor dispensable. Marking a limit between the intrinsic and the extrinsic, it is neither inside nor outside, neither above nor below. Its thickness and depth separate it both from the integral inside of the so-called work itself and from the outside, from the wall or the space in which the work is sited, then, 'step by step, from the whole field of historical, economic, political inscription in which the drive to signature is produced.' The frame thus stands out against the two grounds that it constitutes – the work and the setting – and yet, with respect to each of these, it always dissolves into the other. This oscillation marks its presence and effaces its effect. The frame is all show, and yet it escapes visibility [. . .]. The frame, too, is seen and not seen, disavowed, already at work in fixing the look and the givenness of difference, yet always denied or multiplied to infinity. (Tagg 2009, p. 246, quoting Jacques Derrida)

If we escape visibility through the cut of the frame, we risk being invisible subjects, always escaping the focus and attention of the law. If we are framed in a particular way, on the other hand, we can be seen as criminals, outsiders, dangers to public safety and so forth. The frame and the representation often justify how law approaches us and how legal authority treats us. It can also influence whether we are seen as subjects who can legitimately exercise power. The very recent example of the controversy over representation of history in popular television shows such as *Bridgerton* shows the long-lasting attachment to visually assigned positions in society. Despite the entirely fictional character of the show and the books on which it is based, placing non-white characters in positions of power in the recent depiction of Julia Quinn's books has stirred a debate on 'historical accuracy' (Hackett and Coghlan 2021). For some viewers, non-white characters did not appear to be plausible holders of power or wealth. This example shows that the power of visual representation is lasting and changes slowly and its coding of personhood and power often appears to spectators to be 'natural' or 'normal'. Given such power of the visual register, it is of little wonder that depictions of migrants can influence how their role is perceived in host societies and what kind of migration law is seen as 'legitimate'.

Archetypes and the Figures of Citizen and Migrant

If the notions of legitimacy and legality stretch to how law construes us as different legal subjects, 'visual archetypes' becomes a crucial term to understand. Being seen or being left unseen, being seen in a specific manner or conversely being continuously erased, can have consequences on how law treats us as subjects of its authority. Such depictions can determine whether someone is seen as a part of the community or as a subject that is foreign and thus remaining alien to the community. These depictions are often stereotypical or archetypal, because archetypes are more easily absorbed and accepted by viewers. Dan Schill has demonstrated that archetypal images often play a crucial role in political communication because they 'can quickly make arguments and communicate emotions' and 'are uniquely equipped to create identification, or perceived similarity' (2012, p. 129). Multiple scholars have shown that archetypal imagery often perpetuates racism and other forms of exclusion within the community (Renner 2009; Bakali 2016; Mariolle 2019; Lupton 1999). Nicholas Mirzoeff (2002) illustrated how the nineteenth-century elevation of whiteness to the role of a historical archetype of beauty led to problematic notions of racial supremacy. Such archetypes, once established, tend to live long lives in the visual register and create real-life impacts on subjects who fall within one of them. Deborah Lupton defines an archetype as an act of personalisation, through which people become symbols standing for wider meanings and concerns (1999, p. 37). Once people become symbols, the relationship with them becomes simplified and, rather than approaching them as individuals, we begin fitting them into pre-existing categories (ibid., p. 38). Once archetypes are established, they become increasingly difficult to challenge while at the same time exacerbating exclusion and discrimination.

These visual archetypes can play a crucial role in delineating between inclusion of a citizen and exclusion of a migrant. Just as with portraits of kings or judges, which are coded to convey the power of authority, our visual register is full of representations coded to convey lines of inclusion and exclusion. Sherally Munshi illustrates how being seen as a white member of a community in photographic representations affected naturalisation cases in the United States in the early twentieth century: showing 'assimilability' was crucial for successful recognition as a person who could be naturalised under racially charged provisions on obtaining US citizenship (2018, pp. 174–5). Munshi argues that not only did individual images showing assimilability impact on decisions concerning the persons depicted, but they also revealed how 'the nation maintains its self-image – not only by excluding others but by conscripting bodies capable of serving as a narcissistic mirror reflecting its superiority and universality' (ibid., p. 180). She concludes that the visual archive is a crucial register envisioning and re-envisioning the legal meaning of citizenship (ibid., p. 181).

Similarly to being coded for citizenship, some imagery can code persons depicted for exclusion as a migrant. As outlined earlier, I distinguish five primary archetypes of migrants that circulate in our visual register. The following part analyses those images and shows how these visual archetypes embedded in the selected figures of the migrant play a crucial role in formation of an 'us' and 'them' divide, and how particular figures legitimate legal approaches that criminalise, exclude and attempt to keep migrants away from the territory of the host. These images will often appear 'natural' due to the subtle workings of the optical apparatus. By pointing out the role of the host gaze and its direction, the frame and the field of appearance within the frame, I hope to uncover the often-invisible ethical divide between host and guest and show its impact on how we envision, implement and apply migration law provisions.

Conclusions

Connections between the visual and the legal are deep and intertwined in the interplay between legitimating law, authority and different forms of legal subjectivity. Visual reality impacts on how we understand justice, the role of legal authority and the place of different legal persons in our society. Today's expansion and the easy accessibility of the visual domain create an overwhelming affect that maintains and creates our perceptions of what justice ought to be like and who ought to be included in our societies. Visual reality can code us for power, citizenship or exclusion. Its long-lasting impact and its seeming – although deceptive – objectivity can be hard to challenge once the image is established of who is to be included and who is to be excluded. These established visual archetypes, which are analysed in the following part, often appear 'neutral' and are seen as a part of 'reality'. Yet, as the following analysis shows, most of the time these archetypes of the migrant create a wide gap between host and guest. This gap, rather than being 'natural' or a part of 'objective reality', is instead construed through migration discourse and imagery. Yet, since it is deeply internalised, it plays an enormous role in what kind of migration law is seen as just and what kind of legal solutions are supported by host societies.

References

Althusser, Louis. 'Ideology and ideological state apparatuses (notes towards an investigation) (1970).' In *Cultural Theory: An Anthology*, ed. Imre Szeman and Timothy Kaposy, pp. 204–22. John Wiley, 2010.
Azoulay, Ariella. *The Civil Contract of Photography*. Princeton University Press, 2021.
Bakali, Naved. 'Popular cultural Islamophobia.' In *Islamophobia: Understanding Anti-Muslim Racism through the Lived Experiences of Muslim Youth*, pp. 63–78. Brill, 2016.
Behrmann, Carolin. 'Law, visual studies, and image history.' In *The Oxford Handbook of Law and Humanities*, ed. Simon Stern, Maksymilian Del Mar and Bernadette Meyler, pp. 39–64. Oxford University Press, 2019.

Curtis, Dennis E., and Judith Resnik. 'Images of justice.' *Yale Law Journal* 96, no. 8 (1986): 1727–72.
Dahlberg, Leif, ed. *Visualizing Law and Authority: Essays on Legal Aesthetics*. Walter de Gruyter, 2012.
Douzinas, Costas, and Adam Gearey. *Critical Jurisprudence: The Political Philosophy of Justice*. Hart Publishing, 2005.
Douzinas, Costas, and Lynda Nead. *Law and the Image: The Authority of Art and the Aesthetics of Law*. University of Chicago Press, 1999.
Eagleton, Terry. 'The ideology of the aesthetic.' *Poetics Today* 9, no. 2 (1988): 327–38.
Etxabe, Julen. *The Experience of Tragic Judgment*. Routledge, 2013.
Feather, Norman T. 'Domestic violence, gender, and perceptions of justice.' *Sex Roles* 35, no. 7–8 (1996): 507–19.
Foucault, Michel. 'The confession of the flesh.' In *Power/Knowledge: Selected Interviews and Other Writings, 1972–1977*, ed. Colin Gordon, pp. 194–27. Pantheon Books, 1977.
Goodrich, Peter. 'Maladies of the legal soul: Psychoanalysis and interpretation in law.' *Washington and Lee Law Review* 54 (1997): 1035–74.
Goodrich, Peter. 'The theatre of emblems: On the optical apparatus and the investiture of persons.' *Law, Culture and the Humanities* 8, no. 1 (2012): 47–67.
Goodrich, Peter. *Legal Emblems and the Art of Law: Obiter depicta as the Vision of Governance*. Cambridge University Press, 2014.
Hackett, Lisa J., and Jo Coghlan. 'The history bubble: Negotiating authenticity in historical romance novels.' *M/C Journal* 24, no. 1 (2021).
Hayaert, Valérie. *Lady Justice: An Anatomy of Allegory*. Edinburgh University Press, 2023.
Hirsch, Francine. 'The Soviets at Nuremberg: International law, propaganda, and the making of the postwar order.' *The American Historical Review* 113, no. 3 (2008): 701–30.
Jay, Martin. 'Must justice be blind? The challenge of images to the law.' In *Refractions of Violence*, pp. 97–112. Routledge, 2013.
Jowett, Garth S., and Victoria O'Donnell. *Propaganda & Persuasion*. SAGE, 2018.
Kearney, Michael G. *The Prohibition of Propaganda for War in International Law*. Oxford University Press, 2007.
Larson, Arthur. 'The present status of propaganda in international law.' *Law and Contemporary Problems* 31 (1966): 439–51.
Leiboff, Marett. *Towards a Theatrical Jurisprudence*. Routledge, 2019.
Lupton, Deborah. 'Archetypes of infection: People with HIV/AIDS in the Australian press in the mid 1990s.' *Sociology of Health & Illness* 21, no. 1 (1999): 37–53.
Manderson, Desmond. *Songs without Music: Aesthetic Dimensions of Law and Justice*. University of California Press, 2000.
Manderson, Desmond. *Governor Arthur's Proclamation: Images of the Rule of Law*. Routledge, 2011.
Manderson, Desmond. 'The metastases of myth: Legal images as transitional phenomena.' *Law and Critique* 26, no. 3 (2015): 207–23.
Manderson, Desmond. 'Chronotopes in the scopic regime of sovereignty.' *Visual Studies* 32, no. 2 (2017): 167–77.

Manderson, Desmond. 'Blindness visible: Law, time, and Bruegel's justice.' In *Law and the Visual: Representations, Technologies, Critique*, ed. Desmond Manderson, pp. 23–50. University of Toronto Press, 2018a.

Manderson, Desmond. 'Here and now: From "aestheticizing politics" to "politicizing art".' In *Sensing the Nation's Law*, pp. 175–90. Springer, 2018b.

Marin, Louis. *Portrait of the King*. Springer, 1988.

Mariolle, Tiffany S. 'Combating the harmful effects of gendered racist stereotypes using counter-stereotypical images based in archetypes with African American women.' Doctoral dissertation. Alliant International University, 2019.

Martyn, Georges. 'Inspiring images for judges: Late medieval court room decorations in the Southern Netherlands.' In *The Iconology of Law and Order (Legal and Cosmic)*, ed. Anna Kérchy, Attila Kiss and György Endre Szőnyi, pp. 37–49. Jatepress, 2012.

Miller, John L., Peter H. Rossi and Jon E. Simpson. 'Perceptions of justice: Race and gender differences in judgments of appropriate prison sentences.' *Law and Society Review* 20, no. 3 (1986): 313–34.

Mirzoeff, Nicholas. 'Ghostwriting: Working out visual culture.' *Journal of Visual Culture* 1, no. 2 (2002): 239–54.

Moore, Colin. *Propaganda Prints: A History of Art in the Service of Social and Political Change*. A&C Black, 2010.

Mulcahy, Linda. 'Eyes of the law: A visual turn in socio-legal studies?' *Journal of Law and Society* 44 (2017): 111–28.

Munshi, Sherally. '"You will see my family became so American": Race, citizenship, and the visual archive.' In *Law and the Visual: Representations, Technologies, Critique*, ed. Desmond Manderson, pp. 161–88. University of Toronto Press, 2018.

Rawls, John. *A Theory of Justice: Revised Edition*. Harvard University Press, 1999.

Renner, Eric. *American Disguise*. Flying Monkey Press, 2007.

Richardson, Alice. 'Sir Redmond Barry and the trial of Ned Kelly: Representing the judge and judgment in nineteenth-century Australia.' In *Judgment in the Victorian Age*, ed. James Gregory, Daniel J. R. Grey and Annika Bautz. Routledge, 2018.

Ross, Sheryl Tuttle. 'Understanding propaganda: The epistemic merit model and its application to art.' *Journal of Aesthetic Education* 36, no. 1 (2002): 16–30.

Schill, Dan. 'The visual image and the political image: A review of visual communication research in the field of political communication.' *Review of Communication* 12, no. 2 (2012): 118–42.

Seidman, Steven A. *Posters, Propaganda, and Persuasion in Election Campaigns around the World and through History*. Peter Lang, 2008.

Sherwin, Richard K. *When Law Goes Pop: The Vanishing Line between Law and Popular Culture*. University of Chicago Press, 2000.

Sherwin, Richard K. 'What authorizes the image? The visual economy of post-secular jurisprudence.' In *Law and the Visual: Representations, Technologies, Critique*, ed. Desmond Manderson, pp. 330–54. University of Toronto Press, 2018.

Singer, Peter. 'Democracy and disobedience.' *Philosophy* 49, no. 188 (1974): 215–16.

Tagg, John. *The Burden of Representation: Essays on Photographies and Histories*. University of Minnesota Press, 1988.

Tagg, John. *The Disciplinary Frame: Photographic Truths and the Capture of Meaning.* University of Minnesota Press, 2009.
Tall, Emmanuelle Kadya. 'On representation and power: Portrait of a vodun leader in present-day Benin.' *Africa: Journal of the International African Institute* 84, no. 2 (2014): 246–68.
Welch, David. 'Nazi propaganda and the *Volksgemeinschaft*: Constructing a people's community.' *Journal of Contemporary History* 39, no. 2 (2004): 213–38.
Winter, Irene J. 'What/when is a portrait? Royal images of the ancient Near East.' *Proceedings of the American Philosophical Society* 153, no. 3 (2009): 254–70.
Žižek, Slavoj. *The Sublime Object of Ideology.* Verso, 1989.

PART II
FIGURES OF THE MIGRANT

3

The Janus-Faced Refugee: The Interplay Between the 'Genuine' and the 'Bogus' Asylum Seeker

Introduction

The figure of the refugee, central to further discussions on the spreading paradigms of 'illegality', appears to rely on a somewhat fragmented and Janus-faced set of imagery. Refugee law literature has characterised this as the interplay between two distinct figures, namely those of the 'bogus' asylum seeker and the 'genuine' refugee (Kmak 2015). This chapter focuses on these figures to illustrate that they have informed depictions of migrants and refugees more broadly. This is possible because the dichotomy between 'bogusness' and 'genuineness' applies both to images that communicate negative ideas concerning migration and to those that convey positive depictions of refugees and migrants. While negative imagery may be used by political campaigns or – as shown here – governmental materials, positive depictions are often prepared by artists for NGOs or rights-based initiatives. I intend to show, however, that regardless of their intention, most of these images rely on established ways in which the 'genuineness' of a refugee hinges on depictions of absolute deprivation and destitution. These two figures are pivotal because of the previously noted confusion in categorising between refugees and migrants and the exponential expansion of 'illegality' in migration law more generally. The dichotomy between who is 'genuine' and who is 'bogus' – and, by extension of their bogusness, 'illegal' – has overtaken social, political and sometimes legal discourses affecting all migrants and the conditions for crossing borders or settling in the new community. As I will show in this chapter, this dichotomous framing stems from the interplay between autonomy and refugeehood observed in refugee literature (Zagor 2015). The assumption of limited autonomy underpinning the figure of the refugee has shaped refugee law into a form of charity deserved only by those most victimised and deprived. As a consequence, any form of autonomy displayed by the refugee automatically puts them in a position of a suspected bogus asylum seeker – and potentially illegal migrant. While originating in the realm of refugee law, this faulty distinction has quickly expanded to all migration law, miring all those migrating in the spectacle of illegality.

To show how this dichotomy is depicted visually, this chapter analyses images of refugees in graphic novels and comics released by the Australian Department of Immigration and Border Protection (ADIBP) and the United Nations Relief and Works Agency for Palestine Refugees in the Near East (UNRWA). The ADIBP graphic novel illustrates how bogusness is portrayed in a way that strips the refugee of the experiences of persecution, war or other conflict. Conversely, genuineness is vividly contrasted with bogusness and focused on images of trauma and suffering as shown by the example of the UNRWA comic drawn by Andy Warner (UNRWA 2014). While this comic promotes humanitarian aid and delivering help to existing refugee camps, its sole focus is ultimate and inhumane suffering and an absolute lack of hope, one of the tropes of genuineness.

As this chapter shows, the most problematic consequence of the dichotomy between these two figures relies on the state of absolute hopelessness to justify the need for refugee protection. That dichotomy, as this chapter will illustrate, sets a priori visual frames separating the 'deserving' from the 'undeserving' in terms of the hospitality of the host state and fixes the image of the victim as the only figure worthy of such hospitality. In reference to existing refugee law literature, I will illustrate firstly why this dichotomy is false and secondly how it affects refugees and migrants more generally. I will then move to analysis of the frames, the gaze point and the field of appearance in order to show how the figures used in both graphic novels employ this dichotomy to deter the 'undeserving' and muster commitment to the 'deserving'.

The 'Genuine' and the 'Bogus' and Proving 'Genuineness'

While, as we have seen, the figures of the refugee and the migrant are legally distinct, it is nearly impossible to distinguish between them in contemporary migration debates, whether verbal or visual. The 'genuine' refugee, the 'illegal' migrant and the 'bogus' asylum seeker are often used interchangeably, confounded, and referred to in debates about both refugee protection and immigration more generally (Feller 2006; Crawley and Sklep200 2018). Even the EU free movement debate, as demonstrated during Brexit campaigns (Dennison and Geddes 2018), has been prone to discussion of 'immigrants' as a generality, regardless of their migration background or their reasons for staying. In popular discourse, the legal condition of a well-founded fear of persecution – the core legal requirement of the Refugee Convention – seems frequently to have been omitted in favour of a discussion on economic motivations for migration and construing economic migration as a threat (Innes 2010). While economic motivations for migration have inspired migratory movements across borders throughout human history, the 1990s focus on the so-called economic migrant has sprouted the debate on 'bogusness' and 'genuineness' (Pratt and Valverde 2002). Prompted by the climate of suspicion towards refugees from the Global South, the figure of the 'bogus' asylum seeker has been used to describe those suspected to have left the Global South in pursuit of economic benefit (Scheel and Squire 2014, p. 8). As Stephan Scheel and Vicki Squire (ibid.) have demonstrated, voluntariness versus involuntariness in terms of characterising migration has been replaced with an entirely new dynamic of 'genuineness' versus 'bogusness'. This dynamic has gradually developed into using 'genuineness' as a synonym for the 'legality' of a migrant and 'bogusness' as a synonym for their 'illegality' (Feller 2006; Scheel and Squire 2014; Karakayali and Rigo 2010). As Tazreena Sajjad (2018) has demonstrated, the categories of 'legal', 'illegal', 'migrant', 'refugee' or 'undocumented' migrant have all been in constant flux ever since and have oscillated around perceptions of 'worthiness' and 'unworthiness'. Irregular migrants have gradually been increasingly 'illegalised' (De Genova and Roy 2020) and refugees have increasingly often struggled to prove their 'genuineness' by having to demonstrate increasingly extraordinary forms of persecution (Ticktin 2011). As Miriam Ticktin has persuasively demonstrated, ordinary persecution has often failed to be perceived as genuine, even when meeting the required legal threshold for protection. As a result, refugee law has adopted additional clauses, such as the illness clause (ibid., p. 90), to elicit compassion that allows extending refugee protection.

With ever-greater suspicion towards the refugee, and the increasing impossibility of qualifying for protection, an inherent suspicion of every person crossing borders has crept into the legal discourse on refugees and other people crossing borders. This suspicion has gradually contributed to legal changes justifying ever-harsher forms of treatment of those arriving in irregular ways. These forms have increasingly come to resemble forms of criminal law enforcement at the border (Stumpf 2013; Franko 2019) and further forms of control when within the territory. Illegality as a criterion has grown exponentially (Dauvergne 2008; De Genova 2014), slowly affecting both those in course of migrating and those who have already migrated. Multiple migration regimes have developed character tests (Rimmer 2008) that can affect any already-resident migrant at any time and brand them as 'illegal' as a result of the ever-wider list of behaviours classified as problematic and characteristic of those 'unworthy' of being welcome. The never-ceasing suspicion of illegality has developed into the threat of removal from the country at any point in the future.

With the exponential growth of 'illegality', refugees – many of whom meet the convention requirements – have been under increased pressure to prove their genuineness (Innes 2010). The frame of the undeserving character of those classified as 'bogus' migrants has, on the other hand, turned into suspicion of all refugees (ibid., p. 464). Magdalena Kmak (2015) has persuasively argued that ever since the appearance of the 'bogus' refugee, a somewhat 'schizophrenic' approach has been applied to the motivations underpinning migration. While in the case of some 'desirable' migrants, such as highly specialised experts, economic motivations are rewarded, in the case of refugees and irregular migrants any sign of economic motivation is thoroughly punished. The ideal refugee, as Kmak goes on to demonstrate, must display no agency and has to remain passive in order to be recognised as 'genuine' (ibid., p. 405). The genuine refugee is most often displayed as a subject at the mercy of Western states and their institutions. 'Genuineness' is characterised by patient waiting in a long 'queue' in a refugee camp where refugees are 'rescued' with no external help and without paying anybody for their passage. In reality, though, such a path for seeking refugee status is close to being fictional, partly because of the narrowness of legal entry criteria that force genuine protection seekers to resort to an array of illegal practices in order to secure their flight and protection-seeking (Papadopoulou 2004). Whether in regard to entry (ibid.), obtaining illegal documents or paying for passage (Rowe and O'Brien 2014, p. 184), the reality of passage forces many protection seekers to resort to a combination of illegal practices to escape and be able to claim asylum. Yet the idea of passiveness is pervasive in legal, visual and political discourse. This passiveness has often been characterised as genuineness or authenticity and is synonymous with displaying no autonomy:

> It is not just that those who have breached our borders are 'bad' refugees; they lack an essential quality of genuineness, assessed not by reference not to the law, but to their conduct and its moral dimension (the 'good/bad' refugee) – and thus, implicitly, to their exercise of an authentic moral agency, one informed by cultural values of the queue, of the patience and passivity 'genuine' refugees are expected to demonstrate. Lack of 'genuineness' thus perversely becomes a function of 'inauthenticity', allowing us to deny the irregular arrival recognition of their manifest or latent autonomy. (Zagor 2015, p. 380)

In other words, to escape the often-deadly equating of 'bogusness' and 'illegality', Western states have 'romanticised' passiveness (Zagor 2015, p. 381) and created a binary between the passive, authentic refugee subject and the bogus, 'illegal' migrant who displays symptoms of moral agency – a quality not attributed to those whom we deem worthy of protection. An ideal protection subject is far from a subject equal to us whom we are able to picture as similar to ourselves. An ideal protection subject who can escape the deadly label of bogusness is instead someone whom refugee law and migration discourse have imagined as the ideal victim – one who is passive, who does not take matters into their own hands, and who waits patiently to be 'saved' (ibid.). This ideal victim is someone who can perform a 'template of authenticity' (Murray 2016; Sarı 2020) rather than be seen as finding their own way to resolve the situation (Schindel 2017). This dynamic is palpable as much in visual as in legal representations of refugees and irregular migrants (Bleiker et al. 2013; Fawzy 2019). Those who do not succeed in meeting the narrow criteria set in the templates of authenticity are instead staged in what Nicholas De Genova (2013) calls 'the spectacle of illegality'. Due to the presumed economic motivations of the 'bogus', the spectacle of illegality evaluates everyone in relation to their place in the market and their desirability in market relations. As De Genova reminds us, 'the phantasm of exclusion is essential to that essentially political process of labour subordination' (ibid., p. 1190).

The 'undesirable' migrant – whether seen as 'economic' or 'illegal' or simply failing to present a narrative deemed 'genuine' – is subsequently put in an uneven position vis-à-vis the host. The 'unworthy' migrant is faced with hostility and treated as a threat to the host, seen as an unwanted guest that does not deserve the ethical approach of hospitality and needs to be denied entry at all costs.

Victimhood, Suffering and the Host Gaze

The frame of bogusness is strongly linked to the understanding of refugee law as a form of charitable Western hospitality (Malkki 1995, 1996). This charitable hospitality links back to the narrative of the victim and saviour circulating not only in refugee law but also more generally in the Western conception of human rights. Rights are often exported to other regions seen as 'barbaric' and thus 'unfit' to protect their own citizens (Mutua 2001; Žižek 2011). Similarly, as a form of Western charity extended to those in need, legal refuge is often imagined to be a form of charity owed only to those who fit into the figure of the absolute victim. In Anna Szörényi's words:

> This cultural image is attached to a familiar narrative structure that can be summarised as 'persecution–flight–asylum–resettlement'. The narrative also comes with other characters: the 'persecutors' who deprive the refugee-victims of their human rights and home, and the 'rescuers' who (if the refugees are lucky) save them. In the standard refugee story, or at least the one with a happy ending, the host nation in which the suffering protagonist resettles plays the role of benevolent rescuer and peaceful haven. Indeed,

because a refugee is by definition a person in need of a nation, the characters of refugee-victim and rescuing nation fit together neatly, to the extent that when refugees turn out not to be helpless, the host nation is understood to lose all commitment to benevolence. The equation of 'refugee' with 'victim' is so strong that as soon as those aspiring refugees known as 'asylum seekers' express any agency, any determination to act on their behalf, they seem to undermine their own asylum applications. (Szörényi 2012, p. 300)

Equating 'genuine' refugeehood with victimhood is also prominent in visual representations of refugees. Rania Fawzy (2019) observes that refugee portrayals oscillate between the figures of the 'tragic refugee' and the 'unwanted invader'; while the invader is portrayed in ways inviting negative judgement, the tragic refugee is portrayed in ways in which their suffering and often death are worthy of appreciation. Portrayals of suffering are valorised as 'genuine' and protection-worthy while all others are mired in suspicion. Estela Schindel has further illustrated that 'the asylum regime creates a context in which the qualification for international protection relies on extreme helplessness, and consecrates the moral superiority of the victim above the political or social actor' (2017, p. 21). This helplessness required to qualify as an ideal victim of suffering is quite different from the portrayal of Western experiences of suffering. While Westerners are always individualised, the ideal refugee victim is portrayed as an anonymous and symbolic figure experiencing extreme suffering for the entire refugee cause (Szörényi 2004, p. 13). This image of suffering is also a voyeuristic depiction, which distinguishes between forms of suffering that are not imaginable in the West and other 'authentic' suffering that could 'not happen here' (ibid., p. 20). The search for an 'authentic' victim is thus a deeply orientalised search for depiction of unimaginable barbarity, which can satisfy the Western viewer's disgust with those among the 'uncivilised' who need to be saved and given the charity of 'civilised' Western refuge. Which suffering counts as 'authentic' and which does not is, as Honni van Rijswijk reminds us, a consequence of political, legal and visual discourse responsible for producing recognition of bodily pain (2018, p. 193). This fetishisation of suffering in the host gaze impacts on who and under what conditions can be considered a 'genuine' refugee and who will be deemed a 'bogus' asylum seeker. The host gaze seeks 'authentic suffering' to justify the saviour narrative and allow the deserving migrant to cross the narrow threshold of hospitality.

The suffering-oriented host gaze narrows the scope of ethical duty owed to the refugee. It is not an egalitarian recognition of ethical duty towards the other as envisioned by Emmanuel Levinas, but instead a quasi-ethical approach which is concerned with the host's own authority to protect itself from an unwanted visitor. The suffering-oriented gaze frames hospitality in a way which, as Jacques Derrida warned, 'always in some way does the opposite of what it pretends to do and immobilizes itself on the threshold of itself' (Derrida 2000, p. 14). The search for authentic suffering and 'genuineness' on the part of the refugee creates an a priori distance and hierarchy between host and guest which can hardly be overcome. The need to 'perform' particular refugee stories in order to be recognised as a welcome victim whom the host can save and protect results in a master–saviour hierarchy instead of ethics-based equality. This imagery of the 'genuine' refugee who needs to be 'saved' creates an ethical slip. The refugee is always under suspicion of 'inviting' themselves to the host state, unless they wait patiently for an invitation from a host appalled by the barbarity of the suffering the refugee has experienced. Any stranger who does not meet the host-created criteria for 'authentic' suffering is seen as someone with a suspicious motive, not a guest but an unwanted hostile arrival who can be deemed 'illegal' and kept outside the ever-narrowing threshold of the border.

The dichotomy between bogusness and genuineness not only exploits the motivations of those arriving, but also expects patience and voluntary submission to proving suffering, which the host may deem 'authentic' or 'inauthentic' depending on their own imagery of what it means to be a victim, and what kind of a victim is worth saving. The logic of *hostipitality*, controlled by the host gaze's fetish of refugee victimhood and pain, requires justifications of refuge that are appeasing to the host. When suffering is not recognised as familiar to the host gaze, it can be seen as 'inauthentic'. The analysis of the two comics below shows how these frames of 'bogusness' and 'genuineness' are visually presented and controlled through the frame, the gaze point and the field of appearance.

The Frames of 'Bogusness' in Comics

When it comes to the imagery of 'bogusness' of an asylum seeker, the idea can be captured in several ways. As shown below, the visual frames employed for this purpose often rely on a depiction of hidden or threatening motivations on the part of the subjects. While capturing thoughts and motivations in an image is not easy, one visual form is particularly suited for the purpose. Comic strips and graphic novels form an expansive and interdisciplinary epistemological landscape. More specifically, the medium of the comic strip can bring insight to the relationships between multiple 'ways of knowing' (the visual, the rational, the aesthetic, the textual) that are no longer confined by the walls of epistemological certainty. The format of a comic book is particularly well suited in terms of communicating messages about the authenticity of refugees and can likewise imply what the justifiable law's response ought to be. Comics and graphic novels are powerful visual media that 'resort to exploration of the boundaries between word and image, and between rational and aesthetic ways of knowing' (Giddens 2012, p. 87). As such, they can create a form of strong affect and influence the underpinnings of law. The same applies to the figure of the refugee. A comic, thanks to its approach, can speak powerfully to rational and emotional ways of knowing who a 'real' refugee is.

In 2014, the Australian government released a graphic novel as part of the 'NO WAY' campaign accompanying 'Operation Sovereign Borders', which was aimed at stopping asylum-seeking arrivals in Australia. The core of the operation was the principle of turning back boats and preventing them from arriving in Australian maritime territory, effectively depriving on-board asylum seekers of the possibility to lodge an asylum claim in Australian territory. The graphic novel accompanying this campaign depicted and focused almost exclusively on the alleged 'bogusness' of asylum seekers arriving by boat. As a medium suited for passing and controlling both the visuality and the messaging behind the frames, the graphic novel is a potent medium capable of manipulating the presumptions already underpinning the host gaze. The implied voices and motivations of the alleged refugees presented in the novel and their misrepresented motivations are all the more important in light of the Australian government's policies strictly and systematically controlling the voices of actual refugees (Humphrey 2018, p. 458). While allegedly addressed to refugees and published in numerous languages, including Dari and Pashto, the novel includes multiple depictions reinforcing the host's perception of 'bogusness' and includes very few visual clues familiar to those fleeing persecution.

The entire graphic novel focuses on the process of 'buying' a passage by boat (Figure 3.1). The main protagonist of the novel, an alleged Hazara refugee, buys an illegal (under Australian law) passage by boat. The term 'boat refugees', or more crudely 'boat people', has for decades been used as a term describing irregular migration to Australia (Rowe and O'Brien 2014, p. 172). With Prime Minister John Howard introducing the 'Pacific Solution' in response to the so-called Tampa crisis in 2001, Australia became focused on deterring all arrivals by boat. The Pacific Solution normalised the – legally controversial – off-shore processing, disabling the standard process of arriving in a territory and claiming asylum therein (Peyser 2002). Arriving 'by boat' has become synonymous with deception, stealth and crime, and the term 'illegal' used to categorise those arriving by boat catalysed the fear of asylum-seekers as potentially dangerous outlaws disrupting Australia's rule-governed society (Devetak 2004, pp. 105–6). Eventually, as shown in the following chapter focusing on the figure of the 'illegal', the boat itself has acquired an affective negative significance in Australia.

Figure 3.1 NO WAY graphic novel, Australian Department of Immigration and Border Protection, 2014

To link this allegedly illegal mode of arrival to the motivations of the people on board, the comic focuses on facial expressions that suggest 'bogus' intentions. The refugee in this comic is not presented as a person suffering persecution, war or conflict. Indeed, in one of the frames of this comic the alleged 'bogus' refugee is a man working as a car mechanic in a somewhat orientalised but not dangerous place. What motivates him to board the boat is the image of a better life in Australia. We see the somewhat colonial imagery here reinforcing the contrast between a dirty 'savage' migrant working in a dusty place and the image of a clean, 'saviour' country, presumably Australia, with clean streets and big shops. The colonial undertones paint the figure of the typical 'bogus' asylum seeker from the Global South, seeking a better life in a clean, enlightened and morally superior Western state. To convey thoughts of migrating for economic reasons, the graphic novel uses thought bubbles, commonly used in comic book aesthetics, to unveil thoughts and motivations. The agency of *homo oeconomicus* taking matters into their own hands is spread across several pages. The main protagonist of the graphic novel dreams of and subsequently follows 'illegal' steps in boarding the boat

Figure 3.2 NO WAY graphic novel, Australian Department of Immigration and Border Protection, 2014

to Australia. The economic dream depicted here is supported by this 'bogus' migrant's entire family who put together their savings to pay for the migrant's passage by boat (Figure 3.1). As van Rijswijk succinctly puts it:

> The graphic novel tells the story of the 'economic' refugee who chooses to suffer for potential gain and fails. The first image shows a poor family with a young son. The parents dream of a brighter future for their son, and approach someone – presumably a 'people smuggler' – telling him of their dream. A 'thought bubble' appears above father's head, picturing a bright, wealthy city (Perth). (Van Rijswijk 2018, p. 199; see Figure 3.2)

The recurring thought bubbles invite viewers to examine the hidden motivations of the 'bogus' asylum seeker, as do the close frames depicting the refugee's eyes and cutting away the rest of the context. Focus on the eyes, but not the face, prevents any form of ethical looking. The host gaze obscures the circumstances and cuts away the face, focusing on the suspicion of what is lurking behind the 'bogus' asylum seeker's eyes. The viewer is supposed to second guess what refugees arriving by boat are thinking and question their intentions. The frames' focus on the eyes – the metaphorical window to the soul – does not encourage the viewer's ethical encounter with fellow human beings in need of help (Figure 3.3). Quite the contrary – it invites the spectator to examine the illegal thoughts in the heads of those depicted. The focus on thoughts reinforces the assumption that 'boat people' are not

Figure 3.3 NO WAY graphic novel, Australian Department of Immigration and Border Protection, 2014

'authentic', they are not 'real refugees', because they hide their true thoughts and intentions. The gaze point used here is that of omnipotence and ability to read the thoughts of the guest and thus look at the 'truth' behind boat arrivals. Judgement on those arriving is already presupposed in the frame, in the thought bubbles and in the life-like colours that attempt to represent this depiction as the 'reality'. The embedded suspicion over the motivations of the guest aims at triggering resistance in the host. When the guest is suspected of harbouring illegal intentions, the host can narrow the threshold of hospitality or shut the door entirely to keep their home 'safe'. When such a fear dominates the encounter with the guest, hospitality turns into hostility and refusal and criminalisation of entry.

Naturally the 2014 graphic novel conflates bogusness and illegality – the two closely related categorisations of refugees – in an alleged attempt to warn those wishing to arrive by boat. This warning comes with the promise of suffering inflicted by the Australian government in the process of intercepting the ship, placing refugees in detention. This promise in no uncertain terms communicates a vision of despair and suffering (van Rijswijk 2018, p. 200).

The message directed at anyone thinking of buying a passage by boat is the certainty of detention, pain and anguish. Despite this claim of deterrence and the clear promise of cruelty towards those cast as 'bogus', the message contained in the graphic novel is hard to square with experiences of escaping persecution and death.

This is because, as Aaron Humphrey observes, while emotions are clear, the facts are obscured (Humphrey 2018, pp. 473–4). Naturally, no refugee escaping persecution could possibly find any familiarity with this narrative. Death, war, torture, ethnic cleansing, religious conflict or other circumstances triggering a well-founded fear of persecution are absent from the discursive and visual frame reinforcing the 'bogus' versus 'genuine' dichotomy. The real circumstances of the Hazaras, the group of refugees that this novel was aimed at, are conspicuously absent from the frame. What is present is the visual narrative immediately recognisable by the true audience of this novel – Australian viewers – who are invited to look at the familiar narrative of 'bogusness'. The viewer is invited to examine the motivations confirming the pre-existing conception that a bogus refugee is in fact an economic refugee who is in no danger at all, but instead 'chooses' to buy a passage by boat. The actual refugee in circumstances of terror and persecution is probably unlikely even to see this comic. But if they do, could the imagery of a 'bogus' refugee motivated by very different concerns even resonate with someone forced to flee? That is quite unlikely, but another audience – the one on shore – will find the depiction of 'boat people' in this imagery far more convincing. The story depicts a typical subject of 'bogus' asylum seeker discourse – an 'illegal' who tries to deceive the authorities by hiding their true and solely economic motivation. No genuineness can feature in this strip because, to maintain the criminalisation of boat arrivals, the frame must rely on this dichotomous and simplistic narrative. The frame is necessary to convince the true spectators – the Australian audience – that the draconian Australian boat turn-backs and offshore processing law denying settlement in Australia are both legally unproblematic and necessary. The remainder of the comic justifies this hostile response and gives the host, represented by the Australian government, power to become merciless and unwilling to negotiate the terms of the guest's arrival. It shows how the guest will be punished for their allegedly illegal intentions. The peaceful life which the comic protagonist dreamt about will never happen. Instead, the authorities of the host will take them off the boat, search them and place them in guarded detention where they will suffer illness, mosquito bites and other misfortunes. While a person escaping persecution is unlikely to identify with this phantasm, the host can rest assured that their legal response is appropriate, justified and preventing the arrival of 'bogus' asylum seekers, who take their economic future into their own hands.

The 'Authentic' Suffering of the Genuine

While the Australian graphic novel legitimises the hostile response of the state by reinforcing the figure of the 'bogus' asylum seeker, many other comics rely on the bogus–genuine dichotomy to depict and promote pleas of 'genuine' refugeehood. The comic drawn by Andy Warner for the UNRWA – a body specifically established in 1949 for the purpose of helping Palestinian refugees – is an example of visual art focusing on helping 'genuine' refugees in their struggle to find a peaceful place of refuge (UNRWA 2014). This comic was aimed at promoting humanitarian aid and delivering it to existing refugee camps run by the UNRWA. Although the comic's focus may appear narrow as it depicts a specific group of refugees, below I will show how it reinforces the image of a typical 'genuine' refugee, standing on the other side of the dichotomy discussed in this chapter.

The comic's protagonist is encapsulated in the figure of Hoda, a Palestinian refugee living in a refugee camp in Yarmouk. Despite being a teacher and wife of a prospering engineer in the refugee camp, Hoda is once more forced to leave by unexpected circumstances. While the comic does not go into the details of defining a refugee, such as flight from persecution due to belonging to a particular social group, it strongly exploits another dominant trope present in the refugee discourse, namely the absolute suffering and a feeling of utter hopelessness that cannot be remedied. It is in fact the suffering, not the persecution, that dominates the visual discourse. The comic is drawn in a specific set of colours: reds, yellows and occasional greens. The predominance of these colours exacerbates the heaviness of the refugee's reality; it is not a normal life, presented in a normal palette of colours. The contrast of green and red, exacerbated by the yellows, reinforces the contrasting reality of refugee life where the harshness of circumstances and the always temporary nature of refuge safety are intertwined. This depiction underlines the unpredictability and the suffering associated with the reality of refugee life. The reality is bleak and dark, and oscillates between being safe and being on the run – the only two conditions in which a 'genuine' refugee is imagined to exist. The contrast between the two is sharp and their reality can change at any point; safety can be taken away in the blink of an eye and disappear in the rising smoke captured in one of the frames. A refugee, in other words, is a person without choices, a person at the mercy of constantly changing circumstances, hiding from bombs and raids and fumes. The refugee, like Hoda here, is always at the mercy of someone else: whether it is the mercy of other human beings or the mercy of humanitarian aid or the UNRWA as shown in this comic, the refugee constantly requires help. The 'genuineness' depicted here relies on showing not a person who chooses to go, but a person who is mercilessly thrown from one place to another. The 'genuine' refugee, as we have been reminded before, cannot choose to leave; if they did, they would be suspected of being 'bogus'. They must instead 'adhere to an authentic moral imperative of inaction and passivity which would have seen them stay in the camps' (Zagor 2015, p. 380). Warner's comic, despite promoting help for refugees, powerfully reinforces the host's narrative of genuineness. Refugees cannot choose to fight for their cause by picking up their things and perhaps paying for passage to a safe place. Quite the contrary, a genuine refugee is at the mercy of others who will receive them after they have suffered enough. Genuineness requires protection to be delivered as a saving charity extended by safe havens and organisations such as the UNRWA. Genuineness equals unimaginable suffering and an unimaginable state of hopelessness encapsulated in one powerful slogan featured in the first frame of this artwork: 'There is no future, there is no hope.'

Turning to the frame and the gaze, these are aimed both at reinforcing imagined 'genuineness' and at generating an ethical response. Unlike the previous comic, the majority of the frames include faces of suffering, not merely a narrow focus on the eyes and thought bubbles that would suggest any intentions whatsoever. Quite the contrary, a 'genuine' refugee has no intentions, just bare emotions that are hard to contain due to the surrounding circumstances, which generate tears of desperation. This is particularly true in the frame focusing on the figure of a crying girl. The child, her hopelessness and her tears, her clearly present PTSD are encouraging an ethical response from the viewer. They are appeasing the saviour instinct and prompt the host to act hospitably. As shown in the chapter focusing on the figure of an innocent, the figure of a suffering child as an innocent is often contrasted with a 'bogus' refugee, due to the perceived limited autonomy and choices that children have. This is extremely difficult to portray when it comes to adults, but Warner's comic attempts to achieve this by showing the deserving as victims of absolute suffering, something that refugee law has evolved to expect from those who are to meet the criteria of protection established in the Refugee Convention.

The gaze in Warner's comic is coming from the outside, from the one who is responsible for delivering the charity of human rights to the people depicted. Hence the audience, just as with the graphic novel reinforcing the notion of 'bogusness', is external. The gaze once more speaks to the host, this time reinforcing their role as a powerful saviour. The comic once more is directed not at the refugee, who will often be unable to demonstrate their suffering in accordance with the expectation seen here, but at the one providing the charity of refuge. The comic is directed to the host who is supposed to welcome the stranger without suspicion but instead with open arms.

Legal Responses to Bogusness and the Rising Legal Threshold of Genuineness

When law is faced with a subject that can never be autonomous and must always be a victim of suffering, the response of the legal system is often to resort to a progressive tightening of migration rules to make sure that only the 'deserving' receive protection and only 'genuine' suffering is relieved. Others, who are suspected of being undeserving or who have not demonstrated absolute suffering, cannot be welcomed with hospitality but must be rejected with unmistakable hostility. They are typically those who fit the figure of the 'bogus' asylum seeker and subsequently end up classified as 'illegal'. To prevent a welcome for suspected 'bogus' asylum seekers, migration laws have often actively discouraged people crossing borders from seeking asylum. This happens either through deterrence mechanisms or through more novel solutions, such as boat turn-backs, which make it impossible to claim asylum in the territory of the host state. The Australian policy of boat turn-backs is an excellent example of resorting to ever more progressive deterrence mechanisms.

The Australian comic analysed in this chapter accompanied one of the many steps in the slowly introduced Pacific Solution, the precursor to Operation Sovereign Borders, preventing all asylum seekers arriving by boat from claiming asylum in Australia. The first steps in the progressive tightening of legislation implementing the Refugee Convention were introduced on 27 September 2001. These amendments to the Commonwealth Migration Act 1958, introducing Excision from the Migration Zone, followed as a form of response to the so-called Tampa affair. This incident in August 2001 involved Australian troops intervening in an attempt by the Norwegian freighter MV *Tampa* to rescue asylum seekers stranded on an Indonesian fishing boat off Christmas Island (Fox 2010). As a response to the perception of an 'unmanageable' number of arrivals, the legislation introduced the excision zone, essentially designating certain parts of Australian territory to be 'excised' from Australia's migration zone (Vogl 2015, p. 114). After its suspension in 2007, the policy was reintroduced in August 2012 and became the 'backbone' of the government's response to those arriving by boat (ibid., p. 128). Upon its return in 2012, the policy introduced offshore processing of all asylum applications. The policy became even stricter with the launch of Operation Sovereign Borders, under which so-called boat arrivals were met with a 'zero tolerance' policy. This was accompanied by further amendments to the Migration Act introducing the term 'illegal maritime arrivals', in contrast to the term 'irregular maritime arrivals' as previously applied. This new term relied strongly on the perception of the 'bogusness' and illegality of refugees who arrived by boat. The change of vocabulary shifted the perception of life-threatening escape from persecution and reduced it to a criminal act, contrasted with a fictional and orderly line of patient 'regular arrivals' (Hodge 2015, p. 126). This perception was strongly supported by the visuals analysed here, including the graphic novel illustrated in this chapter and the posters illustrated in the following chapter. The policy of offshore detention, the legal follow-up to this classification, will be further analysed when scrutinising the posters and their relationship with the figure of an 'illegal'.

But even in those jurisdictions that do not deny asylum seekers the right to lodge an asylum claim, the law constantly reinforces the requirement of victimhood, hopelessness and destitution. In recent years, European legislatures, beginning with Denmark, introduced new laws allowing for making those already vulnerable even more destitute. In 2015 the Danish Parliament passed Bill no. 87, including an amendment to the Aliens Act, which gave police the power to search and confiscate the property of asylum seekers. The alleged justification was a 'contribution' to expenses associated with their stay in Denmark (Hartmann and Tan 2016). While previously the police were allowed to search asylum seekers in order to find items or documents that could be of importance when processing asylum claims, Bill no. 87 expanded that power and allowed the police to confiscate property including assets above DKK10,000 (ibid.). Despite attempts to strip asylum seekers of their movable property, seeking asylum from persecution does not legally deprive asylum seekers of the right to property whether movable or immovable. The Refugee Convention specifically requires states to respect asylum seekers' property rights based on the principle of non-discrimination in comparison with aliens generally. This applies to both movable and immovable property. It states specifically:

> The Contracting States shall accord to a refugee treatment as favourable as possible and, in any event, not less favourable than that accorded to aliens generally in the same circumstances, as regards the acquisition of movable and immovable property and other rights pertaining thereto, and to leases and other contracts relating to movable and immovable property. (Refugee Convention, Article 13)

Yet the dynamic of bogusness and genuineness remains so strongly connected with the requirement of victimhood and economic deprivation that stripping those arriving of valuables they bring with them has succeeded in passing as a law in several jurisdictions. A refugee subject owning property appears irreconcilable with the image of those who in our ethical and legal imagination 'genuinely' seek asylum. Having property means they have not suffered 'enough', which in turn automatically equates asylum seekers with suspicious economic – and thus 'bogus' – arrivals. The host used to equating genuineness with deprivation, hopelessness and destitution cannot imagine any form of economic savviness as part of genuineness. Quite the contrary, possessions signal bogusness, and depriving those seeking refuge from whatever they brought with them does not appear unethical. The image of the refugee as a completely destitute legal subject at the mercy of the host is often the only image that the host is ready to accept. The progressively strengthened requirement of victimhood deprives the host of the ability to imagine an asylum seeker as a person just like them, instead of a person at their mercy.

Conclusions

The dynamic of genuineness and bogusness has long been observed in refugee law. As illustrated in this chapter, the visual media often perpetuate these two dominant narratives, equating 'genuineness' with hopelessness and absolute suffering and 'bogusness' with the slightest hint of economic acumen. Only the absolutely deprived are seen as genuine refugees while all others are presented as autonomous persons taking matters into their own hands instead of letting circumstances dictate their fate. Those implicated in the suspicion of bogusness are often precluded from seeking asylum and immediately implicated in the presumption of 'illegality'.

As underlined by Kmak (2015), these two figures of the 'bogus' asylum seeker and the 'genuine' refugee are two faces of the same – albeit fragmented – refugee subject. In reality, they are deeply inter-related and inter-dependent. While the figure deemed genuine must fit into the passive and victimised narrative, those who in any way 'fail' to fit into this narrative cannot be recognised as refugees, even though their need for protection might have a genuine basis (ibid.). In visual depictions, this dynamic often invites the host to look into the motivations of those who arrive in circumstances the host believes are 'illegal' and to feel empathy and the need to extend charity only to those shown to suffer beyond all hope. As a result of this narrative, imaging genuineness is severely limited and affects the lives of those with a genuine basis for protection. This often means inability to arrive and claim protection, or the infliction of further forms of deprivation on those already deprived.

References

Bleiker, Roland, David Campbell, Emma Hutchison and Xzarina Nicholson. 'The visual dehumanisation of refugees.' *Australian Journal of Political Science* 48, no. 4 (2013): 398–416.
Convention Relating to the Status of Refugees (Refugee Convention), 28 July 1951, United Nations, Treaty Series, vol. 189. UN General Assembly.

Crawley, Heaven, and Dimitris Skleparis. 'Refugees, migrants, neither, both: Categorical fetishism and the politics of bounding in Europe's "migration crisis".' *Journal of Ethnic and Migration Studies* 44, no. 1 (2018): 48–64.

Dauvergne, Catherine. *Making People Illegal: What Globalization Means for Migration and Law*. Cambridge University Press, 2008.

De Genova, Nicholas. 'Spectacles of migrant "illegality": The scene of exclusion, the obscene of inclusion.' *Ethnic and Racial Studies* 36, no. 7 (2013): 1180–98.

De Genova, Nicholas. 'Immigration reform and the production of migrant illegality.' In *Constructing Immigrant 'Illegality': Critiques, Experiences, and Responses*, ed. Cecilia Menjívar and Daniel Kanstroom, pp. 37–62. Cambridge University Press, 2014.

De Genova, Nicholas, and Ananya Roy. 'Practices of illegalisation.' *Antipode* 52, no. 2 (2020): 352–64.

Dennison, James, and Andrew Geddes. 'Brexit and the perils of "Europeanised" migration.' *Journal of European Public Policy* 25, no. 8 (2018): 1137–53.

Derrida, Jacques. 'Hostipitality.' *Angelaki: Journal of Theoretical Humanities* 5, no. 3 (2000): 3–18.

Devetak, Richard. 'In fear of refugees: The politics of border protection in Australia.' *The International Journal of Human Rights* 8, no. 1 (2004): 101–9.

Fawzy, Rania Magdi. 'Aestheticizing suffering: Evaluative stance in Pulitzer-winning photos of refugees' crisis in Europe.' *Discourse, Context & Media* 28 (2019): 69–78.

Feller, Erika. 'Asylum, migration and refugee protection: Realities, myths and the promise of things to come.' *International Journal of Refugee Law* 18, no. 3–4 (2006): 509–36.

Fox, Peter D. 'International asylum and boat people: The Tampa Affair and Australia's "Pacific Solution".' *Maryland Journal of International Law* 25 (2010): 356–73.

Franko, Katja. *The Crimmigrant Other: Migration and Penal Power*. Routledge, 2019.

Giddens, Thomas. 'Comics, law, and aesthetics: Towards the use of graphic fiction in legal studies.' *Law and Humanities* 6, no. 1 (2012): 85–109.

Hartmann, Jacques, and Nikolas Feith Tan, 'The Danish law on seizing asylum seekers' assets.' Blog of the *European Journal of International Law*, 27 January 2016, available at: <https://www.ejiltalk.org/the-danish-law-on-seizing-asylum-seekers-assets/>, last accessed 12 May 2021.

Hodge, Paul. 'A grievable life? The criminalisation and securing of asylum seeker bodies in the "violent frames" of Australia's Operation Sovereign Borders.' *Geoforum* 58 (2015): 122–31.

Humphrey, Aaron. 'Emotion and secrecy in Australian asylum-seeker comics: The politics of visual style.' *International Journal of Cultural Studies* 21, no. 5 (2018): 457–85.

Innes, Alexandria J. 'When the threatened become the threat: The construction of asylum seekers in British media narratives.' *International Relations* 24, no. 4 (2010): 456–77.

Karakayali, Serhat, and Enrica Rigo. 'Mapping the European space of circulation.' In *The Deportation Regime: Sovereignty, Space, and the Freedom of Movement*, ed. Nicholas De Genova and Nathalie Peutz, pp. 123–44. Duke University Press, 2010.

Kmak, Magdalena. 'Between citizen and bogus asylum seeker: Management of migration in the EU through the technology of morality.' *Social Identities* 21, no. 4 (2015): 395–409.

Malkki, Liisa H. 'Refugees and exile: From "refugee studies" to the national order of things.' *Annual Review of Anthropology* 24, no. 1 (1995): 495–523.

Malkki, Liisa H. 'Speechless emissaries: Refugees, humanitarianism, and dehistoricization.' *Cultural Anthropology* 11, no. 3 (1996): 377–404.

Murray, David A. B. 'Queer forms: Producing documentation in sexual orientation refugee cases.' *Anthropological Quarterly* 89, no. 2 (2016): 465–84.

Mutua, Makau. 'Savages, victims, and saviors: The metaphor of human rights.' *Harvard International Law Journal* 42 (2001): 201–45.

Papadopoulou, Aspasia. 'Smuggling into Europe: Transit migrants in Greece.' *Journal of Refugee Studies* 17, no. 2 (2004): 167–84.

Peyser, Emily C. '"Pacific Solution"? The sinking right to seek asylum in Australia.' *Washington International Law Journal* 11, no. 2 (2002): 431–60.

Pratt, Anna, and Mariana Valverde. 'From deserving victims to "masters of confusion": Redefining refugees in the 1990s.' *Canadian Journal of Sociology/Cahiers canadiens de sociologie* 27, no. 2 (2002): 135–61.

Rimmer, Susan Harris. 'The dangers of character tests under Australian migration laws.' *ISIL Year Book of International Humanitarian and Refugee Law* 8 (2008): 207.

Rowe, Elizabeth, and Erin O'Brien. '"Genuine" refugees or illegitimate "boat people": Political constructions of asylum seekers and refugees in the Malaysia Deal debate.' *Australian Journal of Social Issues* 49, no. 2 (2014): 171–93.

Sajjad, Tazreena. 'What's in a name? "Refugees", "migrants" and the politics of labelling.' *Race & Class* 60, no. 2 (2018): 40–62.

Sarı, Elif. 'Lesbian refugees in transit: The making of authenticity and legitimacy in Turkey.' *Journal of Lesbian Studies* 24, no. 2 (2020): 140–58.

Scheel, Stephan, and Vicki Squire. 'Forced migrants as illegal migrants.' In *The Oxford Handbook of Refugee and Forced Migration Studies*, ed. Elena Fiddian-Qasmiyeh, Gil Loescher, Katy Long and Nando Sigona, pp. 188–99. Oxford University Press, 2014.

Schindel, Estela. 'Migrants and refugees on the frontiers of Europe: The legitimacy of suffering, bare life, and paradoxical agency.' *Revista de Estudios Sociales* 59 (2017): 16–29.

Stumpf, Juliet. 'The process is the punishment in crimmigration law.' In *The Borders of Punishment: Migration, Citizenship, and Social Exclusion*, ed. Katja Franko Aas and Mary Bosworth, pp. 58–75. Oxford University Press, 2013.

Szörényi, Anna. 'The face of suffering in Afghanistan: Identity, authenticity and technology in the search for the representative refugee.' *Australian Feminist Law Journal* 21, no. 1 (2004): 1–21.

Szörényi, Anna. '"Two dreams in one bedroom": Narrating victimhood and perpetration in Australian refugee history.' *Australian Feminist Studies* 27, no. 73 (2012): 297–306.

Ticktin, Miriam. *Casualties of Care: Immigration and the Politics of Humanitarianism in France*. University of California Press, 2011.

United Nations Relief and Works Agency for Palestine Refugees in the Near East (UNRWA) (UNRWA). *Palestine Refugees in Syria: An Andy Warner Comic.*

UNRWA, 2014, available at: <https://www.unrwa.org/sites/default/files/unrwa_comic_web_final_800px.gif>, last accessed 21 September 2023.

van Rijswijk, Honni. 'From sentimentality to sadism: Visual genres of asylum seeking.' In *Law and the Visual: Representations, Technologies, Critique*, ed. Desmond Manderson, pp. 189–209. University of Toronto Press, 2018.

Vogl, Anthea. 'Over the borderline: A critical inquiry into the geography of territorial excision and the securitisation of the Australian border.' *University of New South Wales Law Journal* 38, no. 1 (2015): 114–45.

Zagor, Matthew. 'The struggle of autonomy and authenticity: Framing the savage refugee.' *Social Identities* 21, no. 4 (2015): 373–94.

Žižek, Slavoj. *Against Human Rights*. Routledge, 2011.

4

The Spectre of the Invisible Illegal

Introduction

The figure of the bogus asylum seeker has become a catalyst for another powerful figure dominating migration law discourses, namely the figure of the 'illegal'. As shown earlier, illegality as a legal category has been proliferating and fear of the illegal underpins regulation of migration across the globe. In this chapter I will illustrate that the illegal is such a vague and ephemeral figure that its appearance in a visual field is often conveyed in the form of the invisibility of an actual migrant. The preference for invisibility is dictated by the uncertainties related to who the illegal is, how they cross borders, and what qualities the illegal represents. But more importantly, as a form of ghostly figure that threatens the viewer with the unknown but powerful illegality of arrival (Gozdecka 2020), their invisibility can result in a more powerful affective and legal response from the viewer.

I will use the Australian 'NO WAY' campaign and the British 'Go Home' campaign to show how those implicitly 'depicted' without a physical appearance become 'ghostly' and threatening entities that can be disciplined, detained and deported with the help of the law. In addition, I will focus on the image from the gallery of US Customs and Border Protection. The visual campaigns and resources analysed below have been used by authorities to directly target migrants and refugees in order to deter them from crossing the border, staying in the territory or claiming asylum and to warn them of harsh treatment on the other side of the border. They have used invisibility as a tool to convey 'fraudulence' on the part of a migrant or asylum seeker rather than seeking to depict them as a specific person. This chapter examines how invisibility reinforces the local population's anxiety about the imagined arrival of 'illegals'. I will also show that visual invisibility often translates into invisibility within the legal system and leads to long-term or permanent inability to access the justice system. I argue that images which use invisibility rely on what I call the 'spectrality' of the migrant (Gozdecka 2020). This spectrality leaves the migrant out of the frame because as an unknown spectre they can powerfully affect the legal imagery of the community. If they are seen as a spectre before our very eyes, the ethical distance between the viewer and the migrant would not be as big as in spectropolitical play with invisibility. Spectropolitics uses invisibility to expel some subjects beyond the compass of compassion and to recast the boundaries of what is permissible in migration regulation. I will argue that being cast as an invisible illegal in a spectropolitical play with images leads to justifying the harshest of migration control measures and perpetuates the political invisibility of those crossing borders irregularly.

Why Illegality Often Remains Invisible

As a legal category, illegality is a broad term with which we describe things, events and persons that stand outside the permissible boundaries of the law. Due to its very breadth, illegality itself is an ephemeral and somewhat ghostly category. Illegality is frequently subject to quick changes (Barak 1990) and can often be unpredictable. Across time and space, multiple jurisdictions have outlawed a range of activities that after a certain time may appear bizarre. From selling alcohol, through participation in suffragette protests to murder, the historical catalogue of outlawed activities is extremely broad and diverse. Illegality can creep in quickly and affect life as we know it overnight. The spread of the COVID-19 pandemic has shown how quickly activities such as walking, hosting friends or travelling beyond the certain parameter of the home can become punishably illegal. Despite its quickly changing nature, illegality is normally targeted by criminal law and penal punishment ranging from fines to much harsher methods using legal violence such as deprivation of liberty or – in some jurisdictions – even life. Criminal law and its penal power exemplify the preserving force of the law in a Derridean understanding of the law as inherently laden with force and violence (Derrida 1990). Despite the harsh consequences that it may bring, illegality is often difficult to portray due to its quickly changing and somewhat ephemeral nature. While law does not change overnight, it evolves constantly and what was illegal 100 years ago may be legal today, and vice versa. Its obvious links with criminal law, however, often result in the use of criminal law imagery or depictions of law enforcement officers or methods as visual proxies for illegality (Gozdecka 2020). Sometimes, all that is necessary to visually capture illegality is the shadow of the law enforcement figure, the figure of a judge or a depiction of some other symbol related to the workings of the justice system.

In terms of migration law, however, illegality has a rather recent history. While it did occasionally appear in the past, its use prior to the 1990s was rare. Its prevalence took hold in the 1990s as a result of the emerging discourse of 'bogus' and 'genuine' asylum seekers (Scheel and Squire 2014) analysed in the previous chapter. As a result of the exponential growth of those classified as 'illegal', the term quickly became attached to those crossing borders as a result of forced migration (ibid.) or those who arrive without proper paperwork (Menjívar and Kanstroom 2014). As shown below, 'illegality' has also been used in particular contexts to describe those crossing borders in a particular manner, such as those arriving by boats in Australia. Illegality in migration law and its expanding boundaries are a result of the workings of the governance of borders (Dowling and Inda 2013) and ever-increasingly restrictive migration regulation. Illegality's ephemeral nature and quickly changing rules result in migrants often shifting between legality and illegality. Due to the problematic character of illegality, its slippery nature and the power it has over those arriving, migration law scholarship has avoided using the term to describe any modes of arrival or any type of migrant (Scheel and Squire 2014). Use of the term 'illegal' results in unavoidable and often irreversible consequences for those arriving. As 'illegals', migrants cease being seen as individuals worthy of ethics or compassion (Hugo 2002) but instead are seen simply as criminals deserving application of criminal law methods despite their having committed no crime: criminal punishment without trial and with no legal recourse (Stumpf 2006). Although migration law was traditionally closer to foreign policy than criminal law, the situation changed in the mid-1990s when the discourse of bogusness resulted in outlawing a range of issues related to arrival and migrant status. Juliet Stumpf reminds us that the merger between migration law and criminal law became possible because both are essentially connected with the process of deciding who does and who does not belong:

> Both criminal and immigration law are, at their core, systems of inclusion and exclusion. They are similarly designed to determine whether and how to include individuals as members of society or exclude them from it. Both create insiders and outsiders. Both are designed to create distinct categories of people – innocent versus guilty, admitted versus excluded or, as some say, 'legal' versus 'illegal.' Viewed in that light, perhaps it is not surprising that these two areas of law have become entwined. (Stumpf 2006, p. 380)

The label of 'illegality' is easy to apply to those depicted as 'other' and results in effectively removing those classified in that way from 'worthiness' status (Stumpf 2006, p. 419). Rather than referring to people as 'irregular' or 'unregistered', the pejorative tag of 'illegal' removes any ethical concerns over the use of harsh forms of legal violence involved in criminal law response. 'Illegality' as a word obscures diverse individual circumstances and encompasses anyone from a visa overstayer, through a *sans-papiers*, to those planning their arrival in a particular manner. Depending on the jurisdiction and local migration laws, illegality can be used as a blanket label to convey an extremely wide variety of circumstances. Once the word 'illegality' appears in the discourse, a migrant effectively ceases to be seen as a fellow human being deserving an ethical response and compassion but instead is put in the position of a fraudster that can and should be targeted with the greatest severity of the law (ibid., p. 395). For these reasons, law enforcement rationalises that it is justified to use more severe methods in targeting 'illegality' than would be the case if instead we spoke of 'irregularity'.

The 'Illegal' Migrant as a Haunting Spectre

The discourse of illegality can be tricky to achieve visually. As shown below, in order to convey the same ethical distance between the figure of the illegal and the viewer, visual campaigns often erase the migrant from the visual field and leave them out of the frame altogether. Instead of seeing the migrant as such, images focusing on migrant illegality often use symbols and images related either to criminality more broadly or to symbols used in specific discussions of migrant illegality. These visual depictions use the symbols themselves as a proxy for migrant illegality, while the actual person they talk about remains outside the frame, cutting the field of appearance. Removing the migrant from the depiction while retaining the symbol of migrant 'illegality' results in haunting the viewer. The words 'ghostly', 'spectrality' and 'haunting' to describe the absence of migrants and refugees from certain images dealing with migration may appear an awkward choice. Yet, as I show below, spectrality – or a haunting-like or ghost-like absence of certain figures from the field of appearance – is often a powerfully emotive method of construing an image and can impact viewers more than a direct depiction. Using the frame to exclude the subject – but retaining its implied ghost-like presence – limits the viewer's ethical response and promotes a refocus of attention from 'ethics' to 'fears'.

Spectrality, apparitions, haunting and ghosts are not entirely absent from theoretical exploration. Jacques Derrida used the vocabulary related to ghostly apparitions in his account of the current position of Marxist thought in *Specters of Marx* (2012). For Derrida, history is informed by what has been, so that it is full of ghostly entities from the past that always 'haunt' the future. This gives history continuity with no before and no after, because the ghosts of history always threaten to return. While Derrida's ghost has little to do with image, its central feature is important for understanding the role of the spectre in spectropolitics. The ghost in Derrida's account is always there, threatening to come, but is never quite here: almost like justice, it is always yet to come (Zacharias 2007). The spectre leaves the imprint of the past both on the present and on the future and its power lies precisely in its invisibility. What cannot be seen is terrifying and fills the spectator with fear:

> Is it the difference between a past world – for which the specter represented a coming threat – and a present world, today, where the specter would represent a threat that some would like to believe is past and whose return it would be necessary again, once again in the future, to conjure away? (Derrida 2012, p. 48)

It is precisely the connection of the spectre with fear that translates into pictorial invisibility. While different from Derrida's ghost, the spectre remains central in terms of instigating the feeling of fear. This fear can be of different kinds. While for Derrida it is the disruption of history, for others the spectre signifies fear of all kinds of disruption of the status quo. Charles Garoian insists that hauntology has a meaning pertaining to the broader interplay between ontology and hauntology or, in other words, being and not being (2002, p. 114). He emphasises that hauntology also applies to the field of appearance, because an image, or the artist behind the image, invites the viewer to consider those who are absent from a work of art (ibid., p. 116). It is those who are invisible that haunt the artwork or even a piece of writing (ibid.). The power of the spectre lies precisely in its invisibility. Julian Wolfreys (2004) insists that hauntology applies to a broader political spectrum altogether because haunting imposes on us an impossible attentiveness. Where spectres lurk, no closure is possible – a lack of closure that applies as much to the arts as to politics (ibid.). Spectrality thus uses the interplay of visibility and invisibility to capture the existence of ghosts that haunt the field of appearance. Removal of the subject from the field of appearance does not entirely remove them from the image. As an invisible spectre, the subject continues to haunt the image by their absence rather than their presence. As such, the one who is removed from the image continues to control the viewer's perception of the image. As a ghost, the subject haunts the viewer's imagination by different means, such as symbols that remind the viewer of the subject, whose presence becomes non-ontological but hauntological and continues to underpin the image even when the viewer cannot directly see them. Nicholas Mirzoeff (2002) reminds us that this hauntological interplay between visibility and invisibility has a different effect on different viewers. While some will see the ghost clearly, others will not. While some will hear the ghost speak, others will not. The ghost is thus always on the spectrum of visibility and invisibility (ibid., p. 239) and is always a threatening and disruptive presence.

The Hauntological Invisibility of the Migrant

When we examine the figure of a migrant, the spectral interplay between visibility and invisibility can be highly intricate, often generating and perpetuating a feeling of fear in the observer. This fear becomes amplified when the figure of the migrant becomes irreversibly connected with criminality and illegality. The mere spectre of the migrant becomes synonymous with a danger to the community, something that the viewer is warned about in the hope they will react by keeping the danger away. Throughout the centuries, the spectre that threatens a community has often been used to characterise the existence of the subaltern and the various efforts to exclude otherness as an imagined threat to the norm. Whether colonial (Cameron 2008), racial (Saleh-Hanna 2015) or migratory (Papailias 2019), the spectre 'has many names in many languages: diasporists, exiles, queers, migrants, gypsies, refugees, Tutsis, Palestinians' (Mirzoeff 2002, p. 239).

Jo Maddern (2008, p. 378) has illustrated that migrants in particular have typically been seen as ghostly entities in what she calls 'spectropolitics'. Spectropolitics is the politics of choosing who can and cannot speak or, as I would like to argue, who can and cannot be seen or even who can and cannot be included. Spectropolitics involves the use of ghostly entities without showing them as subject and often have the objective of terrifying the viewer by the presence of a ghost-like subject. The presence of the spectre of the 'Other', be it Jew, Muslim or migrant, is often construed as a threat and, as Esther Romeyn (2014, p. 89) argues, the logic of haunting is employed to show the 'excess of heterogeneity' and to protect the community from the perceived 'excess'. In the imagery of migration and in subsequent migration regulation, spectropolitics uses the haunting presence of the arriving migrant as a threat to the community of the nation state. In the visual realm, the ghost of the arrival often does not feature in the frame but their presence is always felt on the horizon, pending the arrival's sudden appearance.

According to Penelope Papailias, the use of spectropolitics in relation to migrants forms a part of the nexus between biopolitics and necropolitics and the global power relations that dispossess subjects (2019, p. 1053). In this absolute control over life and death, spectropolitics excludes the migrant from humanness (ibid., p. 1056). In the realm of images, this translates into removal from the field of appearance. When such absolute dispossession happens with the aid of images that generate fear, the legal response that follows is legitimised, no matter how exceptional or extreme a form it may take. Without the presence of the spectre, the law's harsh and often unprecedented response would be difficult to consider as just, and as a result its legitimacy would be in question. But it is precisely the invisibility of the migrant as a human being – and use of the migrant presence as an invisible but threatening ghost – that disestablishes the ethical response of the viewer, replacing it with a fearful response to a haunting spectre. Below, I will analyse the spectropolitics of portraying ghost-like figures of migrants and their exclusionary effects.

British, Australian and American Spectropolitical Imagery of the Migrant

The ever-expanding nature of 'illegality' in migration law allows for diverse use of spectropolitical visualisations of allegedly 'bogus' and 'illegal' migrants. Spectropolitics can best reach their goal of exclusion when the migrant is presented as an invisible presence on the horizon rather than a real person with a face, story, family and a range of reasons for having migrated in a specific manner. The migrant's illegality can be depicted in various more or less sophisticated ways symbolising the threatening status of the migrant who, however, remains hidden from view.

Visually conveying migrant 'illegality' can simply use symbolism directly associated with criminality and the workings of penal law. Prominent recent examples of spectropolitical play with the notion of illegality are the 'Go Home' vans targeting migrants considered 'illegal' in the UK (Jones et al. 2017). This campaign, using connotations with law enforcement symbols, was released prior to the Brexit vote and relied on the image of handcuffs as a proxy to conveying the notion of 'illegality'. The campaign called upon those who might be in the UK illegally to turn themselves in to receive assistance with voluntary return. The vans featured a fairly straightforward image of handcuffs and bold printed letters: 'In the UK illegally?' accompanied by a text box below, informing potential 'illegals' that if they fail to 'go home', they face arrest (for an image, see Hattenstone 2018). The implication of the depiction was relatively straightforward, namely that the shadow of the law will reach those hiding from it. Ghosts living in the shadow of the law will face its enforcing power as symbolised by handcuffs. The presence of the migrant is only implied but is nonetheless powerful. While we see no migrants in the posters, once again we are invited to question their motivations. If 'genuine', migrants should be honest enough to either be in the territory legally or turn themselves in, in response to the campaign. If, however, ghostly and 'illegal' migrants hide from the authorities, they can be legitimately targeted with criminal law methods such as deprivation of liberty. The spectropolitical play with the invisibility of the potentially 'illegal' ghost of a migrant reaches its ultimate exclusionary potential by implying that all migrants have the potential to be 'illegal' and harbour intentions to stay illegally. The viewer may not see them, but is informed that the ghosts will be found and punished.

Conflating the image of handcuffs, a method of restraint used during criminal arrests, with words such as 'go home' paints the shadow of an 'illegal' migrant ghost that may be hiding anywhere in the community and may have arrived in any number of ways. Since the migrant does not appear in the picture, their migrant status itself becomes mired in suspicion. This justifies any potential arrest unless the migrant's presence is proven 'legal', because the viewer's image of the migrant remains open to interpretation. The absence of migrants is replaced by their powerful ghostly haunting of the viewer with the potential of migrant illegality. That illegality, as an invisible threat to the community, powerfully justifies the use of crimmigration methods to target the threatening ghost of migrants allegedly hiding from the law.

Similar imagery where illegality is captured by a proxy of a law enforcement figure features on the website of US Customs and Border Protection. Alongside other images in the same gallery featuring people subjected to prison-like confinement, search procedures and officers pointing guns at them, the spectropolitical imagery of the illegal migrant is captured in the image in Figure 4.1, which is accompanied by the caption 'US Border Patrol agent scans the area into Mexico with binoculars looking for illegal immigrants potentially staging to enter the United States'. The image and caption embody the fact of migrant invisibility and specifically refer to the ghostly potentiality of an illegal spectre. Illegality is conveyed by a proxy of a Border Patrol agent in full uniform. The frame focuses on a fragment of a river, which neatly embodies the idea of the border, which – in this image – is not merely administrative but instead a 'natural' formation. The 'naturalness' of the border is presented from the viewpoint of US soil, inviting US citizens to step into the shoes of the agent. The migrant, while invisible, is on the other hand presented as a constant danger lurking on the horizon, able to appear anytime, anywhere in the wilderness, and threatening to cross the river and the border. The urgency of the threat is captured in the implied 'necessity' to be constantly on the watch. The viewer is not invited even to consider the arrival as a fellow human being, likely harrowed by a life-threatening journey. The invisibility of the migrant is used here in a far more sophisticated manner and combines the imagery of illegality, invisibility and an emphasis on the constant nature of the alleged threat that the spectre poses to the border. The viewer is reminded that there is 'no rest' in awaiting the spectre, because the spectre has an unlimited potential to materialise on the other side of the border. The migrant spectre requires vigilant watch and prevention to keep them on the outside. The image conveys a sense of urgency and embodies a deep ethical gap between the host and the arrival. After all, the spectre cannot be welcome, ever, under any circumstances. Instead, it must be stopped at all costs, no matter the amount of hours required to patrol the wilderness

THE SPECTRE OF THE INVISIBLE ILLEGAL   81

Figure 4.1 US Customs and Border Protection gallery, along US borders, 2016

pictured on the other side of the river. There is no option for hospitality here. The hostility extends to any potential ghost spotted on the other side of the river.

A similar play with invisibility features in the visual material supporting the 2014 NO WAY campaign released by the Australian Department of Immigration and Border Protection. In addition to the previously analysed graphic novel, the campaign – supported by posters and a video – was aimed at promoting 'Operation Sovereign Borders', which in turn aimed at stopping refugee boats from arriving in Australian territorial waters and returning them to offshore detention centres on Manus Island and Nauru (van Berlo 2015).

The NO WAY campaign embodied in the posters contains a sophisticated balancing of the elements of visibility and invisibility in a spectropolitical play intending to remove refugees not only from the compass of compassion, but also from the normal workings of established legal mechanisms. To justify the legally problematic goal of turning back boats, the NO WAY posters remove the refugee from the frame, focusing solely on the image of the boat, which is singled out for affective significance to Australians, standing as a proxy for the visually missing ghost – an allegedly 'illegal' asylum seeker who can violently emerge on the horizon by boat (Figure 4.2). For a long time, Australian political discourse had reframed arrival by boat into a synonym for deception, stealth, crime (McKay et al. 2011) and allegedly 'illegal' jumping

Figure 4.2 NO WAY poster, Australian Department of Immigration and Border Protection, 2014

of the legally non-existent refugee queue (Gelber 2003). Equating the boat with illegality was a gradual process that began during the Howard era, which famously focused on 'deciding who is and is not welcome'. In the past two decades, boat arrivals, mired in the discourse of 'illegality', have been subject to multiple changes in the law. Starting from framing them as 'irregular arrivals' in the 1958 Migration Act (Rowe and O'Brien 2013), those arriving by boat eventually became 'illegal' arrivals (Rowe and O'Brien 2014) in more recent legislation. The boat itself became a symbol permanently associated with illegality. The existence of the fixed symbol of the boat not only effaced the unique experiences of those on board but also irrevocably connected those on board with criminality. This focus erased the criteria recognised as grounds for protection under the Refugee Convention. Persecution and meeting legal protection criteria have been effectively removed from all political and legal discourse, leading to the gradual delegalisation of boat arrivals. Refugees on board boats arriving in Australian territorial waters became 'illegal' by default, regardless of whether they were genuine refugees under the Refugee Convention.

Visually, this sinister turn was captured by none other than the boat in the NO WAY posters employed by the Australian authorities. An image completely removing the refugee from the field of appearance reminded the viewer about the affective association between the boat and 'illegality', at the same time amplifying the viewer's fear of the spectre appearing on the horizon. The hauntological presence of so-called boat arrivals was achieved through the use of a broad frame focusing on the open sea. Amidst raging waves and the dark field of appearance, the viewer is faced with a small boat struggling in the violent ocean waters. Looking at the poster, the viewer cannot see any refugees but is instead invited to focus on the symbolic image signifying 'illegality': the boat itself. The people on board are deprived of their personality, their humanity, their individuality, their legal history, and instead become a part of the boat (Poon 2018). In addition to the small vessel struggling against the waves, the viewer encounters the disproportionately large printed words: 'NO WAY; YOU WILL NOT MAKE AUSTRALIA HOME'. The gaze point is from the Australian shore, looking outwards towards the ocean and thus prompting the viewer to respond emotionally by metaphorically protecting the shore from the 'illegality' of the boat. This positioning and the erasure of the people on board make it abundantly clear that the message in the picture is not directed to the alleged recipients of the message – the people on board – but instead to viewers in Australia watching the fate of the haunting boat from the safe distance of the Australian shore. As Justine Poon observes, when watching the image:

> The real becomes abstract and the abstract becomes real in a substitution that completely removes the asylum seeker bodies from frame, overwriting them for the only body who is permitted at and who rules over the maritime border space – the sovereign. (Poon 2018, p. 114)

In their message supporting the legally problematic treatment of asylum seekers, the images perform a metonymical trick using the image of a boat as a substitute for an asylum seeker (Poon 2018, p. 114). Removal by this metonymy of the affective connection with refugees as human beings completes the spectropolitical act of exclusion. The invisibility of the refugee and replacing the refugee with the boat leads to an amplified fear of the invisible ghostly migrant and thence to a complete inability to truly imagine those on board as people. Desmond Manderson reminds us – in the context of quite another, but equally potent image of a boat – that what follows this disassociation is the impossibility of picturing that the people on board 'have families and communities that cherish their bodies and their memories' (2015, p. 286). The ethical connection between host and guest becomes fully disestablished, and a viewer seeing the boat from the perspective of an

Australian shore can easily justify the intervention of criminal justice methods in approaching threatening 'illegals'. After all, apparitions can materialise at any time, regardless of the distant, roaring waves on the horizon. The viewer haunted by the potentiality of 'illegals' on the distant horizon feels no ethical duty to extend hospitality but instead can easily legitimise harsh methods of returning the boats – a move that would be much harder to accept should the viewer look at the suffering faces of people instead (Galemba 2013). Looking at the boat presented through the spectropolitical frame imposed by the government (Poon 2018, p. 115) can easily also legitimise exclusion of those on board from the normal workings of the law. Stopping ghosts from appearing is only one part of the spectropolitical play with invisibility; the other is the use of offshore detention centres, which cease being seen as exceptional means and slowly become normalised as a new standard of treatment. When confronted with the apparition of the boat and the ghostly, invisible entities on board, the viewer slowly normalises these means because the question the images prompt is not whether the policy potentially contravenes international legal standards. Instead, spectropolitics achieves its fear-fuelled goal: creation of the invisible subject approaching from the broad frame of the horizon, prompting the viewer to ask, 'How can "illegals" be stopped?'

Out of Sight and Outside the Law

Spectropolitical representation is a powerful form of visual removal that can lead to political removal of the depicted subjects from the normal workings of the law. The previously analysed Australian Operation Sovereign Borders was an extension of the 'Pacific Solution', based on keeping refugees in offshore detention processing centres on Manus Island and Nauru. These centres were controlled by the Australian government and relied on a multitude of private contractors for security and other services (van Berlo 2015). The Pacific Solution, reinstated after a brief break in 2012 by the Labor government, originally assumed that the so-called Regional Processing Centres (RPCs) in Nauru and Papua New Guinea (PNG) would process applications and determine which refugees were owed protection. But Operation Sovereign Borders, with its focus on deterrence, changed all that. The backbone of this policy was a new principle insisting that no 'illegal maritime arrivals' – or in other words asylum seekers – arriving by boat could ever, under any circumstances, be resettled in Australia. Instead, if found to be genuine, those granted refugee protection would be resettled in third countries (ibid.). In practice, refugees detained in these centres were often unable to get assessed and were not permitted to leave for countries like New Zealand that offered them a welcome (Kampmark 2017, p. 58). This process was allowed only in 2022, nine years after some of those arriving were detained on Manus Island

and Nauru. During operation of the centres, refugees were not allowed communication with the outside world, and the government restricted access by journalists and visitors (Nethery and Holman 2016). The erasure of the ability to be heard completed the visual erasure. While several refugees lost their lives in the centres (Dehm 2021), release of details was strictly controlled. Eventually, when the centres in PNG were found to be illegal under domestic law by the PNG Constitutional Court (Dastyari and O'Sullivan 2016), Australia decided to open the centres without any legal processes, thus allowing refugees to be processed (Giannacopoulos and Loughnan 2020).

Today, despite slow resettlement in the United States and – more recently – New Zealand, some refugees still remain in legal limbo. They have been brought to Australian territory under medical evacuation laws, but remain in hotel detention often without resettlement options and without the possibility to obtain asylum in Australia (Ruddick 2021). Their detention can in principle continue indefinitely. Under a recently confirmed High Court interpretation of the Migration Act pertaining to detention of refugees, so-called unlawful citizens can be detained until their removal from Australian territory. If, however, removal is not possible, it is not illegal under Australian law to detain them indefinitely (*Commonwealth of Australia v AJL20*). The ghostly existent migrants and refugees are relegated to the workings of spectropolitics, which removes them from both the picture and the law and casts them not only as threatening ghosts, but also as ghosts who cannot access the realm of law reserved for those fully living. They become the epitome of Giorgio Agamben's 'homo sacer' (1998) – subjects so far outside the law that their existence is no longer ghostly in the image only but also within and between legal systems (Grewcock 2017; Dehm 2020). Invisible in domestic migration laws in the places where they are detained, not allowed to be recognised by places willing to host them, barred from accessing legal processes allowing for their recognition in Australia and detained potentially for the rest of their lives, those branded 'illegal' can become the ultimate spectres paying the price of the play with invisibility.

Conclusions

The interplay of visibility and invisibility in representations of migrants often controls the narrative surrounding their legal status. Spectropolitical exclusion in the field of appearance is capable of fusing invisibility and illegality, allowing for masterful manipulation of how the migrant is seen by the potential host. The migrant's hauntological presence and transformation into a threatening apparition of an 'illegal' migrant continues and further modifies the discourse of, on the one hand, genuine, hopeless and deprived refugees and, on the other, autonomous but 'illegal' bogus asylum seekers.

When spectropolitics fuses illegality and invisibility, the migrant as a threatening apparition can also become a ghost without a legal status. When barred from accessing legal recourse, the migrant becomes not only a ghost on the horizon of an image, but a legal spectre that the legal system needs to expel and protect the borders from. As an 'illegal' ghost, the migrant becomes a subject of crimmigration and can be effectively expelled outside the legal system but remain controlled by it with no legal recourse. Spectropolitical play with invisibility can turn into a sinister form of manipulating the aesthetic field of appearance. It removes the migrant from the picture precisely in order to disable the possibility of viewers standing face to face with the migrant as a person who is just like them. Spectropolitics fears such an encounter because it risks preventing viewers from switching off any ethical considerations. But when those considerations cease to operate, repressive migration laws no longer seem inhumane and instead are perceived as necessary. If viewers encountered migrants as people instead of as threatening ghosts, they could perhaps make no sense of the cruelty of the current migration regimes.

References

Agamben, Giorgio. *Homo Sacer: Sovereign Power and Bare Life*. Stanford University Press, 1998.

Barak, Gregg. 'Crime, criminology and human rights: Towards an understanding of state criminality.' *The Journal of Human Justice* 2, no. 1 (1990): 11–28.

Cameron, Emilie. 'Indigenous spectrality and the politics of postcolonial ghost stories.' *Cultural Geographies* 15, no. 3 (2008): 383–93.

Commonwealth of Australia v AJL20 [2021] HCA 2, High Court of Australia, 23 June 2021.

Dastyari, Azadeh, and Maria O'Sullivan. 'Not for export: The failure of Australia's extraterritorial processing regime in Papua New Guinea and the decision of the PNG Supreme Court in Namah (2016).' *Monash University Law Review* 42 (2016): 308–38.

Dehm, Sara. 'Outsourcing, responsibility and refugee claim-making in Australia's offshore detention regime.' In *Asylum for Sale: Profit and Protest in the Migration Industry*, ed. Siobhán McGuirk and Adrienne Pine, pp. 47–66. PM Press, 2020.

Dehm, Sara. 'International law at the border: Refugee deaths, the necropolitical state and sovereign accountability.' In *Routledge Handbook of International Law and the Humanities*, ed. Shane Chalmers and Sundhya Pahuja, pp. 341–56. Routledge, 2021.

Derrida, Jacques. *Specters of Marx: The State of the Debt, the Work of Mourning and the New International*. Routledge, 2012.

Dowling, Julie A., and Jonathan Xavier Inda, eds. *Governing Immigration through Crime: A Reader*. Stanford University Press, 2013.

Galemba, Rebecca B. 'Illegality and invisibility at margins and borders.' *PoLAR: Political and Legal Anthropology Review* 36, no. 2 (2013): 274–85.

Garoian, Charles R. 'The spectre of visual culture and the hauntology of collage.' In Charles R. Garoian and Yvonne M. Gaudelius, *Spectacle Pedagogy: Art, Politics, and Visual Culture*, pp. 99–118. State University of New York Press, 2002.

Gelber, Katharine. 'A fair queue? Australian public discourse on refugees and immigration.' *Journal of Australian Studies* 27, no. 77 (2003): 23–30.

Giannacopoulos, Maria, and Claire Loughnan. '"Closure" at Manus Island and carceral expansion in the open air prison.' *Globalizations* 17, no. 7 (2020): 1118–35.

Gozdecka, Dorota. 'Spectropolitics and invisibility of the migrant: On images that make people "illegal".' *Index Journal* 2 (2020): 195–212.

Grewcock, Michael. '"Our lives is in danger": Manus Island and the end of asylum.' *Race & Class* 59, no. 2 (2017): 70–89.

Hattenstone, Simon. 'Why was the scheme behind May's "Go Home" vans called Operation Vaken?' *The Guardian*, 26 April 2018, available at: <https://www.theguardian.com/commentisfree/2018/apr/26/theresa-may-go-home-vans-operation-vaken-ukip>, last accessed 21 September 2023.

Hugo, Graeme. 'From compassion to compliance? Trends in refugee and humanitarian migration in Australia.' *GeoJournal* 56, no. 1 (2002): 27–37.

Jones, Hannah, Yasmin Gunaratnam, Gargi Bhattacharyya and William Davies. *Go Home?: The Politics of Immigration Controversies*. Manchester University Press, 2017.

Kampmark, Binoy. 'Undermining NZ: Dutton's refugee ploy.' *Eureka Street* 27, no. 23 (2017): 58–60.

McKay, Fiona H., Samantha L. Thomas and R. Warwick Blood. '"Any one of these boat people could be a terrorist for all we know!" Media representations and public perceptions of "boat people" arrivals in Australia.' *Journalism* 12, no. 5 (2011): 607–26.

Maddern, Jo Frances. 'Spectres of migration and the ghosts of Ellis Island.' *Cultural Geographies* 15, no. 3 (2008): 359–81.

Manderson, Desmond. 'Bodies in the water: On reading images more sensibly.' *Law & Literature* 27, no. 2 (2015): 279–93.

Menjívar, Cecilia, and Daniel Kanstroom, eds. *Constructing Immigrant 'Illegality': Critiques, Experiences, and Responses*. Cambridge University Press, 2014.

Mirzoeff, Nicholas. 'Ghostwriting: Working out visual culture.' *Journal of Visual Culture* 1, no. 2 (2002): 239–54.

Nethery, Amy, and Rosa Holman. 'Secrecy and human rights abuse in Australia's offshore immigration detention centres.' *The International Journal of Human Rights* 20, no. 7 (2016): 1018–38.

Papailias, Penelope. '(Un)seeing dead refugee bodies: Mourning memes, spectropolitics, and the haunting of Europe.' *Media, Culture & Society* 41, no. 8 (2019): 1048–68.

Poon, Justine. 'How a body becomes a boat: The asylum seeker in law and images.' *Law & Literature* 30, no. 1 (2018): 105–21.

Romeyn, Esther. 'Anti-Semitism and Islamophobia: Spectropolitics and immigration.' *Theory, Culture & Society* 31, no. 6 (2014): 77–101.

Rowe, Elizabeth, and Erin O'Brien. 'Constructions of asylum seekers and refugees in Australian political discourse.' In *Crime, Justice and Social Democracy: Proceedings of the 2nd International Conference, Volume 1*, ed. Kelly Richards and Juan Tauri, pp. 173–81. Crime and Justice Research Centre, Queensland University of Technology, 2013.

Rowe, Elizabeth, and Erin O'Brien. '"Genuine" refugees or illegitimate "boat people": Political constructions of asylum seekers and refugees in the Malaysia Deal debate.' *Australian Journal of Social Issues* 49, no. 2 (2014): 171–93.

Ruddick, Baz. 'Refugee advocates protest outside Brisbane immigration centre to mark nine years of indefinite detention.' *ABC News*, 18 July 2021, available at: <https://www.abc.net.au/news/2021-07-18/qld-protesters-refugee-immigration-detention-bita-anniversary/100302690>, last accessed 11 September 2023.

Saleh-Hanna, Viviane. 'Black feminist hauntology: Rememory the ghosts of abolition?' *Champ pénal/Penal field* 12 (2015), available at: <https://doi.org/10.4000/champpenal.9168>, last accessed 25 September 2023.

Scheel, Stephan, and Vicki Squire. 'Forced migrants as illegal migrants.' In *The Oxford Handbook of Refugee and Forced Migration Studies*, ed. Elena Fiddian-Qasmiyeh, Gil Loescher, Katy Long and Nando Sigona, pp. 188–99. Oxford University Press, 2014.

Stumpf, Juliet. 'The crimmigration crisis: Immigrants, crime, and sovereign power.' *American University Law Review* 56, no. 2 (2006): 367–419.

van Berlo, Patrick. 'Australia's Operation Sovereign Borders: Discourse, power, and policy from a crimmigration perspective.' *Refugee Survey Quarterly* 34, no. 4 (2015): 75–104.

Wolfreys, Julian. *Occasional Deconstructions*. State University of New York Press, 2004.

Zacharias, Robert. '"And yet": Derrida on Benjamin's divine violence.' *Mosaic: A Journal for the Interdisciplinary Study of Literature* 40, no. 2 (2007): 103–16.

5

The Figure of the Absolute Other

Introduction

While 'bogusness' and 'illegality' underpin much of migration policy discourse, not all figures of the migrant focus on crossing borders. At times, guests already in the host territory experience the power of the host gaze, particularly when it is used in representations aiming at changing existing migration regulation. In this chapter I argue that such frames often operate in the host society for many years or sometimes even decades after the guest's arrival. These deeply entrenched frames through which the host views those recently settled govern the lives of migrants to a substantial degree. Those already living in their new countries are often subjected to the assumption that being a 'migrant' is not just a transitory state, but instead a long-lasting or even perpetual status. Indeed, in certain host societies migrant status can be 'inherited' to the point of speaking of first, second or even third 'generations' of migrants. The host gaze applied to those already living in societies often relies on the presumption of 'inherent' differences between host and guest. These differences are continuously emphasised by the use of the host gaze which reinforces a perception of irreconcilability and inability of those with a migrant background to ever 'truly' belong. The perception of such 'irreconcilable' and 'natural' cultural differences and perpetual exclusion from being a full member of society continue to impact the lives of those who have already settled in the territory and sometimes even those who were born there. As shown in this chapter, the figure of an absolute other is often harder to deconstruct as a migration-related figure but continues to be powerfully effective in controlling discussion of migration law and introducing changes limiting the rights of newer members of society.

In this chapter I will firstly analyse the perception of non-belonging and what I call 'inheriting' migrant status. Secondly, I will show how this perception informs and construes often racialised frames, and why such forms of racialisation are often complex and rely not only on visible physical differences but on a range of other factors used to racialise the newly arrived. And finally, I will illustrate how electoral campaigns employing these racialised figures can affect the host society to the point of introducing both restrictions on migration as well as limitations to the lives of those already living in the host society. I will primarily resort to the images used prior to two Swiss referenda concerning the famous minaret ban and the continuous campaign to limit migration.

Exclusion Within and Inheriting 'Migrant' Status

For many new members of our societies, the experience of exclusion does not stop at the border. Quite the contrary, most migrants in multiple societies – whether traditionally migrant or not – experience barriers to full belonging in their societies (Fangen et al. 2016). Beginning with the language, which is often the first barrier, migrants encounter numerous limitations on their rights or multiple forms of discrimination whether legal or extra-legal. Some of these limitations are imposed simply by the requirements of specific visas or legal provisions differentiating between citizens and denizens. These often affect migrants' right to work and make a living (Fleay and Hartley 2016) or limit their access to public health insurance (Geeraert 2018) and welfare (Bolderson 2011). In some countries, such as Australia, specific visa types require migrants to reside in specific regional municipalities for a specific amount of time before being able to move within the territory of the host state (Hugo 2008). For many citizens these types of limitation would be unthinkable or seen as severely restricting their rights and freedoms. But when it comes to migrants, as Ruth Wodak (2008) illustrates, exclusion is rationalised and built into the political discourse affecting the shape of laws passed by the legislatures of host states and governing the lives of those already arrived and settled. The relationship between host and guest, whether or not entrenched in domestic laws, is typically negotiated by 'knowledge, institutional roles, language, gender, ethnicity, social class or a combination of all of these factors' (ibid., p. 55). All these factors impact on how migrants are represented and viewed and what kind of figures of a migrant circulate in a given community. Few societies report successful migrant stories, and if such reporting occurs, it is usually presented as an exception to the overwhelmingly negative coverage (Gemi et al. 2013).

The typical journey of a migrant from their place of origin does not stop at the border but continues through a strenuous 'integration' process, which may or may not be finally rewarded with the grant of legal citizenship of their new country (Ersanilli and Koopmans 2010). Being awarded citizenship of the host state ought to end any legal discrimination between the original members of host societies and those who arrive as migrants. However, as research in multiple countries has illustrated, this is typically very far from reality. Not only do migrants report never feeling like 'full citizens' (Ghorashi and Vieten 2012), but their children and grandchildren often continue being treated differently from children of native citizens of their countries (Alba 2005). The distinction between 'us' and 'them' is not just a status affecting movement across the border but a form of power that host societies can hold over the descendants of migrants for multiple generations. While the children of new citizens and grandchildren of new citizens typically consider themselves as belonging, they continue to experience multiple barriers to full belonging which are typically no longer legal, but persist through the existence of stereotypes and internal barriers in education (Meier et al. 1989) and employment (Heath et al. 2008). Being the first person from a certain background to celebrate a significant achievement or hold a high function is akin to being the 'first woman' breaking a glass ceiling in her field. Very often this exclusion is strongly racialised, with children of non-white immigrants experiencing discrimination and exclusion longer than children of white immigrants (Kasinitz et al. 2009, p. 342). Inheriting migrant status is often also related to class and perceptions of poverty, even though these perceptions are frequently unfounded as children of immigrants in many societies often perform economically better than children with native backgrounds (ibid., p. 348). To be sure, second and third 'generation' migrants often do not speak the language of their parents' or grandparents' country of origin and have often never visited that country. Yet the lingering discourse about 'generations' of migrants is, as Shirin Hirsch (2019) reminds us, possible because of the very construction of migration law and discourse surrounding migration. Indeed, the very 'figure of a migrant' which is critically approached here, is none other than an extension of racial categorisation and an embedded form of discrimination. Hirsch emphasises that often migration studies – and almost without an exception legal studies of migration – tend to omit the somewhat inconvenient notion of racial discrimination, forgetting that simply speaking of the second generation is merely a veiled form of racism:

> Categories of the 'immigrant', 'race' or indeed 'ethnicity' can often appear to be neutral, descriptive categories because of the evasion of racism through which acts of discrimination disappear and then reappear camouflaged as the victim's alleged difference [...]. For example, there is a significant and burgeoning literature on the 'second generation' immigrant which almost completely ignores racism as shaping experience [...]. Much of this literature runs the risk of reifying the very categories we are seeking to deny; the 'figure of the immigrant' provides a key political and intellectual mechanism through which our thinking is held hostage and this can

be similarly reproduced in researching the children of immigrants [. . .].
(Hirsch 2019, p. 92)

Referring to David Goldberg, Ronit Lentin (2007) calls this lasting focus on the distinction between the host population and those arriving later a 'racial state' in which naturalism and historicism govern contemporary migration regimes (Goldberg 2002, p. 43) and the experience of belonging (Lentin 2007, p. 612). Lentin insists that regulation of immigration and asylum shape the existence of the nation's others. While naturalism conceived of 'natives' as pre-modern, historicism elevates Europeans or descendants of European conquerors over those considered 'primitive', namely indigenous populations and immigrants. The predominant role of historicism in our contemporary nation state ideology 'aims, through amalgamation and assimilation, to assist its racial others conceived as non-white to 'undo their uncivilized conditions' (ibid., p. 612). Borrowing Lentin's and Goldberg's theory, the 'figure of a migrant' is undoubtedly essential for the existence of a racial state. As such, it utilises processes of inclusion and exclusion that create and maintain the existence of an 'absolute other' contrasted with the perception of a historically 'paradigm' citizen. As I show below, this exclusion translates into the modes of gazing and is featured in representations that operate in maintenance of a 'racial state'. This gaze is capable of justifying multiple legal exclusions, which would not be possible if not for the existence of racialised otherness.

Complex Forms of Racism and Visual Othering

As shown by multiple studies (Balibar 2008; Ikuenobe 2011; Virtanen and Huddy 1998), the race and discrimination dynamic is not always as simple as skin colour. Particularly in European societies that often imagine themselves as free from traditional racism, racist exclusion exists in other more complex and veiled forms. Multiple scholars have shown that today's complexity of race dynamics may start with racialised exclusion of a migrant or those traditionally seen as subaltern on the basis of skin colour. But it does not stop there. It continues and finds its way deeply into discourses of ethnicity (May et al. 2004), culture (Brah et al. 1999) or religion (Hopkins 2007; Dunn et al. 2007). Whiteness thus often mutates and traverses beyond skin colour, and emanates into the image of culturally paradigm subjects (Gozdecka 2015) who belong 'naturally' and against whom belonging is measured. Those who do not fit the image of a paradigm subject can be excluded even without specific reference to race or skin colour. Quite the contrary, as I have shown elsewhere (ibid.), exclusion sometimes occurs in the very name of equality and non-discrimination, which can pervert the logic of who counts as included through the figure of the 'barbarian' endangering the values of the community (ibid.). These far more subtle and complex forms of racism traverse boundaries between citizen and non-citizen and allow for exclusion attached to those with specific characteristics, such as 'second' or 'third' generation 'migrants' and their cultural backgrounds, ethnicity or religion. In Lentin's words, the complexity of contemporary racism turns it into a mechanism of governance of the contemporary state where '[r]ace no longer serves one group against another, but becomes a "tool" of social conservatism; a racism that society practices against itself, a tool of constant purification and social normalization' (2007, p. 614). As a result of such complex racialisation, the images used in migration discourse frequently single out migrants and asylum seekers and present them as one coherent group (Rotas 2009, p. 77). Public discourse, on the other hand, appeals to values and emotions, frequently relying on such homogenising imagery blending migrants into an anonymous cohort which is then contrasted with the values, language, religion or culture of the host state.

The discourses of 'natural' belonging and exclusion due to being 'irreconcilably different' seep into visual representations of those whose presumptive differences are exploited for political purposes. These presumptions reinforce existing prejudices underpinned by the historicism of a 'racial state' and create new ones affecting either all migrants or only some targeted groups. When it comes to the racialised figure of a migrant, visual depictions more often than not rely on other distinctions between the historically 'paradigm' citizens and those considered migrant rather than appealing directly to race. Occasionally, however, the visual figures of migrants as the absolute other use directly racist depictions referring more or less to skin colour. Singled out with the help of such racialising frames, representations of migrant lives call for governing perceived difference with special – frequently corrective – measures. Across different contexts, public opinion often associates such imagery with 'common sense' without a deeper analysis of presumptions lying behind such representations. Certain ideas, however, which are implanted through such imagery, encourage thinking, feeling and deciding in a particular way (Entman 2007, p. 164). Images become a hidden ground of rhetoric (ibid.), capable of redefining cultural issues as a realm requiring control and protection through law and order (Lentin and Titley 2011, p. 202). Such representations subsequently become the subject of discussion in legal discourse as well. The community of a nation state is represented by reference to its 'cultural essence' and governed by the sense of protection of that essence. Invoking cultural essence – whether related to language, religion or culture – justifies demanding legal changes aimed at 'excluding and stratifying the less desirable' (ibid., p. 206). The images that trigger these desires reinforce existing cultural power by representing the community as a pre-given and unchangeable unity standing in vivid contrast to those arriving. Below, I analyse Swiss images illustrating how powerful the idea of a culturally homogenous community can be.

Swiss Visual Campaigns on Banning Minarets and Migration

In the past twelve years, Switzerland has been the scene of multiple referenda focusing on controlling otherness and migration. Each of these was accompanied by vivid visual campaigns calling upon citizens to vote in favour of the amendments. The two posters analysed here were circulated by the Swiss People's Party (SVP), a right-wing, anti-immigration party known to support curtailing migration and preserving Swiss 'cultural identity'. While the posters sponsored by the SVP can be considered extreme – indeed, one of them has even been classified as racist by a Swiss court (Miller 2017) – they are a perfect example of the use of the archetypal visual rhetoric of otherness. Visual representations of migrants in both posters selected here exemplify reliance on racial difference and cultural otherness and are parallel to multiple non-visual discourses promoted by extreme right-wing parties across Europe (Kallis 2013; Krzyżanowski 2020).

The first poster was circulated in 2009 before the referendum concerning the ban on building minarets in Switzerland. This poster relied on Islamophobic depictions of minarets as a cultural imposition on the 'local' population. The frame, field of appearance and the gazing point all amplify the discursive notion of absolute otherness and depict it as a threat 'incompatible' with the artificially homogenised notion of 'national identity'. The poster focuses on the Swiss flag pasted across a white background and allowing a bird's-eye view that typically stands for seeing the 'big picture' or the entire picture. The flag pierced by the minarets stands as a proxy for Swiss soil, encouraging the viewer to take a look at the big picture of what – according to the SVP – is happening with Switzerland and its cultural identity. The bird's-eye gaze point invites the perspective of a Swiss citizen, who presumably ought to respond to the image of the flag which is additionally synonymous with Swiss-ness. The redness of the flag corresponds with the redness of blood and serves as a metaphor for nationalistic belonging and national identity (Langlotz and Muazzin 2014, p. 118). Meanwhile the black colour of the piercing minarets symbolises the danger coming from the alleged cultural other. The contrast between black and red in the field of appearance strengthens this metaphor of the purity of blood, which can be tainted with the blackness of the alleged danger – a direct proxy not just for the exclusion of Islam, directly targeted by these posters, but by extension of race, too. The direct danger to this imagined cultural and national purity is depicted by the minarets themselves, which are piercing the flag and presented as bullet-like shapes (ibid.; Kallis 2013). Not only are the minarets presented in a stereotypical way related to Islamophobic rhetoric confounding Islam with 'terrorism', but they are also presented as an alien organism. The presumption of inheritance of otherness, entailed in this metaphor as the 'second' or 'third generation' of migrant descendants, is presented as 'dangerous' stealth organisms waiting to sprout. In the words of Andreas Langlotz and Danièle Muazzin:

> When reading the Swiss flag as an abstract depiction for soil, then the pointed minarets can be interpreted as mushroom-like organisms that have stealthily spread underneath the Swiss flag, that have made use of the rich and fruitful Swiss ground, and that have profited from its protection. (Langlotz and Muazzin 2014, p. 118)

The other in this picture is clearly outlined. It is the woman wearing a traditional chador who stands as a proxy for the alien who cannot be welcomed. The dehumanisation of the other is not atypical of racist depictions of otherness present in both newer and older forms of racism. Those presented as an absolute other are often seen as a 'virus', 'disease' or other form of inhuman menace to the host, who deserves to be protected from such danger. Dehumanisation of this type of course played a significant role in Nazi propaganda (Fackenheim 1985) and it plays an analogical role today. The point of dehumanising rhetoric is to create a deep wedge between the 'pure' and the 'impure' – in the case of the anti-minaret poster, the culturally Swiss and the other characterised by her faith and ability to bear children, who will become the 'second generation' migrants. The direct appeal to faith and indirect appeal to blood perpetuates the perception of inherited 'cultural purity' and the perceived natural difference of the migrant and those with a migrant background. Adherents of Islam are seen as perpetually 'alien' by virtue of blood and contrasted with the rest of the Swiss community regardless of how long they have been living in the territory. They are thus seen as impossible to accommodate not only immediately upon arrival but also in the future. The perception of absolute otherness behind this image perpetuates exclusion of the other for generations to come. The migrant seen as a multi-generational absolute other by blood, culture and religion signifies a threat not only because of her arrival. She is seen as a threat by the very virtue of her origin and the way she leads her life and practises her culture and religion. This alleged danger is then presented as something requiring increased control, including legal bans and limitations. The law is invoked as a means of stopping this imagined threat and protecting the host population from presumably dangerous invaders who were not returned at the border. The large bold letters, 'Yes, stop!', encourage expressing support for the proposed bans.

Aristotle Kallis has summarised this logic of the necessity to eliminate otherness in the following way:

> This mindset rests on the principle that both prosperity and identity are more or less finite resources that the majority group should have privileged access to. Sharing them would involve a loss, but failing to safeguard them altogether could pose a serious existential threat to the majority group in the long run. At the same time, the 'zero-sum' mentality extends to the symbolic capital of national society – its culture, traditions, embedded values and ways of life – that fosters social reflexes deriving from a national and, in some cases, 'European' racist/nativist mindset. Again, failure or reluctance to defend those values actively against 'others' is perceived as conducive to dilution, erosion and, eventually, even extinction. To accept this kind of diagnosis/negative prognosis constitutes the first necessary and crucial step towards subscribing to aspects of the accompanying prescription – that national society should be aggressively protected, that the flow of immigrants must be arrested or even reversed and that 'integration' devices deployed by the state towards ethnic/religious minorities must become more rigid and forceful. (Kallis 2013, p. 60)

As shown by Kallis (2013) and Hans-Georg Betz (2013), this logic has been highly successful, not only in the case of the Swiss referendum but across the continent where a wave of Islamophobic legal bans on facial covering, burkinis and other symbols associated with Islam spread rapidly. The visual and – as shown by Langlotz and Muazzin (2014) – verbal rhetoric has also been extraordinarily successful in the case of the Swiss referendum. In response to the campaign and rhetoric, a significant majority of 57 per cent of voters were in favour of introducing the ban on building minarets, all despite the fact that only four minarets existed in Switzerland when the initiative was launched (Wyler 2017). The image of absolute otherness, however, succeeded in creating the image of an unbridgeable cultural gap between the host society and freedom of worship for those identifying as Muslim.

The other image (Figure 5.1) used by the same party in 2016, and appearing multiple times in different campaigns since 2007 (Quito 2016), combined racialised rhetoric with the discourse of illegality. The 2016 poster was reused by the SVP prior to a referendum on expulsion without trial or appeal of foreigners who commit offences. In this poster, similarly to the one analysed above, the frame cuts out the Swiss flag but this time puts it side by side with a white field symbolising territories outside the Swiss border. The gaze is this time directly focused on the flag and reminiscent of looking at a map. The edge of the Swiss flag represents the border and the whiteness symbolises all other countries outside that border. The gaze is once more presented through

Figure 5.1 'More Security' poster campaign, the Swiss People's Party (SVP), 2007, Alamy

the prism of a – presumably – Swiss national who ought to respond to the presence of a black sheep that occupies half of the image and 'needs' to be kicked outside the national border by the white sheep that is presumably the rightful inhabitant of the territory symbolised by the Swiss flag. The mere size of the two sheep signifies a focus on 'full' capacity, another frequently used argument in anti-migration rhetoric (Wilkes et al. 2008). This presumption assumes finite resources and capacity to accommodate those arriving. This presumption is amplified by the sheer size of the two sheep, which are too big to both comfortably fit within the territory symbolised by the tiny Swiss flag on the left side of the image. The overwhelming size of the sheep in the field of appearance is aimed at triggering an affective response from the viewer to protect the endangered little country from 'overcrowding' as well as from the dangerous other encapsulated by the image of the black sheep. The multiple iterations of this image, which first appeared in 2007, included either three or one white sheep representing the majority kicking out the black sheep representing the minority. These images have been used in campaigns aimed at limiting the rights of foreigners. While the image has been defended by some viewers as a 'figure of speech' (Quito 2016), the racial parallels are impossible to miss. The whiteness of the sheep that 'rightfully' occupies Swiss territory is vividly contrasted with the blackness of the dangerous outsider who presumably is visibly different from the image of the stereotypical white inhabitant of Switzerland. While both figures are sheep, only the white one has the right to belong, while the black one hides its 'true' nature under its sheep-like exterior. Thus the migrant again does not naturally belong and their humanity is, for these racially tainted depictions, merely a disguise for some other, more sinister intent lurking within. These posters utilising whiteness versus blackness were ultimately a subject of interest for the UN Human Rights Council: the Special Rapporteur expressed concern about the campaign and their impact on spreading Islamophobia (Diène 2007, p. 11).

Subsequent Legal Changes

In the aftermath of the campaigns, Switzerland implemented legal changes seriously affecting the rights of migrants and nationals of foreign origin. An unprecedented ban on building minarets was imposed in 2009, introduced thanks to the institution of a 'popular initiative' (Wyler 2017). Under Swiss law, if a popular referendum initiative is accepted, the Federal Constitution is amended by including the text of the initiative. For such an initiative to be adopted, not only does the majority of the Swiss people have to vote in favour, but the initiative must be accepted by the majority of the cantons (ibid., p. 414). Despite the fact that popular initiatives hardly ever pass, the 2009 initiative was adopted with 57 per cent of votes in favour (ibid.). As a result, Article 72 regulating the relationship between Church and State was modified to the following wording:

1. The regulation of the relationship between the church and the state is the responsibility of the Cantons.
2. The Confederation and the Cantons may within the scope of their powers take measures to preserve public peace between the members of different religious communities.
3. The construction of minarets is prohibited.

While the 2016 referendum failed, a previous referendum of 2014 using similar anti-migrant visual rhetoric succeeded in passing an amendment requiring limits on migration, including migration from the EU. The referendum was called an 'initiative against mass immigration' (Milic 2015) and passed by a narrow margin. The result put Switzerland on a 'collision course' with the EU (Abu-Hayyeh et al. 2014), giving the government three years to implement the changes. The text of the constitution was amended to include Article 121a on 'Control of immigration':

1. Switzerland shall control the immigration of foreign nationals autonomously.
2. The number of residence permits for foreign nationals in Switzerland shall be restricted by annual quantitative limits and quotas. Quantitative limits apply to all permits issued under legislation on foreign nationals, including those related to asylum matters. The right to permanent residence, family reunification and social benefits may be restricted.
3. The annual quantitative limits and quotas for foreign nationals in gainful employment must be determined according to Switzerland's general economic interests, while giving priority to Swiss citizens; the limits and quotas must include cross-border commuters. The decisive criteria for granting residence permits are primarily an application from an employer, ability to integrate, and adequate, independent means of subsistence.
4. No international agreements may be concluded that breach this Article.
5. The law shall regulate the details.

As a result of long negotiations, the Swiss government finally reached an agreement with the EU in 2016 (Maurice 2016). Both laws have had severe effects on those presumed legally and culturally alien, raising serious questions on who controls access to rights and to what extent such rights can be limited. While the minaret ban attracted strong criticism from international human rights bodies (UN News 2009), there was relatively little criticism related to the changes limiting migration, despite such essentialising wording as 'ability to integrate' underpinning the constitutional amendment. This wording hints directly at perceived cultural difference and reinforces the presumption that the figure of the migrant is first and foremost an absolute other who can never truly fit the mould of cultural uniformity, yet whose rights can be perpetually regulated and severely limited while they attempt to do so.

Who 'Owns' the Right to Regulate Access to Rights?

The limitations on rights imposed by Switzerland pose two questions: who 'owns' the right to regulate rights; and how far can a democratic community exclude those it considers 'problematic' or 'alien'? I have explored this problem previously (Gozdecka 2015), observing that in spite of liberal theory claiming that each person has an equal claim to a full scheme of equal basic rights and liberties (Rawls 1999), exclusion from rights in liberal democracies is common and often perpetuated in the name of maintaining a consensus and the cultural core of the community. Liberal theory has grappled with the dilemma of rights in culturally diverse societies and for long insisted that rights are of vital importance for cultural accommodation. In Jürgen Habermas's words:

> In multicultural societies, the coexistence of forms of life with equal rights means ensuring every citizen the opportunity to grow up within a world of cultural heritage and to have his or her children grow up in it without suffering discrimination. (Habermas 1998, p. 223)

In an effort to accommodate those culturally different, liberal theorists have proposed expanding the catalogue of rights to include 'rights to cultural membership' (Kymlicka 2003) or rights to be recognised through diverse forms of multicultural jurisdiction (Shachar 2001). But as observed by critics, liberal politics of equal dignity, equal rights and immunities often create an identical standard applicable to everyone, regardless of their unique cultural identity (Taylor 1994). Instead of recognising distinctiveness, rights tend to create a dominant identity of the majority where the presumed neutral set of difference-blind principles is in fact merely a reflection of one hegemonic culture. While the ban on building minarets in Switzerland may affect everyone equally, only a small minority will experience its effects in their daily religious practice. The difference-blind approach, as evident by the aesthetic analysed here, is not in fact a difference-blind approach at all but instead an approach aimed at eliminating visible difference and homogenising cultural expression.

Rights can thus be used to suppress or build a communal sense of identity when they are claimed in the name of 'paradigm humans' (Rorty 2011, p. 122), 'active citizens' (Balibar 2009, p. 59) or 'Eurocentric prototypes' (Mutua 2001, p. 205). When rights are used as corrective tools in battles of cultural recognition, they become carefully controlled and afforded only to those deemed 'paradigm subjects' (Gozdecka 2015). Rights of those classified as falling outside the category of a 'paradigm subject' are controlled and limited because those to whom they are owed are seen as 'bad irrational people' who lack the capacity for qualities such as tolerance and are deprived of 'truth and moral knowledge' (Rorty 2011, pp. 122–3). Control of universal rights is often guaranteed only to those who are seen as having no 'inherent deficiencies' stemming from culture and origin (Balibar 2009, p. 60). When some subjects are framed as threatening to the community and excluded by virtue of their difference, the consequence of such framing results in sealing off the boundaries of the 'community of citizens' and equating that community only with the community of 'paradigm subjects'. Those seen as belonging to cultures and groups of specific origins are in contrast seen as deficient and falling outside. The normalisation of 'deficiencies' is amplified by revering the matrix of affiliations shaped by historical groups and communities and exploiting differences between these affiliations and those in the community who are of migrant or otherwise 'alien' origin. This juxtaposition of two communities eventually leads to constant comparison of those culturally different from their European 'prototype' (Mutua 2001, p. 205). As a result the racial state is maintained with its current set of existing hierarchies. The least harmful exclusion it generates is a limitation of some rights, but at its worst it leads to aberrations such as revocation of citizenship. The historical example of many German Jews losing citizenship prior to World War II is an extreme example showing how far the slippery slope of exclusion can go if the racial state selects a particular group and singles it out as one requiring control with the help of law. Those seen as inferior can be controlled because they are seen as 'savage' and not resembling paradigm and native subjects. The paradigm subject with whom all subjects are compared is not a static category, but instead is constantly evolving by recourse to a 'combination of practices, discourses and representations in a network of affective stereotypes' (Balibar and Wallerstein 1991, p. 18). The problem with 'owning' rights begins when those who consider themselves to be 'paradigm' begin to correct what is seen as 'inherently deficient' by limiting, redefining and controlling access by the other to the catalogue of rights.

The mutation of rights from mechanisms of protection into instruments of correction of identities and eventually cultural coercion reinforces and maintains cultural exclusion of those seen as the 'absolute other' (Gozdecka 2015). Such otherness is typically defined as either 'barbaric' or 'radical' and framed as a threat that requires management (Gozdecka 2018). This can be done in nearly unnoticeable ways, focusing on citizenship and links with a historical 'community of citizens' (Balibar 2009, p. 61) to accentuate the 'natural' difference between the 'paradigm citizen' and those who are culturally alien. This framing was evident in the poster presenting the minarets as a threat to the 'Swiss community'. The emphasis on the difference between the Swiss-ness as represented by the flag and the otherness represented by the piercing, penetrating minarets attempted to define the 'acceptable' boundary of the community itself. When the community is defined in such a way, equating between the community and its majoritarian premises results in the rise of 'domopolitics' (Lentin and Titley 2011). As a consequence, rights are used to reaffirm the place of 'natural belonging' (ibid., p. 206). They can reinforce frames of 'difference' or 'incapability' and endlessly expand the category of foreignness. The foreign is cherry-picked from a set of diverse cultural practices by reference to its difference from majoritarian norms. Thus one can be classified as a second, third or even fourth generation migrant, whose access to rights can be determined by reference to protecting the rights of paradigm subjects and governed by the logic of saving the other from their own 'savagery' (Mutua 2001, pp. 219–27). The community that defines itself by reference only to its paradigm subjects stands for nothing more than a set of power relations excluding, correcting and isolating with the help of law and management of rights.

Conclusions

The visual figure of the absolute other can be employed against refugees, migrants and citizens of migrant origin. It relies on accentuating presumed differences, which are always shown as inalienable and threatening to those seen as 'naturally' belonging. As shown in this chapter, absolute otherness is often racialised. Moreover, its impact reaches far beyond the right to enter: it can also have a serious impact on the exercise of basic rights such as freedom of religion. Reliance on the oft-imagined difference coupled with references to culture, religion or – less subtly – race perpetuates presumptions of otherness as unchangeable and inherent to the migrant and their descendants. This is reinforced by the hosts' presumption of what forms 'natural' belonging and what can be defined as excluded from it. In turn, this leads to a demand for exclusion which often starts with the migrant but with time has the potential to expand to all those bearing certain traits seen as alien such as – in the case of minaret bans – practising a particular religion. When 'natural' difference is narrowly defined through the historicised gaze of the host, ethics fail to come into play and are replaced by control of the boundaries of the community – and of rights. This control often results in legitimating and enacting laws that would otherwise likely be seen to be discriminatory and unnecessary in a democratic society. The figure of the absolute other, as problematic as it is, often does not strike the potential viewer as such because belonging is presented through the lens of citizenship, culture or some other trait defined as 'natural' for the host.

References

Abu-Hayyeh, Reem, Graham Murray and Liz Fekete. 'Swiss referendum: Flying the flag for nativism.' *Race & Class* 56, no. 1 (2014): 89–94.

Alba, Richard. 'Bright vs. blurred boundaries: Second-generation assimilation and exclusion in France, Germany, and the United States.' *Ethnic and Racial Studies* 28, no. 1 (2005): 20–49.

Balibar, Étienne. 'Racism revisited: Sources, relevance, and aporias of a modern concept.' *PMLA/Publications of the Modern Language Association of America* 123, no. 5 (2008): 1630–9.

Balibar, Étienne. *We, the People of Europe?: Reflections on Transnational Citizenship*. Princeton University Press, 2009.

Balibar, Étienne, and Immanuel Wallerstein. *Race, Nation, Class: Ambiguous Identities*. Verso, 1991.

Betz, Hans-Georg. 'Mosques, minarets, burqas and other essential threats: The populist right's campaign against Islam in Western Europe.' In *Right-Wing Populism in Europe: Politics and Discourse*, ed. Ruth Wodak, Majid KhosraviNik and Brigitte Mral, pp. 71–88. Bloomsbury, 2013.

Bolderson, Helen. 'The ethics of welfare provision for migrants: A case for equal treatment and the repositioning of welfare.' *Journal of Social Policy* 40, no. 2 (2011): 219–35.

Brah, Avtar, Mary J. Hickman and Máirtín Mac an Ghaill. 'Thinking identities: Ethnicity, racism and culture.' In *Thinking Identities: Ethnicity, Racism and Culture*, ed. Avtar Brah, Mary J. Hickman and Máirtín Mac an Ghaill, pp. 1–21. Palgrave Macmillan, 1999.

Diène, Doudou. 'Report of the Special Rapporteur on Contemporary Forms of Racism, Racial Discrimination, Xenophobia and Related Intolerance, Doudou Diène, on the manifestations of defamation of religions and in particular on the serious implications of Islamophobia on the enjoyment of all rights.' A/HRC/6/6. United Nations, 2007, available at: <https://digitallibrary.un.org/record/606485?ln=en>, last accessed 17 October 2023.

Dunn, Kevin M., Natascha Klocker and Tanya Salabay. 'Contemporary racism and Islamaphobia in Australia: Racializing religion.' *Ethnicities* 7, no. 4 (2007): 564–89.

Entman, Robert M. 'Framing bias: Media in the distribution of power.' *Journal of Communication* 57, no. 1 (2007): 163–73.

Ersanilli, Evelyn, and Ruud Koopmans. 'Rewarding integration? Citizenship regulations and the socio-cultural integration of immigrants in the Netherlands, France and Germany.' *Journal of Ethnic and Migration Studies* 36, no. 5 (2010): 773–91.

Fackenheim, Emil L. 'The Holocaust and philosophy.' *The Journal of Philosophy* 82, no. 10 (1985): 505–14.

Fangen, Katrine, Kirsten Fossan and Ferdinand Andreas Mohn, eds. *Inclusion and Exclusion of Young Adult Migrants in Europe: Barriers and Bridges*. Routledge, 2016.

Fleay, Caroline, and Lisa Hartley. '"I feel like a beggar": Asylum seekers living in the Australian community without the right to work.' *Journal of International Migration and Integration* 17, no. 4 (2016): 1031–48.

Geeraert, Jérémy. 'Healthcare reforms and the creation of ex-/included categories of patients – "irregular migrants" and the "undesirable" in the French healthcare system.' *International Migration* 56, no. 2 (2018): 68–81.

Gemi, Eda, Iryna Ulasiuk and Anna Triandafyllidou. 'Migrants and media newsmaking practices.' *Journalism Practice* 7, no. 3 (2013): 266–81.

Goldberg, David Theo. *The Racial State*. Blackwell, 2002.

Ghorashi, Halleh, and Ulrike M. Vieten. 'Female narratives of "new" citizens' belonging(s) and identities in Europe: Case studies from the Netherlands and Britain.' *Identities* 19, no. 6 (2012): 725–41.

Gozdecka, Dorota A. 'A community of paradigm subjects? Rights as corrective tools in culturally contested claims of recognition in Europe.' *Social Identities* 21, no. 4 (2015): 328–44.

Gozdecka, Dorota A. '"Barbarians" and "radicals" against the legitimate community? Cultural othering through discourses on legitimacy of human rights.' *No Foundations* 15 (2018): 101–26.

Habermas, Jürgen. 'Struggles for recognition in the democratic constitutional state.' In *The Inclusion of the Other: Studies in Political Theory*, ed. Ciaran P. Cronin and Pablo De Greiff, pp. 203–36. MIT Press, 1998.

Heath, Anthony F., Catherine Rothon and Elina Kilpi. 'The second generation in Western Europe: Education, unemployment, and occupational attainment.' *Annual Review of Sociology* 34 (2008): 211–35.

Hirsch, Shirin. 'Racism, "second generation" refugees and the asylum system.' *Identities* 26, no. 1 (2019): 88–106.

Hopkins, Peter E. 'Young people, masculinities, religion and race: New social geographies.' *Progress in Human Geography* 31, no. 2 (2007): 163–77.

Hugo, Graeme. 'Australia's state-specific and regional migration scheme: An assessment of its impacts in South Australia.' *Journal of International Migration and Integration/Revue de l'intégration et de la migration internationale* 9, no. 2 (2008): 125–45.

Ikuenobe, Polycarp. 'Conceptualizing racism and its subtle forms.' *Journal for the Theory of Social Behaviour* 41, no. 2 (2011): 161–81.

Kallis, Aristotle. 'Breaking taboos and "mainstreaming the extreme": The debates on restricting Islamic symbols in contemporary Europe.' In *Right-Wing Populism in Europe: Politics and Discourse*, ed. Ruth Wodak, Majid KhosraviNik and Brigitte Mral, pp. 55–70. Bloomsbury, 2013.

Kasinitz, Philip, John H. Mollenkopf, Mary C. Waters and Jennifer Holdaway. *Inheriting the City: The Children of Immigrants Come of Age*. Russell Sage Foundation, 2009.

Krzyżanowski, Michał. 'Discursive shifts and the normalisation of racism: Imaginaries of immigration, moral panics and the discourse of contemporary right-wing populism.' *Social Semiotics* 30, no. 4 (2020): 503–27.

Kymlicka, Will. 'Multicultural states and intercultural citizens.' *Theory and Research in Education* 1, no. 2 (2003): 147–69.

Langlotz, Andreas, and Danièle Klapproth Muazzin. 'Unveiling the phantom of the "Islamic takeover": A critical, cognitive-linguistic analysis of the discursive perpetuation of an Orientalist.' In *The Expression of Inequality in Interaction: Power, Dominance, and Status*, ed. Hanna Pishwa and Rainer Schulze, pp. 105–41. John Benjamins, 2014.

Lentin, Alana, and Gavan Titley. *The Crises of Multiculturalism: Racism in a Neoliberal Age*. Zed Books, 2011.

Lentin, Ronit. 'Ireland: Racial state and crisis racism.' *Ethnic and Racial Studies* 30, no. 4 (2007): 610–27.

Maurice, Eric. 'EU and Switzerland agree on free movement.' *EU Observer*, 22 December 2016, available at: <https://euobserver.com/justice/136398>, last accessed 25 September 2023.

May, Stephen, Tariq Modood and Judith Squires, eds. *Ethnicity, Nationalism, and Minority Rights*. Cambridge University Press, 2004.

Meier, Kenneth J., Joseph Stewart and Robert E. England. *Race, Class, and Education: The Politics of Second-Generation Discrimination*. University of Wisconsin Press, 1989.

Milic, Thomas. '"For they knew what they did" – What Swiss voters did (not) know about the mass immigration initiative.' *Swiss Political Science Review* 21, no. 1 (2015): 48–62.

Miller, John. 'Swiss high court rules anti-immigration SVP ad broke racism laws.' Reuters, 14 April 2017, available at: <https://www.reuters.com/article/us-swiss-racism-svp-idUSKBN17F1UT>, last accessed 11 August 2021.

Mutua, Makau. 'Savages, victims, and saviors: The metaphor of human rights.' *Harvard International Law Journal* 42 (2001): 201–45.

Quito, Anne. 'Switzerland's largest political party insists on depicting foreigners as black sheep.' *Quartz*, 16 February 2016, available at: <https://qz.com/617050/switzerlands-largest-political-party-insists-on-depicting-foreigners-as-black-sheep>, last accessed 17 October 2023.

Rawls, John. *A Theory of Justice: Revised Edition*. Harvard University Press, 1999.

Rorty, Richard. 'Human rights, rationality and sentimentality.' In *Wronging rights? Philosophical Challenges for Human Rights*, ed. Aakash Singh Rathore and Alex Cistelecan, pp. 107–31. Routledge, 2011.

Rotas, Alex. '"A soft touch": Racism and asylum seekers from a visual culture perspective.' In *Racism Postcolonialism Europe*, ed. Graham Huggan and Ian Law, pp. 77–91. Liverpool University Press, 2009.

Shachar, Ayelet. *Multicultural Jurisdictions: Cultural Differences and Women's Rights*. Cambridge University Press, 2001.

Taylor, Charles. *The Politics of Recognition*. Princeton University Press, 1994.

UN News. 'Swiss minaret ban discriminates against Muslims, says UN expert.' *UN News*, 30 November 2009, available at: <https://news.un.org/en/story/2009/11/322742-swiss-minaret-ban-discriminates-against-muslims-says-un-expert>, last accessed 11 August 2021.

Virtanen, Simo V., and Leonie Huddy. 'Old-fashioned racism and new forms of racial prejudice.' *The Journal of Politics* 60, no. 2 (1998): 311–32.

Wilkes, Rima, Neil Guppy and Lily Farris. '"No thanks, we're full": Individual characteristics, national context, and changing attitudes toward immigration.' *International Migration Review* 42, no. 2 (2008): 302–29.

Wodak, Ruth. '"Us" and "them": Inclusion and exclusion – discrimination via discourse.' In *Identity, Belonging and Migration*, ed. Gerard Delanty, Ruth Wodak and Paul Jones, pp. 54–77. Liverpool University Press, 2008.

Wyler, Dina. 'The Swiss minaret ban referendum and Switzerland's international reputation: A vote with an impact.' *Journal of Muslim Minority Affairs* 37, no. 4 (2017): 413–25.

6

The Migrant as an Inhuman Mass

Introduction

Racialisation of the figure of the migrant examined in the previous chapter is not the only dehumanising frame that can be applied to those arriving. Another way in which the host gaze frames migrants and obscures their humanity is to present those arriving as a homogenous mass, often metaphorised as a flow or flood. This chapter analyses depictions of the figure of the migrant as a faceless and dehumanised homogenous mass. As a semi-alien threatening organism, those presented as a nameless cohort are seen as a danger even greater than the racialised other. While the racialised other is presented as a danger to the culture, history and perceived national values of host states, the anonymity and the large-scale threat of the mass is often presented as a multifaceted burden that exceeds the capacity of the host to absorb it. This perceived burden is both socio-cultural and economic in its framing. The economic burden is related to the first figure examined in this book, namely the 'bogus' asylum seeker or the unwanted form of *homo oeconomicus* that allegedly competes with the local population for resources, access to social welfare, and employment. While the racialised other is alleged to threaten the cultural foundations of the host state, the anonymous mass threatens all forms of community survival, including economic survival. Together, these figures are often used as a powerful tool in the political arsenal of migration critics. Combined, they constitute a threat so great that not only do they motivate voters to elect right-wing and anti-immigration parties that implement ever stricter forms of migration control (Langlotz and Muazzin 2014), but they also have the capacity to enter the mainstream discourse and become increasingly normalised (Betz 2013; Kallis 2013). What follows from that normalisation are unprecedented legal changes shifting the foundations of existing consensus and legal principles regulating migration.

In this chapter I show how the host gaze frames those arriving as a mass and illustrate how the ultimate dehumanisation expressed in this figure of the migrant impacts on the extraordinary effort to prevent migrants from arriving in the host territory. The focus is on how individual people with their personal histories – often involving war or conflict – become framed as an inorganic, dehumanised and uncontrollable danger that ought to be carefully scrutinised at the border and rejected whenever possible. To show the figure of a migrant as an anonymous mass, I use the example of media portrayals emerging during the so-called European refugee crisis and posters used during the Brexit campaign, where the figure of the racialised migrant and the figure of the mass featured prominently in visual campaigns. Such campaigns have been shown to likely have a decisive impact on the outcome of a referendum (Gietel-Basten 2016; Creighton and Jamal 2022). These depictions are barely a few amongst many, but as imagery distributed either by political parties or by major news outlets across the political spectrum, they were aimed at shifting preferences and challenging existing laws. As such, they are an ideal exemplification of how the popular discourse frames the figure of the mass.

The Flood and *Homo Oeconomicus*

The image of the 'flood' or 'incontrollable flow' of migrants has been prominently employed in anti-migration rhetoric, particularly in discourses involving economic threats to the local population. This way of framing migration discourse has dominated right-wing rhetoric in particular, gradually influencing law and policy across the globe (Hogan and Haltinner 2015; Innes 2010). As Jackie Hogan and Kristin Haltinner (2015) illustrate in the context of Australia, this threat is often construed as manifold economic competition. Firstly, migrants are seen as competition for jobs that 'rightfully' belong to native-born citizens. Secondly, migrants are associated with bringing wages down and increasing unemployment. Finally, anti-migration rhetoric also resorts to seeing migrants as a burden on public healthcare and welfare systems (ibid., p. 528). Unsurprisingly, Australia is not unique in framing the debate in this manner. Desirée Schmuck and Jörg Matthes (2015) have shown the same dynamic visible in the context of Europe, as has Jessica Brown (2016) in the context of anti-migration rhetoric in the USA. The central principle underpinning such framing is the presumption of scarcity of resources (Lucassen and Lubbers 2012) and competition between the host population and those arriving – regardless of their legal status or purpose of arrival. As we have seen – in the discourse about the 'bogus' asylum seeker, the first archetypal figure analysed here, and discussions about unwanted EU migration during the Swiss referendum – the principle of scarcity can be used in discussions on any type of migrant. Such framing is often an effective way of convincing the local (native) population of the need to limit overall migration or a specific segment of migration. If resources are presented as scarce, the notion of a 'flow' or 'flood' works as an affective trigger of those attitudes. The discursive perception of being overrun by an anonymous 'swarm' of migrants – regardless of their profession, experience or reason for stay – presents all arrivals as a uniform type of danger regardless of their potential contribution to the local economy and society or their legal status.

The idea of the mass can be metaphorised in multiple ways. Regardless of the form the mass takes, it is always imagined as an uncontrollable and non-human element. If the mass is metamorphosed into the form of a 'flow', 'river' or 'sea', it creates a distinction between the human (members of the local population) and the non-human (anonymous flow of unknown and threatening migrants). As Heather Johnson observes, wherever we find the vocabulary of 'floods', 'flows' and 'hordes' in the context of refugees, '[r]ather than individuals, refugees began to represent masses of people moving across borders – not fleeing persecution, as outlined in the Convention, but fleeing violence and war, intimidating in their numbers' (2011, p. 1023). Imagery of this kind, as Johnson points out, aims to intimidate and threaten with sheer numbers. However, Elspeth Guild reminds us that such imagery is not unique or rare, but instead quite common and that governments tend to operate with the discourse of the mass even when the numbers of refugees are relatively small:

> the language of mass means that people cease to be individuals with specific needs, entitlements, and demands – including an individual assessment of the merits of their claims – and instead become a group, irrespective of how varied they feel from one another. Often the individuals may be parts of very different ethnic groups, or political opponents to one another, but for the official watching 'them,' they are mass migration. (Guild 2017, p. 193)

Such a discourse operates in the political as well as in the legislative sphere (Van Der Valk 2003). The mass in the form of a flow distorts, exaggerates, homogenises, so that individual arrivals at the border are treated not as people but instead as part of an anonymous danger that needs to be stopped before it even has a chance to materialise. This danger needs to be carefully controlled, monitored and curtailed. The figure of the mass leads to constant narrowing of the catalogue of rights (Gündoğdu 2014), suspicion, and blanket policies aiming at preventing arrival altogether (Drake and Gibson 2017). In this imagery, any shred of humanity becomes presented as an entirely non-human force, allowing for increased control of not only the borders but also the bodies of those who arrive at the borders (Guild 2017). Rejection of the mass perceived as a foreign element results in policies of assigning numbers to those in migration detention and biopolitical management of migration (Radziwinowiczówna 2022).

Non-human People: Viruses and Bodies Without Organs

The image of the 'flow' or 'flood' is one of the many forms presenting the figure of an inhuman mass danger. The key principle behind the figure of the mass is the ultimate dehumanisation of those arriving. This dehumanisation occurs through a fusion of human bodies and non-human elements imagined as the mass. The flood appears to be unstoppable unless the 'right' kind of migration controls are put in place. Even worse, if those arriving are presented as a virus, a shapeless and uncontrollable entity that spreads on a mass scale, the sense of danger prompts the viewer or recipient of such framing to ramp up all possible protections. The figure of the mass relies on the construct of human–non-human assemblage framed as a danger far more sinister and harder to control than each migrant with their individual culture, their own religion or personal intentions. While a figure imagined as human – even if framed as 'bogus', 'illegal' or 'other' – can be imagined as 'controllable', the fusion of human and non-human appears to be far less within the capability of any kind of control. Curiously, the dehumanised figure of a mass of any type, while lacking human features and human dignity, at the same time is seen as featuring human-like agency. The mass – or the virus – can thus 'outsmart' the systems put in place to stop it. Its agency does not stem from the agency of an individual but from the very fusion between human bodies and a non-human form such as the flow or mass.

The idea of a fusion between human and non-human elements has been prominent in twentieth-century thought. It resembles the connection between the body and the machine developed by Gilles Deleuze and Félix Guattari (1987), who worked on the notion of a body without organs. Daniel Smith (2018) reminds us that a body without organs is for Deleuze and Guattari more than simply a connection between a lifeless machine and human vitality but that it becomes something that surpasses both, creating a new form of being, and that reworking the concepts in Deleuze and Guattari's writings leads them to a very different understanding of the relation between the two elements. A body without organs represents neither a classical mechanism nor a classical vitalism but rather a merger of both. The vitalist element informs the notion of the mechanism's understanding of reality as predictable and measurable. But also, vice versa, the mechanist elements share a distrust of vitalism's idea of a special kind of matter particular to the organic. As a result, the construction represents an intertwining of the '"good" – a creative, spontaneous organism – and the "bad" – an inert, lifeless machine' (Smith 2018, p. 96).

Such a fusion is a form of assemblage. In an assemblage, the mass ceases to exist as individual organisms (Dewsbury 2011, p. 148). Instead, an assemblage acquires a variety of new capabilities and capacities. As J.-D. Dewsbury points out, the Deleuzian idea of an assemblage combines 'machinic content and collective expression' (ibid.). As a result, assemblages operate as a form of a matter itself (ibid.). This matter can take on many guises, resulting in multiple possibilities of fusions between the human and the non-human. This fusion can take the form of a flood, but equally the form of a virus. The human and the non-human have often been fused in a discussion of migrants as 'parasites' or 'viruses'. This type of fusion is an ultimately disparaging view of those arriving, which is not uncommon in right-wing discourse (Hogan and Haltinner 2015). Miriam Ticktin points out that such framing is not historically new and that it allows for shifting debate beyond solutions that would be acceptable when the threat is presented as human:

> The treatment of people like animals became the treatment of people as animals. Similarly, during the Second World War, as Bridget Anderson reminds us, German chemical company IG Farben bought the patent for Zyklon B, which was used in the extermination camps of the Holocaust; it had originally been used as an insecticide, licensed for delousing Mexican migrants to the United States in the 1930s. Here again, the notion of 'invader' gets carried from one context to another, justifying the use of the same technologies. (Ticktin 2017, p. xxv)

Ticktin observes that treating people as invaders, animals or other inhuman forms creates a slippage between ontological categories and leads to treating people like viruses, insects or other parasites. The effort to control these invaders begins with subtle ways of 'protecting' the local population and ends with extreme aberrations of ethics such as extermination (Ticktin 2017, p. xxv). The intention to protect the local population from such an inhuman danger enables creation of the notion of a sanctuary to describe the host territory – a place free from potential invaders (ibid.).

When the figure of a mass is seen in this way, the border becomes impenetrable, because the host territory and its boundaries become an untouchable sanctuary from 'invaders'. These invaders form a non-human assemblage constructed from human bodies endowed with a new form of autonomy capable of challenging existing legal systems. While in a human-to-human encounter some forms of ethical duty can be established – even in an increasingly hostile welcome at the border – no such ethical encounter is possible in a meeting with a non-human assemblage. When the guest is presented as a flood or a virus, ethics are not only disrupted but entirely disabled. When faced with a non-human assemblage, the host is inclined to 'defend' its territory from the non-human invader, who is never seen as a guest but instead always as an uncontrollable threat with its own intentions, purposes

THE MIGRANT AS AN INHUMAN MASS

Figure 6.1 'Breaking Point' poster campaign, UKIP, 2016, Alamy

and goals. When those arriving are framed in such a manner, hostility – not hospitality – becomes the norm in an encounter at the border and ethics are ultimately disrupted.

The Figure of the Mass in Visual Discourse

The idea of an unstoppable threat to host states has been expressed in multiple images used by political parties across the globe that propose an anti-migration agenda as well as in the wider media. For the purposes of this analysis, I will use two images. One was intentionally used to manipulate migration discourse, while the intention of the other was to 'simply' report. As I will illustrate, both of these images – regardless of their intention – are framed through the prism of the host gaze; and both result in a narrowing of the threshold of hospitality, turning it into open hostility.

The first image (Figure 6.1) was used by the UK Independence Party (UKIP) during the Brexit campaign. The 'Breaking Point' poster features a long torrent of refugees, which in its curved shape seeks to resemble a human river. While the individual facial features of those forming the crowd are mostly blurred, it is clear that the poster features primarily non-white refugees who were likely photographed during the so-called refugee crisis in Slovenia in 2015. This perception of the flow is further amplified by the accompanying caption in bold red letters: 'BREAKING POINT' and the subtitle in white just below it: 'The EU has failed us all'. Further, at the bottom the image proclaims: 'We must break free of the EU and take back control of our borders.' This problematic visual representation has been characterised as a form of hate speech (Reid 2019) and has even been reported as such to the police (Stewart and Mason 2016).

While the racialisation of refugees is also visible in this image, I would like to primarily focus on the dehumanising effect of the figure of the mass as used here. Starting from the gaze point, the image is clearly directed to the host and delivered through the prism of the host gaze. The first row of people featured, while somewhat blurred out, appears to nearly pop out of the image, giving the host the impression that the 'flow' is not just a distant threat, but is instead already here, right before the host's eyes. It is no longer a spectre on the horizon as used in spectropolitical play with invisibility, nor an abstract alien element like the sheep in the racialising Swiss posters. The threat from the flow is imminent and present, requiring the host's full attention. This perception is amplified by the aggressively positioned captions. The 'BREAKING POINT' caption urges the host viewer to take immediate action to stop the flow. This proposed action purports to empower the viewer and – in case the viewer has any doubt as to 'how' the threatening flow could be stopped – the captions further specify that the vote to leave the European Union could do just that. Regardless of the legal inaccuracy of such a statement and the selective presentation of migration from outside the EU as the key focus of EU law, the image is undoubtedly successful in creating a sense of urgency. The flow is supposed to 'speak for itself' and show a threat beyond control – unless immediate action is taken. If we consider the frame, it is also evident that the people in the field of vision are captured in a particular way, strengthening the perception of an endless torrent of people. The image does not focus simply on the front row, but instead is focused slightly above it, to convey the idea of a multitude of people in the form of a tremendous queue, snaking like a river on the horizon. As quickly pointed out on social media (Stewart and Mason 2016) the formation captured and presentation of a 'river' of people is reminiscent of a Nazi propaganda video, shown in one of the episodes of the BBC documentary *Auschwitz: The Nazis and The Final Solution*. The framing utilises the image of the flow, flood or river together with the intentional blurring of the field of vision, to effectively remove all humanity from each of the individual faces, replacing it by the non-human association with an uncontrollable flow.

Additionally, however, the field of vision fuses not only the human and the non-human river, but goes further into incorporating the viral element as well. The mass – captured in mid-flight, looking messy with their luggage, plain, grey, worn-out clothes and tired by the ordeal they are undergoing – signifies the 'danger' of dirt, pollution or disease, which much of Nazi

Figure 6.2 Syrian refugee influx reporting, 2018, Alamy

propaganda employed in its anti-Jewish rhetoric (Proctor 1995). Vulnerable people carrying their property on their back references not just a torrent but moreover a 'dirty torrent', which in turn acts as a strong affective trigger for the host. Faced with this figure of a 'dirty' mass, the host is encouraged to think of the country's boundary as the boundary of a sanctuary. Faced with such an inflammatory representation of the mass, the sanctuary is of course not intended ever to welcome or host these arrivals. Instead, the host society itself is invited to think of needing its own 'sanctuary' from the arriving flow.

The image of the mass in the 'Breaking Point' posters is a particularly problematic way of presenting the migrant. Not only is the mass inhuman, immediate and threatening, but it also appears to carry other hidden dangers, all urging the host to pull up the drawbridge and use state boundaries as a barricade against anyone arriving in the mass. Dehumanising the migrant in the figure of the mass employed here is total and insidious. The only response can be hostility, instead of hospitality, as the mass appears to be non-human and harbouring unknown intentions. While in this case the mass is also racialised, the figure of the mass does not require use of the racial element as a form of affective trigger. The affective response of immediate denial of hospitality can be achieved without presenting any humans at all and prior to any actual encounter with people.

The second image (Figure 6.2) is one of many used while reporting on the refugee influx from Syria in 2015. Branded the 'European refugee crisis', the arrival of a large number of refugees from the Syrian war prompted circulation of multiple press stories, videos and photographs. Unlike the politically charged image used by UKIP, these photographs were not intended to trigger anti-migration sentiments, but instead only to convey the reality of the refugee influx, often without an underlying political message. The image selected here does not differ from the multiple others in which the frame simply captures what is supposed to be seen as the actuality of the refugee crisis. Within the frame of this image, the viewer is confronted with a mountain of left-over safety vests abandoned by refugees who arrived in Greece after their sea journey. Within multiple iterations of these photos, their frame frequently captures nothing but the vests and a background of sky or soil. Very often there is no other background, no people, nothing against which one could scale the image. The viewer does not know whether the jackets are a fragment of a collection of thousands or hundreds of thousands, or whether they are just abandoned on the beach or located in a designated area. The context and the background are missing from the frame. Instead, the frame cuts out the magnitude of the number. What this lack of scale prompts is, of course, the fear of this unknown mass of people. Whether looking at thousands or millions, the viewer facing these anonymous abandoned objects has no information other than a large number of vests with no further context. The vests merge into a new form of shapeless body, one that exists outside the bodies of their wearers. They become a symbol of their wearers as much as an entity of their own. This imagery blends both the idea of a shore 'flooded' by vests and the idea of something new and sinister created by a mountain of lifeless objects. The vests appear to create a new 'organism', which – while not mechanical – blends human-made objects with their human wearers in the form of a new 'body without organs'. In some of the images this body without organs is examined by a lone blond woman, who appears to be examining its foreignness and its lifeless shape. This examination, while not intended to be racial, urges the viewer to consider all differences between them and this new lifeless form appearing on their shores. The mountain of vests appears to be both lifeless and full of life, non-human but full of human agency, countless and at the same time symbolising each and every wearer. It becomes the ultimate new form of being which threatens the host through its duality, its complexity and its unstoppable nature. It reminds the viewer of competition for resources with the new arrivals. Each and every wearer, while invisible, can be imagined as a potential economic competitor. The wearers are anonymous but numerous, unknown but also 'unstoppable'.

The mountain of vests is again put uncomfortably close to the host's gaze point. It is placed at the forefront of the image, 'right before the eyes', so that the host cannot avert their gaze to look elsewhere or position this new form of being against any bigger picture. The inescapable imminence of the 'human non-human' entity of the vests justifies not only fear of the monstrous, as identified in the chapter focusing on illegality; it also urges the host to take precautions to prevent the 'pollution' associated with this new organism. All the viewer is allowed to know is the many unknowns associated with this dualistic entity without bodies. The entity is large and threatens to grow uncontrollably and with no possibility to stop it. It appears to have an uncontrollable agency of its own, the capacity to overflow, to mushroom, to extend in any direction like a Deleuzian rhizome. While, of course for Deleuze, this new type of ontology signified liberation from established structures and the ultimate new form of ontological being which can challenge the established reality through multiple lines of flight, for the viewer of an image employing this new ontology it signifies a shapeless danger. Visualising this new entity triggers not just the image of a ghost that one can picture at the back of one's mind, not just the almost tangible image of the 'bogus' asylum seeker and not just a racialised caricature of those the viewer fears. Quite the contrary, this form of threatening mass with a new form of agency – to grow, spread, multiply and take over – signifies a monster of an entirely new kind. One that can, in the host's view, justify the harshest methods of control, the greatest resistance, and the most inhumane of treatment. By combining the most threatening elements of the human and the most threatening elements of the anonymous mass, this entity appears to be slipping away from its confines, overflowing beyond boundaries put in place by the host gaze. What results is thus a sense of urgency to keep the entity as far away from the shore as possible. With the urgency of preventing the invader from entering, the image urges the viewer to 'rethink', 'recast' and 'fortify' the established boundaries to keep this body without organs at a safe distance.

While the bogus asylum seeker triggers the need to control the boundaries of territory, the ghost triggers the need to control the horizon, while the racialised other triggers the need to control one's own territory, and the body without organs urges the viewer to push the danger to beyond the horizon and to refuse to humanise arrivals altogether. As a result of dehumanisation, coupled with the threat of a new kind of non-human agency, the arrivals are seen not just as human competitors, but instead as another form of being which can take over and endanger life as the viewer knows it. The affect created by this image prompts the viewer to justify new and innovative measures of protection of the sanctuary within one's borders, urging the viewer to keep this new monster without organs at bay, safely away from the boundary of the sanctuary. As a result of this newly triggered fear, unimaginable changes become possible. These changes can go to the very heart of the existing legal status quo and demand new legal solutions to 'protect' the host's sanctuary. In an encounter with the shapeless mass, no ethical connection can be made and no hospitality can be contemplated. The default response becomes entrenched in hostility. Below, I will analyse the legal response to the Brexit campaigns and the emerging legal deals with Turkey, which both aim at keeping migrants – imagined as a mass – at bay. The figure of the mass effectively disestablishes any ethical considerations. Instead, it reinforces the host's need to extend hostility beyond the border, so that the imagined danger never arrives at all.

Brexit and the EU–Turkey Agreement: Keeping the 'Mass' at Bay

Seeing migrants as an inhuman mass can result in denial of rights, as observed by Guild (2017). But the legal response does not necessarily end there. The shift away from the possibility of hospitality to outright hostility triggers the need to 'strengthen' borders beyond the already punitive and extraordinarily controlling methods which most countries have developed for the purposes of managing migration. Yet the figure of the mass – with its overwhelming affective form of a threat – appears to trigger the need for even more profound types of change. When the host's perception of migration as a potentially unmanageable and uncontrollable problem becomes the focal point of law and politics, the legal solutions proposed to tackle the problem are not only punitive but frequently radical. They often seek to overthrow the current legal status quo even though such novel solutions are often costlier to the host state than hosting new migrants (Springford 2018; Fetzer and Wang 2020). In recent years we have witnessed two prime examples of such a radical overthrow: in the form of Brexit and the novel solutions proposed in the EU–Turkey Agreement concerning processing of refugees heading towards Europe. Below, I analyse both in light of management of the affective threat of a mass.

Turning to Brexit, studies have shown that the primary motivation for the public's vote to leave the EU was the attitude towards migration (Goodwin and Milazzo 2017). While free movement within the EU attracted primarily highly educated and competitive migrants, who hardly arrived in overwhelming numbers, the local population's perceptions were vastly different from the legal reality. The perception of the 'Breaking Point', while not founded in legal reality, resulted in a warped sense of lack of 'sovereignty' over borders. In Adrian Favell and Roxana Barbulescu's words, the need to reinstate perceived sovereignty resulted in the power to name, normatively classify, identify and delimit the 'true' British population and those 'foreign' to it against the functional reality of the mobile and highly integrated face of migrant populations (2018, p. 120). Despite not truly depicting the reality of migration, the notion of the mass, or flow, was sufficient to obscure the legal complexities of the common market principles concerning freedom of movement and the fact that the UK always exercised relatively strong control over migration from outside the EU (Outhwaite 2019). It seems, however, that the figure of an anonymous, homogenous and overwhelming mass of migrants resulted in the perception that 'immigrants' are responsible for lack of jobs, poor wages, inadequate public services and shortage of affordable housing (Gough 2017, p. 367). Jamie Gough points out further that research conducted before the referendum suggested 'that most working-class leavers believed that Brexit would reduce immigration to Britain and thereby reduce competition for jobs, public services and housing' (ibid.). William Outhwaite notes that the majority of Brexit voters did not distinguish between different types of migrants; and stopping migration from countries such as Afghanistan or Pakistan was quoted alongside stopping migration from Eastern Europe as a reason for voting to leave the EU (2019, p. 94). Legally, of course, EU freedom of movement applied only to migration from Eastern Europe, but one of the primary qualities of the figure of the mass involves obscuring differences and presenting those arriving as one coherent, uncontrollable and overwhelming cohort. Legal nuances become lost when the figure of the mass enters the picture. As Outhwaite also observed, EU workers, third country nationals and refugees became moulded into one in the perception of those supporting a 'Leave' vote (ibid.). Legally, of course, very different rules applied to each of these categories. Moreover, the UK – due to its long list of exceptions to provisions on control of movement from outside the EU (Ette and Gerdes 2007) – was in a relatively strong position to impose its own regulations on everyone arriving from outside the EU.

The desire to control migration and keep the perceived 'mass' at bay without sacrificing any other benefits of EU membership was also visible during the long and turbulent negotiations on the terms of future cooperation between the EU and the UK after Brexit. While it is hard to suspect high-level British negotiators of a lack of understanding of what Brexit truly involved, in contrast a lack of such understanding was visible in the British press, which repeatedly accused the EU of ill-will or the will to 'punish' the UK for taking control of its borders (Boffey 2021; Forsythe 2021). For those versed in the complexity of EU law, its subsidiary nature and its complex division of competences, these accusations appeared unsubstantiated; however, those backing the vote simply labelled them 'Project Fear' (Hobolt 2016). These arguments – while having little to do with the legal reality of a complex international organisation operating with its own legal regime such as the European Union – could hardly be ignored in the lengthy process of preparing the post-Brexit deal. Multiple threats of no-deal Brexit became a real prospect even weeks before the official day of exit. Until today, the full consequences of the vote remain unknown and continuously manifest themselves in import crises, border queues and other forms. Reports from EU citizens in the UK experiencing difficulties in applying for settled status or being put in detention have multiplied. In addition, EU citizens have begun 'slipping through the net' and are increasingly at risk of deportation (Davies 2021). Meanwhile, the economic reality, particularly in the phase of post-COVID recovery, means that the UK is unable to end its reliance on a migrant labour force and so new migration regulation is necessary to revive multiple sectors relying on a migrant workforce (Rolfe 2017; Milbourne and Coulson 2021). Yet the figure of the mass not only overflows the visual reality but also tends to dilute the nuances of the law and create a new legal reality often not suiting local circumstances and needs.

Another legal solution corresponding with the fear of preventing the arrival of the mass is the EU–Turkey Agreement signed during the period of the so-called European refugee crisis. This deal, which mirrors the Australian offshore solution discussed in the previous chapter, was aimed at preventing the arrival of Syrian refugees in Europe. The objective of the Agreement was to ensure that all new irregular migrants crossing from Turkey to the Greek islands from 20 March 2016 would be returned to Turkey. As Roman Lehner (2019) observes, the idea was quite simple: Turkey would take all refugees crossing to Greece in consideration of a strong commitment to take half a million Syrians from Turkey. This would legally supplement European asylum law as well as international refugee law by applying the safe third country principle by the Greek authorities in returning people to Turkey (ibid., p. 177). While the agreement was initially only a political statement based on the Joint Action Plan, it was soon followed by agreements between Turkey and Greece of 2001 and between Turkey and the EU of 14 December 2013 (Council Decision 2014/252/EU). Further legal obligations stemming from the agreement included a resettlement mechanism for 20,000 people (Commission Recommendation C(2015) 3560), a relocation decision on a distribution mechanism for refugees stranded in Italy and Greece (Council Decision 2015/1601) and a voluntary humanitarian admission scheme with Turkey (Commission Recommendation C(2015) 9490). As Gloria Arribas points out, the central principle of returns underpinning the agreement was at the same time 'undoubtedly the most controversial point' (2016, p. 1098), since it has a serious impact on compliance with international refugee law, EU law and human rights law – particularly the prohibition of collective expulsions and respect for the *non-refoulement* principle. The fact that the agreement challenging these principles came to be discussed and signed in an attempt to bypass the central principles of several legal regimes speaks of the affective power of the mass to overthrow even the most complex and central legal principles that have developed over many years. The discursive element behind the motivation to sign the agreement played a crucial role:

> In sum the deal [. . .] prioritises the protection of national interests over helping those in need of asylum. Supporters have repeatedly emphasised that it was brokered in response to warnings of an imminent humanitarian crisis in Greece and in reaction to the increasing popularity of right-wing exclusionary politics and calls to dismantle the Schengen zone. (Haferlach and Kurban 2017, p. 85)

This agreement, strikingly resembling Australian policies of returning refugees to Indonesia, attempts to shift the responsibility to another country for those arriving and the determination process in refugee decisions. Employing such solutions allows for the 'mass' to be stopped before arriving. It prevents triggering of any actions required for asylum processing and does not require input by local authorities. Such a solution – despite raising difficult legal questions regarding the threshold of what a 'safe country' is, nevertheless contravening the European mass expulsion ban and challenging the standards around *non-refoulement* – appears feasible when the figure of the mass informs considerations. The law becomes fluid and bendable, its principles become tentative rather than set in stone, and gradually, under the guise of necessity, the international legal norms underpinning the governance of legal refugee and migration law become slowly changed. The unacceptable becomes gradually normalised, the questionable becomes possible, and slowly but surely new forms of control and new legal principles begin to form entirely new legal standards. The normalisation of exceptions to existing rules begins with acceptance of one extraordinary solution. For instance, when Australia began its controversial offshore processing, the mechanism raised multiple concerns. When a similar mechanism was introduced in the EU–Turkey Agreement, it was already normalised as a controversial but acceptable exception. Finally, when Denmark followed the same path, in the final year of my writing this book, legislating an analogical external processing mechanism through which those arriving will be sent to a non-European country, there were few raised eyebrows as the solution had already become an acceptable weapon in the legal arsenal of migration control methods. The overhaul of legal principles regulating asylum-seeking and migration, in response to the perceived danger of the 'mass', begins by slightly eroding legal foundations until it eventually establishes itself as a new, acceptable form of legal standard for welcome and protection.

Conclusions

The figure of the mass may be one of many figures dehumanising the migrant. However, it appears to be the one that triggers the most extreme forms of socio-political and legal responses. Direct referenda legitimising dire changes not only to domestic but also to international and regional legal systems show the power wielded by the threat of the mass. What follows from employing this figure are legal changes aimed at keeping 'migrants' at bay. While radical at first, they gradually become normalised, slowly eroding – and eventually changing – standards of legal protection. This is because the figure of the mass is so overwhelming that no other solutions appear 'sufficient'. To control the alleged economic threat morphed with the perception of an alien organism, the law is deployed to control a non-human 'takeover'. The figure of the mass is able to mobilise local populations to do what they perceive as 'necessary' to keep the mass entirely at bay, regardless of the complexity of the law involved. The depth of the actual law with all its ramifications becomes lost and absent when the logic of a sanctuary from the mass becomes the driving force behind the turn from hospitality to complete hostility. The threat of the mass co-opts the legal aspect and triggers unprecedented paradigm shifts, laying entirely new legal foundations, even if those foundations risk being unbeneficial to the host. Fear in host populations can trigger responses modifying long-established rules in highly regulated areas of migration law, such as refugee reception rules. The EU–Turkey Agreement as well as Australian offshore processing have been changing the consensus on what is permissible in refugee law. Keeping refugees away from the territory where they can lodge their claim no longer appears exceptional, and the legal problems surrounding such solutions become brushed under the carpet of necessity 'to protect' those territories from unnecessary, unwelcome and unwanted arrivals. The figure of the mass has a sweeping effect on various legal regimes controlling freedom of movement. The fear it triggers obscures the legal distinctions between different legal categories of those arriving and different legal regimes regulating those arrivals. This existential fear, just as the image of the mass itself, blends all migrants and all law regulating migration into one negotiable and changeable morph. With its fear-driven logic, the mass triggers an overthrow or a transformation into new rules and new ways of rejecting those arriving at the border.

References

Arribas, Gloria Fernández. 'The EU–Turkey Agreement: A controversial attempt at patching up a major problem.' *European Papers – A Journal on Law and Integration* 2016, no. 3 (2016): 1097–104.

Betz, Hans-Georg. 'The new politics of resentment: Radical right-wing populist parties in Western Europe.' In *The Migration Reader: Exploring Politics and Policies*, ed. Anthony M. Messina and Gallya Lahav, pp. 384–401. Lynne Rienner Publishers, 2006.

Boffey, Daniel. 'Ursula von der Leyen says EU could punish UK over Brexit breaches.' *The Guardian*, 27 April 2021, available at: <https://www.theguardian.com/world/2021/apr/27/ursula-von-der-leyen-says-eu-could-punish-uk-over-brexit-breaches>, last accessed 25 September 2023.

Brown, Jessica Autumn. 'The new "Southern Strategy": Immigration, race, and "welfare dependency" in contemporary US Republican political discourse.' *Geopolitics, History, and International Relations* 8, no. 2 (2016): 22–41.

Council Decision (EU) 2014/252/EU of 14 April 2014 on the conclusion of the Agreement between the European Union and the Republic of Turkey on the readmission of persons residing without authorization, L 134, 7.5.2014. European Union: Council of the European Union.

Council Decision (EU) 2015/1601 of 22 September 2015 establishing provisional measures in the area of international protection for the benefit of Italy and Greece, L 248/80. European Union: Council of the European Union.

Creighton, Mathew J., and Amaney A. Jamal. 'An overstated welcome: Brexit and intentionally masked anti-immigrant sentiment in the UK.' *Journal of Ethnic and Migration Studies* 48, no. 5 (2022): 1051–71.

Davies, Cemlyn. 'Brexit: EU citizens in the UK "at risk of deportation".' *BBC News*, 17 February 2021, available at: <https://www.bbc.co.uk/news/uk-wales-politics-56092237>, last accessed 25 September 2023.

Deleuze, Gilles, and Félix Guattari. *A Thousand Plateaus: Capitalism and Schizophrenia*. Trans. Brian Massumi. University of Minnesota Press, 1987.

Dewsbury, J.-D. 'The Deleuze-Guattarian assemblage: Plastic habits.' *Area* 43, no. 2 (2011): 148–53.

Drake, B. Shaw, and Elizabeth Gibson. 'Vanishing protection: Access to asylum at the border.' *City University of New York Law Review* 21, no. 1 (2017): 91–142.

Ette, Andreas, and Jürgen Gerdes. 'Against exceptionalism: British interests for selectively Europeanizing its immigration policy.' In *The Europeanization of National Policies and Politics of Immigration: Between Autonomy and the European Union*, ed. Thomas Faist and Andreas Ette, pp. 93–115. Palgrave Macmillan, 2007.

European Commission. Recommendation on a European resettlement scheme, C(2015) 3560. European Commission, 8 June 2015.

European Commission. Recommendation for a voluntary humanitarian admission scheme with Turkey, C(2015) 9490. European Commission, 15 December 2015.

Favell, Adrian, and Roxana Barbulescu. 'Brexit, "immigration" and anti-discrimination.' In *The Routledge Handbook of the Politics of Brexit*, ed. Patrick Diamond, Peter Nedergaard and Ben Rosamond, pp. 118–33. Routledge, 2018.

Fetzer, Thiemo, and Shizhuo Wang. 'Measuring the regional economic cost of Brexit: Evidence up to 2019.' Warwick Economic Research Paper 486/2020. CAGE Research Centre, 2020.

Forsythe, James. 'The EU needs to stop punishing Britain for Brexit.' *The Spectator*, 19 February 2021, available at: <https://www.spectator.co.uk/article/the-eu-needs-to-stop-punishing-britain-for-brexit/>, last accessed 25 September 2023.

Gietel-Basten, Stuart. 'Why Brexit? The toxic mix of immigration and austerity.' *Population and Development Review* 42, no. 4 (2016): 673–80.

Goodwin, Matthew, and Caitlin Milazzo. 'Taking back control? Investigating the role of immigration in the 2016 vote for Brexit.' *The British Journal of Politics and International Relations* 19, no. 3 (2017): 450–64.

Gough, Jamie. 'Brexit, xenophobia and left strategy now.' *Capital & Class* 41, no. 2 (2017): 366–72.

Guild, Elspeth. 'The right to dignity of refugees: A response to Fleur Johns.' *AJIL Unbound* 111 (2017): 193–5.

Gündoğdu, Ayten. *Rightlessness in an Age of Rights: Hannah Arendt and the Contemporary Struggles of Migrants*. Oxford University Press, 2014.

Haferlach, Lisa, and Dilek Kurban. 'Lessons learnt from the EU–Turkey refugee agreement in guiding EU migration partnerships with origin and transit countries.' *Global Policy* 8 (2017): 85–93.

Hobolt, Sara B. 'The Brexit vote: A divided nation, a divided continent.' *Journal of European Public Policy* 23, no. 9 (2016): 1259–77.

Hogan, Jackie, and Kristin Haltinner. 'Floods, invaders, and parasites: Immigration threat narratives and right-wing populism in the USA, UK and Australia.' *Journal of Intercultural Studies* 36, no. 5 (2015): 520–43.

Innes, Alexandria J. 'When the threatened become the threat: The construction of asylum seekers in British media narratives.' *International Relations* 24, no. 4 (2010): 456–77.

Johnson, Heather L. 'Click to donate: Visual images, constructing victims and imagining the female refugee.' *Third World Quarterly* 32, no. 6 (2011): 1015–37.

Kallis, Aristotle. 'Far-right "contagion" or a failing "mainstream"? How dangerous ideas cross borders and blur boundaries.' *Democracy and Security* 9, no. 3 (2013): 221–46.

Langlotz, Andreas, and Danièle Klapproth Muazzin. 'Unveiling the phantom of the "Islamic takeover": A critical, cognitive-linguistic analysis of the discursive perpetuation of an Orientalist.' In *The Expression of Inequality in Interaction: Power, Dominance, and Status*, ed. Hanna Pishwa and Rainer Schulze, pp. 105–41. John Benjamins, 2014.

Lehner, Roman. 'The EU–Turkey-"deal": Legal challenges and pitfalls.' *International Migration* 57, no. 2 (2019): 176–85.

Lucassen, Geertje, and Marcel Lubbers. 'Who fears what? Explaining far-right-wing preference in Europe by distinguishing perceived cultural and economic ethnic threats.' *Comparative Political Studies* 45, no. 5 (2012): 547–74.

Milbourne, Paul, and Helen Coulson. 'Migrant labour in the UK's post-Brexit agri-food system: Ambiguities, contradictions and precarities.' *Journal of Rural Studies* 86 (2021): 430–9.

Outhwaite, William. 'Migration crisis and "Brexit".' In *The Oxford Handbook of Migration Crises*, ed. Cecilia Menjívar, Marie Ruiz and Immanuel Ness, pp. 93–110. Oxford University Press, 2019.

Proctor, Robert N. 'The destruction of "lives not worth living".' In *Deviant Bodies: Critical Perspectives on Difference in Science and Popular Culture*, ed. Jennifer Terry and Jacqueline Urla, pp. 170–96. Indiana University Press, 1995.

Radziwinowiczówna, Agnieszka. 'Bare life in an immigration jail: Technologies of surveillance in US pre-deportation detention.' *Journal of Ethnic and Migration Studies* 48, no. 8 (2022): 1873–90.

Reid, Andrew. 'Buses and breaking point: Freedom of expression and the "Brexit" campaign.' *Ethical Theory and Moral Practice* 22, no. 3 (2019): 623–37.

Rolfe, Heather. 'It's all about the flex: Preference, flexibility and power in the employment of EU migrants in low-skilled sectors.' *Social Policy and Society* 16, no. 4 (2017): 623–34.

Schmuck, Desirée, and Jörg Matthes. 'How anti-immigrant right-wing populist advertisements affect young voters: Symbolic threats, economic threats and the moderating role of education.' *Journal of Ethnic and Migration Studies* 41, no. 10 (2015): 1577–99.

Smith, Daniel. 'What is the body without organs? Machine and organism in Deleuze and Guattari.' *Continental Philosophy Review* 51, no. 1 (2018): 95–110.

Springford, John. 'The cost of Brexit to June 2018.' *Insight*, 30 September 2018, available at <https://www.cer.eu/insights/cost-brexit-june-2018>, last accessed 25 September 2023.

Stewart, Heather, and Rowena Mason. 'Nigel Farage's anti-migrant poster reported to police.' *The Guardian*, 17 June 2016, available at: <https://www.theguardian.com/politics/2016/jun/16/nigel-farage-defends-ukip-breaking-point-poster-queue-of-migrants>, last accessed 25 September 2023.

Ticktin, Miriam. 'Invasive others: Toward a contaminated world.' *Social Research: An International Quarterly* 84, no. 1 (2017): xxi–xxxiv.

Van Der Valk, Ineke. 'Right-wing parliamentary discourse on immigration in France.' *Discourse & Society* 14, no. 3 (2003): 309–48.

7

The Figure of the Innocent

Introduction

When the body of a young boy washed ashore in Turkey in 2015 the world temporarily held its breath and the humanity of our migration laws was – for a short while – put on moral trial. The image of young Aylan Kurdi, who tragically perished during the perilous passage by sea, appeared to be an exception among the continuous coverage showing people crossing borders as different forms of imagined threats. As an image of the innocent, the photograph of Aylan Kurdi had a significant impact in the shape of a temporary softening of some migration regulations. As this chapter will further show, that impact was possible because images of migrant children, in the right circumstances, are able to challenge the otherwise arid ethical landscape of the border. Unlike most figures we have seen thus far, the figure of a child conjures strong feelings and emotions and for many is a signifier of innocence, vulnerability, as well as the ultimate need for care (Wells 2007, p. 59). Therefore, images of children are capable of triggering a unique ethical response in viewers and are often used to elicit empathy (O'Dell 2008; Höijer 2004; Moeller 2002). As emphasised by Anna Larsen, conceptions of children as vulnerable and innocent make them ideal victims in news media coverage (2017, p. 894). Imagery of this kind is used to elicit sympathy, engagement and action. This explains why international organisations and media often use stories and faces of children when covering tragic events such as famine or war (ibid.). The image of Aylan Kurdi was no exception to this rule, because empathy stirred by depictions of suffering children prompts most viewers to respond ethically (Höijer 2004) in a visual landscape where the average viewer suffers from what many have termed 'compassion fatigue' (Moeller 1999; Tester 2001). Images of children break through compassion fatigue – a state in which too many images of suffering people results in emotional indifference to further portrayals of people in dire circumstances – because children signify innocence and typically harbour no ill intentions (imagined or otherwise). Even if, in some news areas, fatigue about – for example – abuse of children has also been observed (O'Dell 2008; Kitzinger and Skidmore 1995), typically the image of a suffering child remains one of the few effective visual tools capable of injecting ethical elements into the legal and political sphere (Wells 2007, p. 60).

As shown here, images of the innocent are so potent that in the right circumstances they are capable of refocusing a hostile response at the border and reignite the ethical potential of the encounter between host and guest. Due to its emotive qualities in the form of the image of a suffering child, the abstract focus on the potentially suspicious figure of a migrant is replaced with an unsettlingly palpable response to the suffering of the innocent. However, as this chapter illustrates, migrant children typically face a higher threshold of innocence when compared with the children of the host. This is because their autonomy is fragmented and can work similarly to the autonomy of the Janus-faced figure of the 'bogus' or 'genuine' asylum seeker. When lack of autonomy is unquestionable, migrant children enjoy the privilege of innocence. However, when the slightest suspicion of autonomy occurs, migrant children – just like their adult counterparts – can be accused of harbouring fraudulent intentions.

This chapter will analyse the image of Aylan Kurdi and its impact on interim challenges to the rigid rules of refugee reception in the EU. I will argue that the image of a migrant child challenges our ethical imagination in ways in which other figures of the migrant cannot. Not only does it make us see the migrant as a person, but it also injects ethical imagination into the ethically arid area of migration law. This is possible because children present ideal victims (O'Dell 2008; Wells 2007; Höijer 2004; Moeller 2002) in the hierarchy of innocence and, as such, are capable of challenging the foundations of the legal and ethical approaches we take. When they do, they trigger unprecedented ethical responses – even leading to suspension of existing laws in favour of ethics.

The Image of a Child and Ethics: The Puzzle of Children's Autonomy

When facing the image of a suffering child, the viewer typically exhibits compassion for even the most remote stranger, as opposed to seeing an abstract political subject who can be treated with the anonymity of the law and excluded from the workings of ethics (Höijer 2004, p. 522). As observed by Birgitta Höijer, when faced with images of children our preoccupation with abstract rights and rules is frequently replaced by a more immediate concern for the ethical recognition of the other (ibid., pp. 525–7). Such recognition triggers a hospitable response and broadens the threshold of welcome.

This is possible because the figure of a child possesses but a fragmented autonomy and is often perceived as a figure at the mercy of their parents, their carers – and indeed circumstances in general. In the Western construction of childhood (Gittins 2004), the figure of a refugee or migrant child shares with figures of host children the typical presumption about incomplete autonomy. The figure of a child makes us relate to our own childhood (Moeller 2002, p. 44), the childhood of our own children and the potentiality of the future (Cockburn 2005, p. 77; O'Dell 2008, p. 385). As a result, the figure of a migrant child is easier for the host to see as an equivalent to their own children and easier to treat ethically as a guest rather than as an unwanted alien. The autonomy of a child, however, is a complex notion (Freeman 2007; Hafen and Hafen 1996). Indeed, as Bruce and Jonathan Hafen have argued, the presumption of childhood innocence is possible because we often imagine children as both autonomous in terms of making some choices and simultaneously as figures in need of protection (1996, p. 37). While we allow children a level of autonomy to express their will or opinion, Freeman emphasises that we are not willing to allow them to behave in such a way as might damage their chances in adult life (Freeman 2007, p. 325). Allowing children autonomy, according to Selma Sevenhuijsen, would overlook and potentially neglect their vulnerability, their dependence and their ways of dealing with individual conditions and circumstances (2003, p. 28). Barbara Woodhouse observes that children's rights and needs are inextricably intertwined (1993) and rather than defining them as stemming purely from children's autonomy, we often see them as stemming from children's needs. This focus on needs uniquely predisposes us to see children not only as figures in need of an ethical response but also as figures that require both ethics and care.

Tom Cockburn stresses that children's worlds occur in relationships and it is necessary for us to recognise children as actors within those networks (2005, p. 77). With that recognition comes the acknowledgement of our diverse legal duties towards children as subjects with a complex notion of autonomy and often dependent on the fine network of societal relationships providing the care that they require. That recognition has typically been legally translated into the notion of the 'best interest of the child'. We typically focus our legal and ethical response to children in distress with a focus on securing their best interest. The innocence of a child can make the host prioritise this best interest instead of prioritising a judgement on their worthiness to enter host territory. This is particularly true of suffering children. When children become victims of wrongdoing, we are often capable of making ourselves scrutinise our laws and sometimes even identify malevolence and hostility in our legal system (Moeller 2002, p. 39) as the very cause of children's suffering. Such an unprecedented response is possible because – as Lindsay O'Dell reminds us – 'abused or "damaged" children' stand as icons of an ideal childhood and referents of how that childhood has been destroyed by circumstances (2008: 383). When we imagine ourselves in the situation of the child, we are capable of imagining how our own future would have been shaped had we been placed in an analogous situation. For these reasons, the viewer looking at a 'damaged child' (ibid., p. 384) is more likely to recognise this visualisation as a subject requiring an ethical response and care. Susan Moeller asserts:

> The image of an endangered child is the perfect 'grabber'. It is so powerful that it short-circuits reasoned thought. Children dramatise the righteousness of a cause by having their innocence contrasted with the malevolence (or perhaps banal hostility) of adults in authority. (Moeller 2002, p. 39)

This association between childhood and innocence, however, does not always apply to children crossing borders. Because of the fragmented nature of children's autonomy, migrant children can often be suspected of in fact being autonomous rather than innocent.

The Threshold of Innocence and Migrant Children

At first glance, migrant children are no exception to being seen as subjects with partial autonomy who require care and representation by adults (Masson 2000). When migrant children are seen as part of a family, their autonomy remains limited and linked with that of the adult family members. However, as soon as children are unaccompanied, suspicion appears of their actually being autonomous (Drywood 2010, pp. 315–16). This results in a situation where some migrant children are seen as subjects deserving an ethical approach while others continue being marred by suspicion of wrongful intentions. I would like to argue that migrant children are often excluded from the mechanism triggering an ethical response because of this constant suspicion of in fact being autonomous and thus having to be assessed in terms of their innocence. Rather than simply being viewed as partially non-autonomous subjects who require care much like 'our' children, migrant children are constantly assessed as to whether they are in fact 'bogus' like their adult counterparts. This suspicion leads to the possibility of their being viewed as fraudulent and thus cast in the spectrum of illegality. This is possible because the logic of care too often relies on a presumption of dependence of those receiving care, who 'must profess incompetence even when they are more competent than those offering care' (Cockburn 2005, p. 80). The same dynamic underpins the logic of genuineness and bogusness analysed in Chapter 3. While an ethical approach to children may be seen as a remedy for the blindness of the border, nonetheless this remains conditional on an assessment of the 'genuineness' of the innocence of a migrant child. When such genuineness of suffering is confirmed, then the charity of welcome, ethics and care can be extended to the innocent who is similar enough to 'our own' children. But if any suspicion of autonomy occurs, migrant children, just like their adult counterparts, are implicated in the constant classification of some subjects as deserving and others as undeserving of a charitable response. As we have already seen in Chapter 3, the logic of charity requires those who 'qualify' for protection of rights to be ultimately so deprived that rights are granted to them as a matter of necessary charity. While host subjects enjoy rights by virtue of belonging and as fellow citizens equipped with dignity, rights and autonomy, those who receive rights in the form of charity (Rancière 2004; Mutua 2001; Malkki 1996) must be 'absolute victims' (Rancière 2004, p. 309) or victims of 'legitimate' suffering (Ticktin 2011, pp. 25, 132) that classifies them as worthy of protection. If no such victimhood is demonstrated, rights could be withheld on the grounds of the victim not having gone through hardships substantial enough to warrant such a charitable response. Within the realm of rights and regimes of legal protection, refugee protection in particular has for long been seen as a form of charity by Western states owed to those most vulnerable (Kronick and Rousseau 2015, p. 552).

Within this construction, subjects worthy of our charity are placed in a 'hierarchy of innocence' (Moeller 2002) where the ultimate 'innocent' embodied in the person of a tortured, deprived or victimised child is the first figure to whom a charitable response is owed. While some refugee children will qualify as victimised innocents (Kronick and Rousseau 2015, p. 566) who lack autonomy, others will be treated with suspicion so that their migrant or refugee status will take precedence over their status as children (Drywood 2010, p. 315). Compared with 'our own' children, who in most – though not all – circumstances qualify as ideal subjects of rights by virtue of their citizenship (Mustasaari 2016; Bhabha 2009) or for our care by virtue of their non-autonomy that makes them vulnerable, migrant children usually face a higher threshold in proving their place in the hierarchy. Indeed, Jacqueline Bhabha observes that migrant children often fail to qualify for rights at all, constituting a precariate amongst an already precarious population (2009, pp. 413–15). This is because migrant children – in particular, refugee children – are always seen firstly as asylum seekers and only later as children (Drywood 2010, pp. 315–16).

As emphasised by Rachel Kronick and Cécile Rousseau, refugee children's rights are conjoint with the general perception of migrants and refugees and seen as a danger to the taxpayer's rights (2015, p. 557) and thus as the other, very different from the self. They are always in danger of being cast under the spectacle of 'bogusness'. To cross this threshold of compassion and to be able to be classified as truly innocent, refugee children – just like 'genuine' refugees – must be seen as completely non-autonomous subjects whose innocence, lack of intention and being left at the mercy of circumstance is beyond any doubt. A migrant child can only cross the threshold of compassion if the power of their 'innocence' is juxtaposed with the general image of the fraudulent migrant. As Kronick and Rousseau put it, 'In a logic of compassion, justice becomes a zero-sum game dependent on the creation of the suffering child as much as the false refugee' (ibid., p. 562). Such a shift in imagery and avoidance of suspicion is possible only until a certain age (Huijsmans 2011). When suspicion is raised of a migrant child in fact being autonomous, they – including refugee children – are subjected to often humiliating age verifying procedures (Aynsley-Green et al. 2012) and stripped of all protections, much like their adult counterparts. When children project autonomy, they can be treated like potential juvenile delinquents or as a danger to the taxpayer or simply as abusers of charity rather than as children deprived of adequate protection. Nobody can tell when exactly this change of perception occurs but it is generally associated with entering puberty. It is around that time that children begin to lose their privilege of innocence (Fass 2005; Scott 2000). Only when young enough does a migrant child enjoy a chance of escaping the discourse of illegality, criminality and fraudulent intentions and may be treated as the ideal victim deserving an ethical response and protection of rights. These children are not blamed for making autonomous choices in the same way as adult migrants and enjoy a different portrayal by the media:

> As opposed to irregular migrants in general, [. . .] the topic of irregular migrant children was particularly newsworthy: the topic had previously received little public attention and concerned a particularly innocent and vulnerable group that could hardly be blamed for the choices of their parents or the rigidity of the immigration system. (Larsen 2017, p. 901)

It is precisely the idea of the dual nature of children's autonomy that gives children a chance of crossing the threshold of innocence and qualifying for the compassion underlying and underpinning the charity of rights and care. When the non-autonomous element outweighs the autonomous element, children cannot be blamed for choices or intentional abuse of the migration system. This perception of non-autonomy is linked tightly to the visual perception of innocence and special vulnerability. As long as the perception of innocence holds, the figure of a child with their inter-dependent, non-autonomous status is automatically placed closer to the ideal victim requiring a charitable response. Our legal understanding of a child's autonomy as partial and not fully developed and its amalgamation with the perception of innocence may protect children from a cruel response from those legal regimes that treat with suspicion any signs of autonomy projected by adults.

Figure 7.1 Aylan Kurdi on a banner during a protest in Athens, original photograph, Nilüfer Demir, 2015, Alamy

Aylan Kurdi's Image: The Ultimate Innocent and the Challenge to Refugee Reception Laws

While migrant children face a higher threshold in proving their place in the hierarchy of innocence, some images featuring children carry such affective power that in rare circumstances they challenge even the rigidity of legal rules. A challenge of this kind to refugee reception rules occurred when a photograph of Aylan Kurdi's dead body covered the front pages of the worldwide press. Aylan, a two-year-old Syrian boy escaping the war together with his family, died on 2 September 2015 when attempting to cross the Mediterranean Sea and reach Greece. Unlike other dominant images of refugees analysed earlier in this volume, the picture of Aylan's dead but somehow life-like body washed up on a sandy Turkish beach spread around the globe within hours. It caused moral outrage and a compassionate response unprecedented at the time of the so-called refugee crisis (Kingsley and Timur 2015). The visual representation capturing the image of his lost innocence and the links that depiction had with the limited autonomy of children immediately crossed the affective threshold of compassionate response. Thanks to the aesthetic qualities of the image itself, the visual representation of Aylan cut through compassion fatigue.

Aylan's dead body lying ashore was framed unlike most figures of refugees or migrants. His tiny figure was not depicted as part of an anonymous mass or unspecified danger to the community, but instead shown closely and at no distance. The frame remained narrow and cut away much of the surroundings. As a result of the narrowness of this frame, the viewer was not allowed a gaze far from the boy or to put a distance between the viewer and the figure of the dead boy. Instead, the image remained immensely individual and focused on nothing other than the child's humanity and innocence. The gaze point was close, allowing for a face-to-face encounter. A person faced with Aylan's photograph was not positioned in any particular social or legal setting, but instead on a nameless sandy beach – a sight of human tragedy without borders or some pre-imposed place the viewer should take. There were no buildings, no national flags and no authorities to convince of the child's genuineness as a refugee. The only border remained that between land and sea: the boundary between the danger of the water and the safety of the land. The deceptive calm of the waves and the shore appeared almost idyllic but for the knowledge that the child in the frame had lost his life during his journey to safety. Of the little victim of the sea passage, half of the face was visible to nearly every person on the globe. Not only did the picture humanise Aylan but it also emanated a sense of a tangible tragedy. The spectator placed directly vis-à-vis the tragic, lifeless body of a little boy could not, in any way, anonymise the tiny refugee who drowned. They could not escape, nor could they deflect their gaze to the sand and the waves in the frame. This allowed for a nearly face-to-face experience, calling law to justice, preventing narratives dehumanising the arriving cohort. The tragedy was there to see, to watch closely, although the spectacle of this border tragedy was both direct and anonymous. Aylan's half-visible but half-obstructed face allowed for recognition of the innocence of any child but also identification with the future of 'our own' children, as the light tone of his skin served as a proxy for predominantly white European children (El-Enany 2016). Thanks to these qualities, Aylan the tragically lost little refugee child was not just part of a nameless migrant flow crossing the sea, but an embodiment of the innocence of a child that remained innocent and so much like 'our' children. Thanks to these features qualifying for ultimate innocence, he was immediately deemed worthy of the charity of care. In addition – thanks to his similarity to 'our' children – he also qualified to resemble an ideal subject of care: a helpless child with no autonomy, at the mercy of circumstances and the sea. The untimely death of this little boy became palpable, signifying the stolen opportunities we imagine when faced with images of suffering children.

These lost chances and childhood innocence captured in the image did not allow for questioning of Aylan's motives as a refugee and did not impose preconceived judgements that await adults arriving on European shores. There were no thought bubbles, no hidden motives, no adults that could be accused of manipulation or insincere intentions. His tender age and his diminutive body spoke to a lack of autonomy and a need for care from adults. It was suddenly clear beyond doubt that something was missing in terms of the required care. And it was not lack of care by his parents, who protected him from war, but instead something else. Thanks to taking a place at the innocence end of the innocent child/fraudulent migrant spectrum for a brief moment, Aylan could stand as a symbol for the pleas of other refugees for whom – as the innocent – he paid the ultimate price. Thanks to this narrow frame and a close gaze point, the perilous journey was suddenly not the blame of a refugee but instead a consequence of lack of empathy on the part of the Western refugee reception system. In other words, the judgement implied in the visual elements was suddenly implicitly focused – not on the refugee but on the legal refugee reception system itself. A viewer of the image was suddenly challenged to abandon the question usually posed: 'Why do these people board those boats knowing it's dangerous, risky and likely unsuccessful?' Instead, it was turned into: 'What is our ethical responsibility in this crisis? Was it not our negligence, our complacency and the blindness of our laws that led to this? Are our laws to blame?' Owing to all these visual elements, the dead refugee boy ceased being an anonymous other but instead became a concrete subject of legal and ethical duties – both by virtue of charity and simultaneously by virtue of resembling 'our' children. The image circulated on social media and generated unprecedented artistic response in which people attempted to return lost dignity to the human child (Vis and Goriunova 2015) – not a refugee, not an abstract other, but a concrete human child. Images of Aylan playing in the sand, images of Aylan as an angel and other iterations of the original photograph spread quickly, loudly announcing global outrage at the tragic fate of the boy, now a proxy for the pleas of other refugees.

Challenging the Cruelty of Existing Legal Systems

Without a doubt, this dramatic shift in the collective spectator's experience also triggered an unprecedented legal response. Even before Aylan's death, Germany's Federal Office for Migration and Refugees (BAMF) was considering opening the borders to Syrians stranded at the Hungarian border to relieve the crisis caused by the Orban government (Fry 2015; Blume et al. 2016). But, until that point, political willingness to make any concessions was limited. Two days after Aylan's death, however, on the night of 4–5 September 2016 the German Chancellor took the unprecedented decision to allow refugees stranded at the Hungarian border to enter Germany and apply for asylum without any limits on numbers (Wendel 2016). It was as if the image were a tipping point shifting the discussion from the abstractness of legal requirements to the concreteness of the need for care. After Germany, Austria temporarily followed suit in what was seen as a 'suspension' (Fry 2015) of the EU Dublin III regulation requiring the processing of asylum applications in the first receiving country. The principle of applying for asylum at the point of entry (Regulation (EU) No 604/2013, Article 13.1) and the possibility of being returned to the country of entry (Regulation (EU) No 604/2013, Article 23.1) became temporarily non-operational. Speculation whether the decision was a violation of EU law and the Dublin III regulation or whether it was an exercise of the right to assume responsibility under the Directive produced a mixed response (Wendel 2016). Regardless, however, of whether we see the step as remaining within the realm of law or contrary to it, the universality of the legal refugee reception machinery and the central principles underpinning the Common European Asylum System (CEAS) were suddenly shaken by the reappearance of not only legal but also ethical considerations. Viewers, including those responsible for regulating the threshold of the border, were called upon to make their hospitality available. In response to the ultimate sacrifice of an innocent who immediately crossed the imagined threshold of compassion, refugee law was challenged to do what had seemed for a long time to be impossible: taking responsibility and providing care for all refugees requiring protection, not only those who proved especially victimised. In her thesis on the ethics of care in the European refugee crisis, Anne Sophie Eberstein pictures this shift in the reasoning in the following way:

> Merkel acts on the assumption that the refugees coming to Europe and [...] European citizens, institutions and governments are interdependent. By understanding the close interdependence between herself and [...] people in need, she takes on responsibility for their needs, shows empathy and caring behaviour towards them. This originates from the relational ontology of caring ethics that incorporates all human beings beyond differences. (Eberstein 2016, pp. 32–3)

Temporarily, the violence of the law (Benjamin 1996; Derrida 1992) became moderated by the ethics of care, going beyond the language of law or rights. Images of smiling soldiers welcoming refugees on train platforms once again humanised refugees, making them people with their faces, their stories and their suffering. For a short while they were no longer an anonymous cohort, nor were they put in the equation between the 'good' and the 'bogus' refugee. Instead, for that brief moment they took precedence over the malevolence of the law and its stringency. When the ethics of care stirred a strong hospitable response, it was no longer the refugee who was suspect, but the law and the way we regulate arrivals at our borders. This unprecedented turn was triggered by the appearance of the image of the innocent child. Suddenly, it was not refugees but the universalism, objectivity or rationality of the law that became challenged and replaced with *Willkommenskultur*, embracing at the minimum rights and indeed reaching far beyond them. What was unimaginable when viewers were faced with images of thousands fleeing the conflict in Syria unprecedentedly turned out to be possible when viewers had to grapple with the image of a lifeless little boy washed ashore during a perilous journey. Reminding the viewers of the concreteness of the other who had lost all his chances for the future, Aylan passed the threshold of innocence because he was presented as yet another innocent child – someone who could not possibly be accused of choosing or picking a destination country. Instead, he became a victim of the EU refugee reception system turning a blind eye to human suffering.

At moments when the law faces the extremity of suffering directed at the figure of the ultimate innocent – the child – it can for brief moments meet with its ethical counterpart. In those moments, hiding behind the blindness and impartiality of the law no longer suffices, and the blindness of justice appears ridiculous and ill-suited for the occasion of dealing with ultimate innocents deprived of their innocence. This is because the host approaches the guest as a subject requiring an ethical response similar to that we would owe our own citizens. How could we ever remedy the suffering of the child if we kept our legal blindfolds on? How could we ever recognise the uniqueness of their suffering if we refused to look closely and take sides? The suffering of an innocent child and their pain that is portrayed visually can for just a brief moment challenge the legal and ethical boundaries between a refugee, a migrant and a citizen child. An assault on innocence in the form of injury, physical pain, hunger or even death is capable of calling into question the legitimacy of the entire legal machinery controlling the lives of foreigners – something that an assault on the dignity of an adult refugee has for long been unable to do. For that brief moment, and that moment only, the legal system meets its ethical counterpart.

Other Images of Migrant Children

The image of the child as an innocent has of course been used since Aylan's tragedy. The separation of children from their migrant parents under the Trump administration also caused moral outrage (BBC News 2018). The executive order of 'zero tolerance' signed in April 2018 allowed for detaining children and parents separately and likewise resulted in calling the policy into question. Outrage was possible for similar reasons: children as a symbol of innocence and as subjects who are seen as lacking autonomy were neverthe-

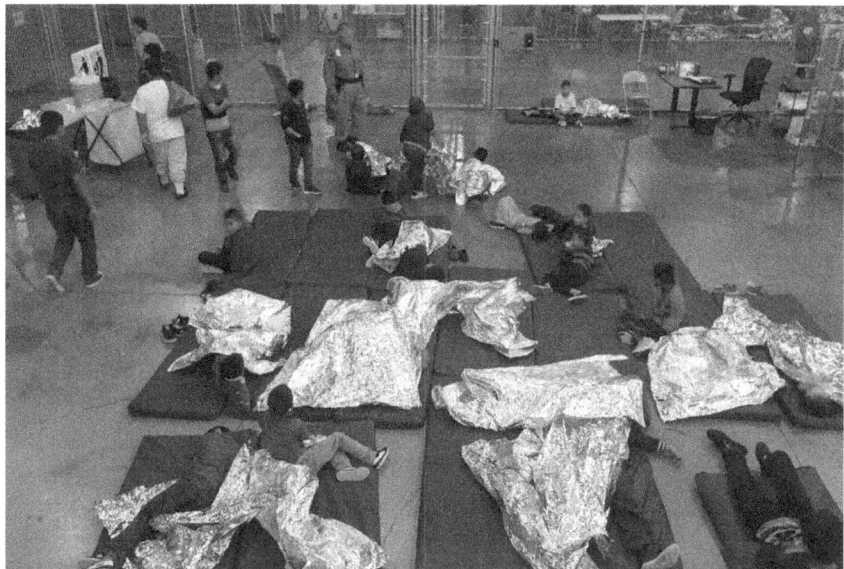

Figure 7.2 Photo provided by US Customs and Border Protection to reporter on tour of Ursula detention facility in McAllen, Texas, 2018, Alamy

less separated from their parents, who typically provide care. Pictures of children in holding cages, behind wire and in other inhumane circumstances, similarly to images of Aylan, shook Americans' moral imagination. But these photos in many ways also differed from images of Aylan. They were less personal and showed children in large groups. In those images, innocence was tainted and undoubtedly prioritised their migrant status. These images have illustrated a more typical pathway of the migrant child to proving their innocence, showing them either as part of a mass when pictured in larger groups or mixed with the suspicion of illegality when pictured behind wire or inside holding cages.

The viewer of the image provided by US Customs and Border Protection (Figure 7.2) was invited to question whether such innocence was in fact 'real'. The frame was wide and showed merely one among many holding cages. The gaze point from above emphasised the large numbers, making a face-to-face encounter with children impossible with their faces in fact blurred, presumably for protection of their identity. Nonetheless, instead of focusing on their individuality and potential as children, this image focused on the numbers and immediately triggered suspicion of the mass. The field of appearance was saturated with the presence of holding cages, inside which children, barely visible as tiny little bodies on the floor, were mixed with the imagery of law enforcement. The mixing of the cages, officers present in the cages, and the reality of the holding cells resembling prison rather than circumstances where children are typically seen prompted viewers to ask whether their innocence was in fact 'genuine' or whether these children were simply 'illegals'. The dull colours dominating the picture did not allow for romanticising childhood, but instead mixed it with the messy reality of the flight, including none of the bright colours or artefacts typically seen around children. This field of appearance made it harder to imagine these children as identical or similar to 'our' children. In many ways this photograph embodies the more typical pathway of a migrant child to innocence. Before being deemed innocent, a migrant child is often firstly seen as one other of the figures: the mass, the illegal or the other. Only after proving their innocence, showing ultimate deprivation or ultimate sacrifice, can they be seen as closer to 'our own' children. The unique framing that occurred in the image of Aylan Kurdi is rare. The unique focus on migrant children's childhood is an exception. Aylan's tender age also left his innocence beyond doubt, because no child of two is seen as truly autonomous. The children captured in the image in Figure 7.2 are older and mostly boys, immediately triggering the question whether they are in fact autonomous and thus suspicious. With multiple similar images emerging, finally the pressure became too strong and the 'zero tolerance' order was modified allowing for families to be detained together. This reaction, however, was slower than in the case of Aylan and allowed only for modifications to the policy, not its reversal. Ultimately, under the modifications, children remained seen mainly as migrants rather than as innocents. Seen primarily as migrants in the pictures, their migrant status legally trumped their innocence. The imagery dominating the news did not allow them to reach the top in the hierarchy of innocence but merely allowed them to be innocent enough not to be separated from their parents.

Conclusions

With the inherent otherness of the non-citizen underpinning them, migration and refugee law regimes have recently proven almost impenetrable to ethical arguments. The refugee – the ultimate other of migration law, as shown earlier in this volume – is being increasingly regulated, securitised and scrutinised. The dominant figures of refugees recurring in visual and legal discourses perpetuate many tropes that allow for these securitised approaches to appear legitimate. The envisioned refugee typically becomes a figure ever further removed from the community and ever less deserving of the charity of legal protection. The figure of a persecuted, injured or deceased child provides a rare counterbalance on the ethically arid horizon of migration laws. In circumstances where such a child is presented as just another child, a child that could be one of 'our' children, this figure may – just as in Aylan's case –

cross the threshold of innocence and compassion, resulting in unprecedented suspicion towards existing laws or even in their temporary suspension. Yet, in circumstances where their migrant status trumps their innocence, cruel policies such as separation from their deported parents by the Trump administration take longer to reverse and do not grant them a welcome at the border. Many migrant and refugee children never cross the threshold of innocence sufficiently for a welcome. Suspicion over their migrant status typically places them only somewhere higher than their parents in the hierarchy of innocence. The case of Aylan and images of his death are exceptional in showing just how powerful the response can be when visual representation focuses solely on innocence, the hardship and the sacrifice that refugee children must bear, rather than their anonymity, potential 'illegality' and projected autonomy in migration choices.

References

Aynsley-Green, Albert, Tim J. Cole, Heaven Crawley, Nick Lessof, L. R. Boag and Rebecca M. M. Wallace. 'Medical, statistical, ethical and human rights considerations in the assessment of age in children and young people subject to immigration control.' *British Medical Bulletin* 102, no. 1 (2012): 17–42.

BBC News. 'Trump backs down on migrant family separations policy.' *BBC News*, 21 June 2018, available at: <https://www.bbc.co.uk/news/world-us-canada-44552852>, last accessed 25 September 2023.

Benjamin, Walter, 'Critique of violence' (1921). In *Selected Writings, Volume 1: 1913–1926*, ed. Marcus Bullock and Michael W. Jennings, pp. 236–52. The Belknap Press of Harvard University Press, 1996.

Bhabha, Jacqueline. 'Arendt's children: Do today's migrant children have a right to have rights?' *Human Rights Quarterly* 31, no. 2 (2009): 410–51.

Blume, Georg, Marc Brost, Tina Hildebrandt, Alexej Hock, Sybille Klormann, Angela Köckritz, Matthias Krupa, Mariam Lau, Gero von Randow, Merlind Theile, Michael Thumann and Heinrich Wefing. 'The night Germany lost control.' *Zeit Online*, 30 August 2016, available at: <http://www.zeit.de/gesellschaft/2016-08/refugees-open-border-policy-september-2015-angela-merkel>, last accessed 25 September 2023.

Cockburn, Tom. 'Children and the feminist ethic of care.' *Childhood* 12, no. 1 (2005): 71–89.

Derrida, Jacques. 'Force of law: The "mystical foundation of authority".' Trans. Mary Quaintance. In *Deconstruction and the Possibility of Justice*, ed. Drucilla Cornell, Michael Rosenfield and David G. Carlson, pp. 3–68. Routledge, 1992.

Drywood, Eleanor. 'Challenging concepts of the "child" in asylum and immigration law: The example of the EU.' *Journal of Social Welfare & Family Law* 32, no. 3 (2010): 309–23.

Eberstein, Anne Sophie. 'Why care matters: Analysing the German response to the European refugee crisis from a global ethics of care perspective.' Lund University Student Papers (2016), available at: <https://lup.lub.lu.se/student-papers/search/publication/8878465>, last accessed 25 September 2023.

El-Enany, Nadine. 'Aylan Kurdi: The human refugee.' *Law and Critique* 27, no. 1 (2016): 13–15.

Fass, Paula S. 'Children in global migrations.' *Journal of Social History* 38, no. 4 (2005): 937–53.

Freeman, Michael. 'Why it remains important to take children's rights seriously.' *The International Journal of Children's Rights* 15, no. 1 (2007): 5–23.

Fry, Luke. 'Refugee crisis timeline: How the crisis has grown.' *The Independent*, 15 September 2015, available at: <http://www.independent.co.uk/news/world/europe/refugee-crisis-timeline-how-the-crisis-has-grown/10502690.html>, last accessed 25 September 2023.

Gittins, Diana. 'The historical construction of childhood.' In *An Introduction to Childhood Studies*, ed. Mary Jane Kehily, pp. 25–38. Open University Press, 2004.

Golec de Zavala, Agnieszka, Rita Guerra and Cláudia Simão. 'The relationship between the Brexit vote and individual predictors of prejudice: Collective narcissism, right wing authoritarianism, social dominance orientation.' *Frontiers in Psychology* 8 (2017): art. 2023.

Guild, Elspeth. 'The right to dignity of refugees: A response to Fleur Johns.' *AJIL Unbound* 111 (2017): 193–5.

Hafen, Bruce C., and Jonathan O. Hafen. 'Abandoning children to their autonomy: The United Nations Convention on the Rights of the Child.' *Harvard International Law Journal* 37, no. 2 (1996): 449–91.

Höijer, Birgitta. 'The discourse of global compassion: The audience and media reporting of human suffering.' *Media, Culture & Society* 26, no. 4 (2004): 513–31.

Huijsmans, Roy. 'Child migration and questions of agency.' *Development and Change* 42, no. 5 (2011): 1307–21.

Kingsley, Patrick, and Safak Timur. 'Stories of 2015: How Aylan Kurdi's death changed the world.' *The Guardian*, 31 December 2015, available at: <https://www.theguardian.com/world/2015/dec/31/alan-kurdi-death-canada-refugee-policy-syria-boy-beach-turkey-photo>, last accessed 25 September 2023.

Kitzinger, Jenny, and Paula Skidmore. 'Playing safe: Media coverage of child sexual abuse prevention strategies.' *Child Abuse Review* 4, no. 1 (1995): 47–56.

Kronick, Rachel, and Cécile Rousseau. 'Rights, compassion and invisible children: A critical discourse analysis of the parliamentary debates on the mandatory detention of migrant children in Canada.' *Journal of Refugee Studies* 28, no. 4 (2015): 544–69.

Larsen, Anna Grøndahl. 'Protection or participation? Editorial evaluation of two news serials concerning irregular migrant children.' *Journalism Practice* 11, no. 7 (2017): 893–908.

Malkki, Liisa H. 'Speechless emissaries: Refugees, humanitarianism, and dehistoricization.' *Cultural Anthropology* 11, no. 3 (1996): 377–404.

Masson, Judith. 'Representation of children in England: Protecting children in child protection proceedings.' *Family Law Quarterly* 34, no. 3 (2000): 467–95.

Moeller, Susan D. *Compassion Fatigue: How the Media Sell Disease, Famine, War and Death*. Routledge, 1999.

Moeller, Susan D. 'A hierarchy of innocence: The media's use of children in the telling of international news.' *Harvard International Journal of Press/Politics* 7, no. 1 (2002): 36–56.

Mustasaari, Sanna. 'Best interests of the child in family reunification – a citizenship test disguised?' In *Subjectivity, Citizenship and Belonging in Law: Identities and Intersections*, ed. Anne Griffiths, Sanna Mustasaari and Anna Mäki-Petajä-Leinonen, pp. 135–57. Routledge, 2016.

Mutua, Makau. 'Savages, victims, and saviors: The metaphor of human rights.' *Harvard International Law Journal* 42 (2001): 201–45.

O'Dell, Lindsay. 'Representations of the "damaged" child: "Child saving" in a British children's charity ad campaign.' *Children & Society* 22, no. 5 (2008): 383–92.

Rancière, Jacques. 'Who is the subject of the rights of man?' *The South Atlantic Quarterly* 103, no. 2/3 (2004): 297–310.

Regulation (EU) No 604/2013 of the European Parliament and of the Council of 26 June 2013 establishing the criteria and mechanisms for determining the Member State responsible for examining an application for international protection lodged in one of the Member States by a third-country national or a stateless person (recast), 29 June 2013, OJ L. 180/31–180/59. European Union: Council of the European Union.

Scott, Elizabeth S. 'The legal construction of adolescence.' *Hofstra Law Review* 29, no. 2 (2000): 547–98.

Sevenhuijsen, Selma. *Citizenship and the Ethics of Care: Feminist Considerations on Justice, Morality and Politics*. Routledge, 2003.

Tester, Keith. *Compassion, Morality and the Media*. Open University Press, 2001.

Ticktin, Miriam. *Casualties of Care: Immigration and the Politics of Humanitarianism in France*. University of California Press, 2011.

Vis, Farida, and Olga Goriunova, eds. *The Iconic Image on Social Media: A Rapid Research Response to the death of Aylan Kurdi*. Visual Social Media Lab, 2015.

Wells, Karen. 'Narratives of liberation and narratives of innocent suffering: The rhetorical uses of images of Iraqi children in the British press.' *Visual Communication* 6, no. 1 (2007): 55–71.

Wendel, Mattias. 'The refugee crisis and the executive: On the limits of administrative discretion in the Common European Asylum System.' *German Law Journal* 17, no. 6 (2016): 1005–32.

Woodhouse, Barbara Bennett. 'Hatching the egg: A child-centered perspective on parent's rights.' *Cardozo Law Review* 14, no. 6 (1993): 1747–866.

PART III
THE COMPLICITY OF THE PICTURE

8

The Challenge of Navigating the Ethics of Law in the Pictorial Era

Introduction

Despite the growing importance of images in our contemporary world and the ease with which we can share, look at and use pictures, photographs and visual media of all kinds, sceptics may continue to remain unconvinced that imagery has much to do with law. After all, if we focus on the idea of competition for gaze, presence of recurring imagery may be considered irrelevant as long as competing imagery is emerging and attempting to speak to viewers. Yet, in spite of the wide variety of visual media available today, the influence of certain depictions of migrants has had an extraordinary power to convince voters (Matthes and Schmuck 2017). However, in this pictorial era – as W. J. T. Mitchell (1995) called it – we are still often unaware of the framing, the gaze and the affect created by the visual field. The way in which we look often goes unnoticed and is rarely treated as a form of power shaping societal bonds and relations. Meanwhile, growing reliance on the visual field in communication more generally makes it all the more important to understand that the way in which we look shapes our understanding of duties we have towards ethical and legal subjects. This book has shown that the visual field communicates messages and presumed relationships between host and migrant through elements such as the frame, the gaze point and the field of appearance. In the overwhelming visual presence of certain figures, the ethical distance between the viewer and the figure of the migrant has become so normalised that exclusion of the migrant from a range of rights and societal participation appears to be 'natural'. Awareness of the role of these archetypal images and their impact on forming individual decisions and normative standards can help us understand why migration law has been progressively moving in the direction of increased hostility, and why hospitality is increasingly withdrawn and remains conditional on meeting numerous special requirements.

This chapter focuses on the relationship between law and the image in the pictorial era. It asks whether we can challenge existing archetypes and shows the impact of the current archetypes on legitimating normative shifts. Finally, the chapter goes back to the question of ethics in law. It shows that while the gap between law and ethics exists and is difficult to bridge, awareness of the influence of the gaze is crucial in order to avoid perpetuation of othering and exclusionary discourses.

Can We Challenge the Broader Archetypes of Foreignness?

As Bonnie Honig pointed out, the enduring and somewhat xenophobic way of thinking about foreignness is so embedded in our daily reality that foreignness is treated as a problem that needs to be constantly managed and reflected in legal, judicial and political decisions (2001, p. 2). While Honig insists that foreignness is related to our concept of a democratic nation state, she invites us to rethink the question 'how to solve the problem of foreignness' as 'what can foreignness solve for us' (ibid., p. 4). As Honig further elaborates, ideas of democracy, which she traces back to Jean-Jacques Rousseau's ideas of the social contract, appear to have a deep relationship with foreignness (ibid., p. 22). Yet, as she argues further through examples of foreigners as founders, it is often those arriving in a new place that draft the rules of new social contracts (ibid., pp. 15–40) and the role of foreigners in building the community is overlooked.

This book agrees with Honig's premises and focuses on the fact that the idea of foreignness as a 'problem' is hard to eradicate. This is supported by the wider ideological apparatus and reinforced by the optical apparatus maintaining and continuously shaping the social contract and the position of those we perceive as 'foreigners'. Thinking of some people as foreigners who need to be controlled and managed, and whose lives require strict regulation through the law, stems from the way we picture foreignness and imagine the 'migrant'. As the five archetypal images analysed here have revealed, the fundamental distance between host and guest in the imagery of migrants establishes a wide – and often unbridgeable – ethical distance that often perpetuates and strengthens feelings of threat and eliminates focus on the shared humanity of those arriving. When we see the migrant through such frames, it becomes hard, if not impossible, to imagine a different relationship with foreignness and the figure of the migrant. Thinking of foreignness as a threat results in imagery deeply reliant on emphasising the threat through different types of representation and gives a foundation to legalising the imagined gap between host and guest. Challenging the archetypes of the migrant is difficult, if not impossible, because the way we look at those arriving already embeds and fortifies the distance between 'us' and 'them'. As a consequence of this distance, the difference in treatment between hosts and guests not only appears 'normal' but presents itself as necessary. Therefore, going back to the idea of the social contract, we need to be able to envision a different social contract, one where foreignness is not perceived as a danger but perhaps as an opportunity to change, evolve and rethink our foundations. While such an approach would certainly alleviate the suffering of thousands of people crossing borders, it is hard to achieve when the current aesthetic and ethical imagination is shaped so powerfully by the host gaze. Exclusion of foreignness has become so deeply embedded in our democratic systems that those born on the wrong side of the border are treated as a perpetual 'problem', regardless of how egalitarian our democracies purport to be and what kind of ethical values they embrace. Challenging the notion of foreignness is a difficult process dependent on challenging the broader societal perception of migrants and their position vis-à-vis the host. This perception is hard to challenge because, as this book has shown, it is tightly linked to the frames through which we approach migrants and the multiple assumptions about what migrants look like, the circumstances in which they arrive, and what they bring with them. If the archetypes we live with are to be challenged and a more ethical vision of migration law is ever to replace our current approaches, we need to learn to look at migrants and their foreignness differently and learn to depict that foreignness through better and less divisive frames. Currently, however, we are experiencing a period of a widening gap between host and guest and the normalisation of further hostility towards those arriving.

Do Pictures Really Influence Viewers?

A question often posed in discussions on law and the image is whether we can really know to what extent images and recurring frames and tropes actually influence viewers. After all, in the visual competition for gaze, certain images may be easily ignored and quickly replaced by others. Robert Entman has illustrated, however, that the role of bias in communication has a clear impact on distribution of power and that different forms of media have a powerful role to play in shaping societal relations. According to Entman (2007, p. 164), framing – which this book has focused on – assembles narratives and forms moral judgements through activating schemas that encourage audiences to think, to feel and to decide in a particular way. Jörg Matthes and Desirée Schmuck (2017) have shown that visual communication – in particular through widely distributed posters concerning migration – is usually highly successful. Such images use affective responses such as group anxiety, response to symbolic threats, including cultural and economic threats, and reinforcement of negative stereotypes. Anti-migrant imagery increases heuristic processing and activates negative stereotypes and intergroup anxiety, leading to cognitive approval of the various hostile arguments presented (ibid., p. 557). Another study showed that stereotypical right-wing anti-immigration posters influenced implicit stereotypes even in critical recipients (Arendt et al. 2015). Such a stereotypical response was observed even in those viewers who negated the stereotypical content. Despite the presence of critical knowledge, anti-migration visuals were able to activate implicit stereotypical thinking, and even informed recipients were found to be somewhat defenceless against implicit media effects (ibid.). While critical recipients were not affected by explicit stereotypes, the impact on an implicit level showed that visual power is hard to ignore even for those aware of general discourse trends. The study demonstrated that stereotypical associations in memory can become automatically activated regardless of whether someone considers them to be accurate (ibid.). The study used zero, two, four and six images and – somewhat surprisingly – the results were already visible upon exposure to only two images.

With such a powerful impact, the visual becomes an undeniable part of contemporary legal and political discourse. The imagery reinforcing the position of the migrant in host societies is absorbed and normalised every day across different legal contexts. Michał Krzyżanowski (2020) created a model showing that discourse, once introduced into the public domain, spreads and settles across diverse social fields. He distinguishes three stages of that process, namely enactment, gradation and normalisation. According to Krzyżanowski, the first phase strategically introduces certain discourses and ideas (including visual), or in other words enacts them. These discursive elements establish key links and contexts promulgating wider ideas and concepts (ibid., p. 508). In the next stage, gradation – also called perpetuation – further diffuses and reinforces the messages introduced across various social fields, spaces and genres. This process relies on reinforcing key arguments and features of a discourse and allowing for its gradual spread and perpetuation (ibid., pp. 508–9). In the last stage of normalisation, we can typically observe a discursive shift which is visible in a deeper change in terms of public norms. This process leads to rationalisation of even the most radical ideas and views and pre-legitimisation of discriminatory action against specific social groups (ibid.). Andrea Bohman emphasises that this is particularly visible when certain rhetorical choices are made and normalised by traditional political parties (2011, p. 470). Bohman illustrates that people respond to this rhetoric; indeed, such articulation has a particularly strong effect on anti-immigrant attitudes.

This book has analysed not only images circulated by political parties but also those issued by governments and international organisations, who enjoy a high level of authority. At the same time, the majority of the figures analysed here have either already undergone all three stages of normalisation or are in the phase of perpetuation leading to a normative shift in the approach to migrants. Each of the migrant figures has also been slowly evolving, allowing for further racialisation, othering and exclusion. The ever-wider gap between hosts and guests is seen as something 'natural', 'unproblematic' and even 'desirable'. Stricter controls, increased criminalisation of those arriving and increasingly punitive measures do not appear out of place because normalisation – as Krzyżanowski (2020, p. 510) points out – is an inherently gradual process starting from the introduction of certain norms and leading to the gradual eradication of old ones. This happens through the slow legitimisation of a new normative order up to the point when previously 'unacceptable' or 'deviant' norms are seen as perfectly acceptable patterns and ways of doing and thinking (ibid.). In today's world, focused on migration as crisis, a problem and something to be curtailed and managed, it is ever harder for viewers to see migrants simply as people who are owed a similar ethical duty as other fellow citizens. It is even harder to see them as persons who could in a valuable way contribute to society and participate in the continuous renegotiation of the social contract.

Borders as Spaces Penalising Ethics

With such an exclusionary approach to the migrant, it is not surprising that law so powerfully restricts the workings of ethics in our bordered spaces. In recent years this already restrictive power of the law has expanded further and resulted in penalisation of those who attempt to stand up to ethically deficient law and help those arriving by extending basic life support tools such as food or water. These situations where basic ethics are penalised with the help of migration law resemble the classic conflict between law and ethical duty captured in Sophocles' *Antigone*. The frequently discussed ethical and legal dilemma of Antigone (Hirvonen 2000; Etxabe 2013) highlights the question: 'What can a legal subject or a judge do if law requires unethical conduct and results in injustice?' The premise of Antigone focuses on civil disobedience against what she perceives as unethical law. Moreover, as I have argued elsewhere (Gozdecka 2021), Antigone's conflict with Creon powerfully encapsulates the conflict between the legal and the ethical that also recurs in multiple contexts and configurations today. As someone speaking against the injustice of the law, Antigone is an archetype of a dissident or a protester; indeed, as Susan Tiefenbrun insists, she is 'one of the first great heroines of civil disobedience and the inspiration of resistance movements against tyranny' (1999, p. 35). Today's migration law, which singles out migrants as subjects to whom no ethical duty is to be owed, generates multiple ethical conflicts between the legal duties that the state puts on its officials and citizens when dealing with migrants as strangers and ethical duties towards migrants as fellow human beings. It is thus a stage of multiple Antigonean conflicts where the chasm between law and ethics becomes deeply perceptible.

Recently, these Antigonean conflicts have become highlighted by cases of prosecution of those attempting to save and help migrants as fellow human beings. In recent years several cases against those aiding migrants and refugees have emerged across different legal contexts and in entirely different legal systems, illuminating the vast chasm between ethical concerns and legal regulation of movement across borders and the need to respond to human beings in need. In January 2018, the famous case against a No More Deaths volunteer, Dr Scott Warren, was initiated after US Border Patrol agents arrested Warren while he was providing help to two young migrants at a humanitarian aid station in Ajo, Arizona. Just a few hours earlier, No More Deaths, a humanitarian volunteer organisation providing water, food and clothing to migrants crossing the US–Mexico border, released a report showing Border Patrol agents abusing migrants and vandalising water, food and medical supplies left by volunteers (Kuykendall 2020). In the action that was conducted in response, Warren was arrested and charged with the felony of harbouring illegal aliens, which carried a potential penalty of twenty years' imprisonment. Additionally, he was charged with the misdemeanour of 'littering', by leaving water for migrants along the trail of death (ibid.). The indictment specified that 'beginning on or about January 14, 2018, and continuing to January 17, 2018, at or near Ajo, in the District of Arizona', Warren, 'knowing and in reckless disregard of the fact that a certain alien, [] 1, had come to, entered, and remained in the United States in violation of law, did knowingly conceal, harbor, and shield from detection said alien in any place [. . .] to avoid said alien's detention by immigration authorities' (*US v. Warren*). Interestingly, Warren's motion for dismissal employed a defence of religious freedom based on the Religious Freedom Restoration Act of 1993 (RFRA) and the Act's protection of action he took on the grounds of conscience. The motion for dismissal asked the court to consider that he 'did in fact give the migrants food, water, beds, and clean clothes as the government alleges' but 'his conduct cannot legally constitute a crime because the government cannot prosecute any individual for exercising his sincerely held religious beliefs in the necessity to provide emergency aid to fellow human beings in need' (*US v. Warren*).

The case was a vivid example of the classic Antigonean conflict between the legal and the ethical, and Warren's line of defence illuminated the chasm between the dictates of the law and the dictates of ethics and conscience. While the case was not dismissed and proceeded to hearing with a jury, the jury deadlocked during the first trial. Eventually, however, Warren was acquitted by a federal jury during the second hearing. Within this contemporary Antigonean conflict, the language used in court proceedings to describe people crossing the border illuminates the key problem observed in this book, namely the growing ethical void of bordered spaces. The word 'alien' signifies absolute otherness and deprives those crossing borders of any vestiges of humanity. People risking lives on a perilous journey through the desert are not described as people in any part of the deliberation, but instead simply as 'aliens'. Alien organisms, just as the viruses described in the previous part of the book, are anonymous, threatening and non-human. They simply signify a threat that is juxtaposed with the constructed legality of the border. As such, they bear no humanity and are owed no human response. In the eyes of the law, the legal space of the border becomes a space of ethical void – one where we do not owe an ethical or humane response to those arriving on the other side of our jurisdictions. Even more, it becomes a space where we are denied the possibility of facing those on the other side as human beings and are punished by the law if we do so.

A similar ethical dilemma was highlighted in an entirely different jurisdiction, in the case of a German captain, Carola Rackete, who undertook rescue operations in the Mediterranean Sea. The captain was arrested on her way into the Sicilian port of Lampedusa while carrying forty migrants and refugees she had rescued off the coast of Libya and brought to the port on board her ship. The Court of Agrigento was requested to validate the arrest on grounds of offences pertaining to Article 1100 Naval Code and alleged acts of resistance or violence against a warship as well as resistance to public officials when entering the port of Lampedusa. In addition, the charges included breaking through a naval blockade. The decision of the court rejected the grounds for arrest and invoked the United Nations Convention on the Law of the Sea (UNCLOS). Referring to Article 98 UNCLOS the decision underlined that these provisions had been transposed into Italian domestic law, which imposes criminal sanctions on masters of ships that do not render assistance to ships found in difficulty. At the same time, however, the decision emphasised the obligation on the state authorities and commanders of ships to extend assistance and rescue foreigners that have entered the territory of the state even in an irregular manner following rescue-at-sea operations. While in this case an attempt was made to penalise ethics and extending solidarity under the guise of prosecuting irregular entry into port, the ultimate decision in the case referred back to the very obligations of those performing rescue operations to provide rescue and assistance. While migrants were not defined purely as aliens with no human qualities, as in Warren's case, Ana-Paula Penchaszadeh and Senda Sferco (2019) remind us that in Rackete's case they were also not treated as equal human beings to whom we owe solidarity and ethical response. Indeed, as the authors argue, they were depicted as typical foreigners who are usually defined by hosts through negative stereotypes. As such, even though the court findings acquitted the captain, the generalised and de-individualised relationship between the host and the foreigner was nonetheless reinforced. The discourse dominating the decision reinforced the image of migrants as purely 'objects' of rescue, but not as subjects to whom we owe solidarity and an ethical response.

Penalisation of ethical actions at the border shows just how extreme exclusion of the migrant from shared humanity can be. The law insists that the migrant framed simply as an alien is to be treated without ethical consideration and left to the forces of nature, be it the sea or the desert. The migrant is prevented from ever facing the host as an equal, simply asking for help necessary to save their life, such as water or food. Instead, the law requires that the migrant is first apprehended by the authorities and evaluated on the scale of worthiness or unworthiness of being welcome. The space of the border and the current construction of the figure of the migrant creates an unbridgeable chasm between host and migrant where no ethics can be born and no ethics can survive. Within this void, migrant otherness and alienness becomes so absolute that no space remains for any care shown towards those arriving. The legal distinction between the citizen and the denizen becomes a source of powerful and fundamental division between those to whom we owe any rights, care and duties at all – typically our fellow citizens – and those whom law dehumanises and excludes from such privileges. The simple classification based on citizenship becomes the dominant logic operating in the space of the border. In the ethically void space of the border, human tragedies encountered while crossing are not to be empathised with and human circumstances are not to be responded to. Thirst, hunger, exhaustion and other threats to survival are to be disregarded. As the above cases analysed have demonstrated, any show of compassion, any attempt to extend solidarity to migrants as fellow human beings is not only discouraged but can be actively penalised with all the severity of the law.

Criminalising fundamental care for another human being or extending ethical conduct should be a wake-up call signifying that our laws have crossed a dangerous boundary – a boundary of arbitrariness where the call of justice and the call of law are far removed from each other. Yet, the normalisation of migrant alienness, which permeates all our encounters with the migrant, results in the opposite – acceptance and proliferation of these fundamentally problematic legal rules. The fundamental distinction of citizenship, which is extended over us in an arbitrary manner from the moment we are born, can lead to legitimisation of the most inhumane policies. These policies, which often dehumanise those arriving as simply 'migrants', 'aliens', 'illegals' or 'illegal arrivals' – objects at the mercy of the law – leaves those crossing borders in a precarious position. Under the guise of the law, we can seize and separate migrants from their families, deprive them of their resources, detain them indefinitely or perpetuate other acts of cruelty which would be ethically unimaginable – and likely illegal – if applied to fellow citizens. The space of the border with its chasm between the citizen and the denizen brings about the ultimate breakdown of ethics. The migrant, after all, stands on the other side of the threshold of the border and, when they arrive uninvited, no ethics are due to them. This chasm between the citizen and the denizen can become so deep and so pervasive because the discourse of illegality, bogusness, invisible threat or a threatening mass gradually creates the perception of a migrant as someone who is not the same kind of human as the host. The migrant's status in the form of a threat almost always takes precedence over their humanity and justifies increasing hostility at the border. Meanwhile, host citizens standing up against the exclusion from humanity of those arriving and instead extending ethical and lifesaving help challenge this rift and attempt to reframe this relationship. Hence law, which has normalised, accepted and absorbed this host–guest chasm, attempts to punish any such challenge to its status quo. The question of course remains whether there is any potential for reinjecting justice and ethics into our dominant paradigms operating in many migration law systems across the globe.

Conclusions

Finalisation of the first draft of this book coincided with the release of an image and a video of a Red Cross volunteer hugging an exhausted Senegalese migrant who had just managed to cross the sea and reach Ceuta. In the aftermath of the video's publication, Luna Reyes, the worker in the picture, received a wave of abuse from supporters of anti-migration party Vox (Kassam 2021). The fact that an image representing one human being extending support to another suffering human being attracted abuse simply because the person receiving support was a migrant speaks volumes about the breakdown of ethics in contemporary bordered space. It shows that people to whom a human and ethical response is extended are no longer treated as human. Their alienness takes priority over their humanity, and a substantial number of citizens of the potential host state would accept their death and suffering before accepting their vulnerability, humanity and need for care. This trend is not only disturbing and shocking but it signals potential for an even darker future than the one many migrants are facing today. It also illustrates how powerful is the impact of replicating the archetypal imagery of migrants. The ethical gap established and normalised through distancing and dehumanising frames can lead to the gradual disassociation of the figure of the migrant from humanity. Instead, the figure of the migrant has become synonymous with a threatening outsider that needs to be stopped, rejected and, if not, controlled and treated with all the caution and severity of the law unless they meet narrowly defined criteria for legality and welcome. Unless we dare to create different frames and gaze points and restore seeing migrants as fellow human beings with the same claim to equality, rights and belonging, exclusion of migrants will progressively deepen. If we do not recognise migrants as fellow legal subjects rather than simply as objects before the law, then perpetuation of practices of cruelty and disregard towards those arriving and depriving them of dignity and humanity will become harder to challenge. Migrant lives have already become framed and normalised as typically 'worthless' unless proven 'legal', 'worthy' or otherwise useful to the host. This book has illustrated that this way of looking is not without impact on what becomes legally permissible. This of course raises questions as to how far we can go in our legally justified exclusion and whether such exclusion has a potential to expand indefinitely. Despite increased awareness of racial, gender and other dynamics of power, the figure of the migrant remains the last one that can a priori be excluded from the discourse of recognition and whose life can remain legally controlled in a variety of ways.

In order to change our contemporary approaches and imagine the migrant as a legal subject rather than as a legal object, we need to develop different and better forms of looking. We need not only to normalise images of migrants being hugged, but also to see migrants as an integral part of our communities and cultures. We need to dare to see migrants as economically successful employees and even employers, and certainly as people who can possess material and immaterial goods or display economic savvy much in the same way as citizens. We need to see migrant bodies and migrant faces on boats crossing the seas rather than anonymise them simply as 'boats' or 'rafts'. We need to be able to look and see individual stories in reports of a dehumanised mass and challenge the presumptions of historically homogenous communities. We need to stop suspecting wrongful intentions and imagine that innocence is not just a quality of children who die during passage. We need to adopt smaller, more individualised frames that focus on migrants as humans, and develop gaze points that emphasise our connectedness rather than our separateness. We also need to hear, see and accept stories, images and films produced by migrants about their life and their humanity. At the moment, even when such stories or images emerge, they often remain on the margins of reporting (Chouliaraki 2017). While these often grainy, poor-quality images bring a new quality and a new aesthetic trend in trying to stop 'aesthetic criminalization of migrants' (Nail 2020, p. 156), they are typically underreported or even not reported at all and instead replaced with imagery familiar to the host. They exist in their own world of migrants sharing their stories with other migrants, often on social media. Only a few representations written and presented by those crossing borders receive recognition from mainstream critics and presence in the mainstream media. Behrouz Boochani's acclaimed book *No Friend but the Mountains* (2018) – a harrowing account of experiences in the detention centre on Manus Island – is one such notable exception. The Victorian Prize for Literature awarded to Boochani has brought this remarkable work closer to mainstream readers who encounter the figure of the refugee through a close, face-to-face encounter which focuses not on the chasm of the border but instead on the cruelty of the border regime. It shows the humanity of the author and experiences of human suffering, loss of hope and perseverance through trauma and deprivation. Despite the well-deserved recognition of Boochani's work, other accounts of migration stories rarely reach the mainstream and are typically featured in local refugee or migration film festivals or art festivals. This labelling as 'migrant' artwork or writing, while intended to support, assigns any such accounts to a niche reserved for advocates, human rights lawyers and migrants themselves. And yet, this work and these perspectives are desperately needed if we are to tackle the deep chasm created by the host gaze. In addition, we also need new forms of the host look rather than the host gaze, which does not single out migrants but which focuses on their shared humanity and belonging. Initiatives to present such perspectives are rare and, again, reserved for specialised organisations and speakers aware of the ongoing negative coverage that migrants face every day. The National Rural Women's Coalition and Migration Council Australia 2020 webinar on positive stories of migrant and refugee women in rural Australia is a good example of such initiatives but, once more, is largely limited to academic and specialised audiences (see Migration Council Australia 2020). All in all, such accounts with a perspective avoiding the host gaze or attempting to shift the host gaze remain rare and few reach wider audiences. This puts them into vivid contrast with the governmental or political imagery analysed in this volume.

Yet, without greater prominence given to such literary and aesthetic perspectives, changing the way we look may remain no more than wishful thinking. Challenging the male gaze, observed and deconstructed half a decade ago, is still an ongoing process with constantly recurring backlashes against those who complain about sexist advertising and stereotyping of women in films or who struggle for greater representation of diversity of female experience. Changing the way in which we look at migrants may be an even longer and more difficult process – firstly, due to the presumption of the unequal position of the citizen and denizen fundamentally embedded in our democratic regimes and international legal order; and secondly, due to limited recognition and distribution of imagery and accounts produced by migrants or those attempting to shift the paradigms of the host gaze. The pervasiveness of our current host gaze is intimately connected with notions of citizenship, borders and international travel. Although our nation states as we conceive of them today are historically relatively recent, their existence has become deeply embedded in our collective psyche. As a form of international legal order, the current system of citizenship and denizenship is unlikely to change in the near future. Unlike the legal system, however, which changes slowly and progressively and responds to normalisation of attitudes and societal values, the way we look can change. As shown in this volume, the way we look at each other matters enormously in terms of our ethical imagination. The more often we ethically dare to face each other, the more we are able to accept a change in our collective social contract. If we dare to look ethically and challenge the 'us' and 'them' divide, we are likely also to dare to challenge the terms through which our democratic communities regulate and govern foreignness and border regimes. Looking differently, if included in the mainstream media and other easily accessible visual campaigns, could slowly reduce the chasm between host and guest. Seeing migrants as neighbours, friends, local entrepreneurs, teachers, parents and so forth without constant emphasis on distance, difference, challenge and threat can be a counterbalance to an overwhelming acceptance of the expanding exclusion of migrants. That exclusion is visible daily and reflected in legislation and interpretation of migration law across the globe. Daring to look differently can eventually also challenge our legal imagination and allow us to picture a different kind of laws and legal 'norm' as legitimate. This author cannot speculate whether, at the point when hugging a migrant attracts abuse, such a different way of looking is truly possible. With other factors reinforcing and fortifying our current border regimes even further, such as the restrictions brought about during the COVID-19 pandemic, finding another way of looking may be challenging. At the same time, I am convinced that finding such a different way of looking is pivotal for a more balanced and less cruel system of regulating borders. If we continue on our current visual and legal course, gradually anyone crossing borders could become a suspect at risk of inhumane treatment or indefinite detention without recourse to justice.

References

Arendt, Florian, Franziska Marquart and Jörg Matthes. 'Effects of right-wing populist political advertising on implicit and explicit stereotypes.' *Journal of Media Psychology: Theories, Methods, and Applications* 27, no. 4 (2015): 178–89.

Bohman, Andrea. 'Articulated antipathies: Political influence on anti-immigrant attitudes.' *International Journal of Comparative Sociology* 52, no. 6 (2011): 457–77.

Boochani, Behrouz. *No Friend but the Mountains: The True Story of an Illegally Imprisoned Refugee*. Trans. Omid Tofighian. Picador, 2018.

Chouliaraki, Lilie. 'Symbolic bordering: The self-representation of migrants and refugees in digital news.' *Popular Communication* 15, no. 2 (2017): 78–94.

Convention on the Law of the Sea (UNCLOS), UN General Assembly, 10 December 1982.
Entman, Robert M. 'Framing bias: Media in the distribution of power.' *Journal of Communication* 57, no. 1 (2007): 163–73.
Etxabe, Julen. *The Experience of Tragic Judgment*. Routledge, 2013.
Gozdecka, Dorota A. 'Antigones of contemporary theatre: Capturing problems of today's civil disobedience in a theatre play.' *Law Text Culture* 25 (2021): 204–26.
Hirvonen, Ari. 'Oikeuden käynti: Antigonen laki ja oikea oikeus.' Doctoral dissertation. University of Helsinki, 2000.
Honig, Bonnie. *Democracy and the Foreigner*. Princeton University Press, 2001.
Kassam, Ashifa. 'Spanish aid volunteer abused online for hugging Senegalese migrant.' *The Guardian*, 21 May 2021, available at: <https://www.theguardian.com/world/2021/may/20/spanish-aid-volunteer-luna-reyes-abused-online-for-hugging-african-migrant>, last accessed 26 September 2023.
Krzyżanowski, Michał. 'Discursive shifts and the normalisation of racism: Imaginaries of immigration, moral panics and the discourse of contemporary right-wing populism.' *Social Semiotics* 30, no. 4 (2020): 503–27.
Kuykendall, Greg. 'Defending those who protect refugees.' In *Proceedings of the ASIL Annual Meeting*, vol. 114, pp. 113–16. Cambridge University Press, 2020.
Matthes, Jörg, and Desirée Schmuck. 'The effects of anti-immigrant right-wing populist ads on implicit and explicit attitudes: A moderated mediation model.' *Communication Research* 44, no. 4 (2017): 556–81.
Migration Council Australia. 'Rural settlement: Positive stories of migrant and refugee women.' YouTube, 1 December 2020, available at: <https://www.youtube.com/watch?v=AQzlnHqsGH0>, last accessed 21 September 2023.
Mitchell, W. J. T. *Picture Theory: Essays on Verbal and Visual Representation*. University of Chicago Press, 1995.
Nail, Thomas. 'Migrant images.' In *Moving Images: Mediating Migration as Crisis*, ed. Krista Geneviève Lynes, Tyler Morgenstern and Ian Alan Paul, pp. 147–64. Transcript Verlag, 2020.
Penchaszadeh, Ana-Paula, and Senda Sferco. 'Philosophical-political thoughts on the criminalization of solidarity practices towards migrants and refugees today: The case of Carola Rackete (2019).' *Historia y Sociedad* 39 (2020): 213–40.
Tiefenbrun, Susan W. 'On civil disobedience, jurisprudence, feminism and the law in the Antigones of Sophocles and Anouilh.' *Law & Literature* 11, no. 1 (1999): 35–51.
United States of America v. Scott Daniel Warren. No. MJ-17-0341-TUC-BGM, 2018.

Conclusion

This volume has argued that the way we see the world shapes the way in which we organise and legislate the lives of our communities. The surrounding imagery has a deep influence on the ethical and legal duties we envision towards others and the relationship between them. In our contemporary world, as our reliance on visual communication increases, so too will the prominence of visual imagery. Deconstructing the way in which we gaze at others can help us uncover multiple presumptions hidden behind the irresistible allure of the image. After all, despite being bombarded by thousands of images every day, we often remain unaware of the frames, gaze points and messages encapsulated in the field of appearance in the pictures we look at. Surrounded by visual campaigns and often glued to the screens of our mobile phones, we too often assume that this visual reality exists in separation from the social contract we constantly negotiate and has little to do with the laws we live by. Yet – as I hope this volume has shown for lawmakers, lawyers dealing with migration cases, human rights activists or scholars teaching migration law – understanding the visual presumptions behind images of migrants may be crucial for understanding why, despite decades of arguing in favour of recognising the rights of migrants, we are steadily moving away from rights-based approaches and towards a heavily crimmigration-based system regulating migration.

This book has focused primarily on the ethical distance that archetypal images of migrants establish between host and guest. It has shown how archetypal representations of those arriving at the border perpetuate dominant perspectives shaped by the host gaze and reinforce the host's existing presumptions about those arriving. These presumptions, as this volume has shown, approach foreignness primarily as a problem requiring elimination through progressively harsher regulation. The same presumptions lead to constant measuring of migrant 'worthiness' and translate to multiple exclusionary measures regulating the lives of those arriving. At the same time, this surrounding visual imagery does little to emphasise legal nuances but bundles all those arriving into a problematic cohort signifying all kinds of dangers to the host. This book has also shown that shifting these dominant perspectives is difficult, and possible only in exceptional circumstance. It mostly applies to those considered the most 'innocent', such as suffering migrant children. In our current visual economy of migration, only those seen as absolute victims can occasionally challenge the suspicion surrounding their arrival. Typically, however, as host societies we treat the figure of those arriving with suspicion and frame them as different forms of threat. The figure of the mass, the invisible illegal, the bogus and genuine asylum seeker or the absolute other, visible both in pro- and anti-migrant rhetoric, can be seen daily by billions of people encountering the world through the screens of their mobile phones and the discourses they perpetuate on social media. Additionally, they are accompanied by posters issued by their governments, political parties or news agencies which consciously or unconsciously replicate existing biases and presumptions. As this volume has shown, similar frames operate despite different contexts. As a consequence, different local laws – despite dealing with different types of migrants – head in a similar crimmigratory direction, partly because circulating imagery focusing on migration perpetuates a similar vision of 'reality' – one seen solely through the prism of the host gaze. This perspective of the host is so deeply internalised by audiences scattered across the globe that it creates similar forms of affect across different social and legal contexts: the perception that more regulation is needed and that migration is a growing 'problem'. As a result, ever-harsher laws aimed at stopping migrants by means of incarceration, deprivation or at the very least incredibly harsh regulation become reality in different corners of the globe.

Imagining a more ethical approach towards migrants is slowly becoming difficult if not already impossible to imagine. As shown by the most recent example of abuse directed at a Red Cross worker hugging a Senegalese migrant, migrants and refugees are often no longer seen as fellow human beings but instead as objects at our mercy that do or do not deserve an ethical response depending on the mode of their arrival, their legality and their visibility as humans. As these problematic objects need to be deterred at all costs, our empathy and ethics wane and our laws move ever further away from considerations of justice and fairness. While lawyers will be trained to avoid the suggestive nature of dominant imagery but to rely instead on the intimate details of the workings of their migration law system, nevertheless images matter even for those trained in the arcane knowledge of the law when it comes to legitimating solutions considered just or fair. After all, interpretation, justification and application of the law which lies at the heart of our legal profession can be affected by dominant imagery shaping the perception of how far we can push migration law without it being considered cruel and fundamentally unfair. This is possible because the omnipresent and hardly noticeable visual apparatus recreating the dominant visual imagery is so fundamentally embedded in our legal imagination that it appears to be 'natural' and purports to simply reflect 'how things are'. Even those trained in law may be influenced by the dominant presumptions passed in images and have them influence their legal reasoning, decision-making or advice on legislative drafts. As sociological research cited here has shown, exposure to just two negative images of migration has an influence on even those viewers who are aware of the frames they are looking through.

Deconstructing the presumptions behind the images is thus crucial for both those trained and those untrained in law so that we can all imagine migrants as equal legal subjects rather than simply objects whose lives we can decide on freely and without consequence. This shift in framing requires bringing migrant perspectives, frames and gaze points to the fore. More imagery focusing on our shared humanity can be crucial for shifting our perception of fairness and justice of laws that deeply and intimately affect people crossing borders. Shifting the visual perspective from the host towards the guest may also help in imagining migration differently and daring to think of less punitive and more nuanced approaches to regulating regular and irregular ways in which people cross borders. Changing the way in which we look may be difficult; but unpacking it is necessary for an understanding of why we currently are where we are legally. I hope that this volume has contributed to the plethora of emerging literature focusing on explaining why certain seemingly cruel legal proposals in the area of migration often become laws against the advice of legal experts and advocates. I hope that it also has illustrated that legitimacy and the perception of justice are deeply affected by surrounding discourse including visual discourse. In the times of populist politics and the increasing role of visual media, I hope this book has helped to understand how often populist discourses take root and eventually become acceptable as mainstream and fair solutions. I leave it to my readers to use this knowledge in their practice, discussions and research and to answer the question whether we can imagine better ways of facing the migrant and develop more ethical ways of regulating their arrival and stay.

Bibliography

Abali, Oya S. 'German public opinion on immigration and integration.' In *Migration, Public Opinion and Politics: The Transatlantic Council on Migration*, ed. Bertelsmann Stiftung and Migration Policy Institute. Bertelsmann Stiftung, 2009.

Abu-Hayyeh, Reem, Graham Murray and Liz Fekete. 'Swiss referendum: Flying the flag for nativism.' *Race & Class* 56, no. 1 (2014): 89–94.

Agamben, Giorgio. *Homo Sacer: Sovereign Power and Bare Life*. Stanford University Press, 1998.

Alba, Richard. 'Bright vs. blurred boundaries: Second-generation assimilation and exclusion in France, Germany, and the United States.' *Ethnic and Racial Studies* 28, no. 1 (2005): 20–49.

Alcoff, Linda Martín. *Visible Identities: Race, Gender, and the Self*. Oxford University Press, 2005.

Althusser, Louis. 'Ideology and ideological state apparatuses (notes towards an investigation) (1970).' In *Cultural Theory: An Anthology*, ed. Imre Szeman and Timothy Kaposy, pp. 204–22. John Wiley, 2010.

Althusser, Louis. *On the Reproduction of Capitalism: Ideology and Ideological State Apparatuses*. Verso, 2014.

Anderson, Benedict. *Imagined Communities: Reflections on the Origin and Spread of Nationalism*. Verso, 2006.

Anderson, Bridget. *Us and Them?: The Dangerous Politics of Immigration Control*. Oxford University Press, 2013.

Arendt, Florian. 'Cultivation effects of a newspaper on reality estimates and explicit and implicit attitudes.' *Journal of Media Psychology: Theories, Methods, and Applications* 22, no. 4 (2010): 147–59.

Arendt, Florian, Franziska Marquart and Jörg Matthes. 'Effects of right-wing populist political advertising on implicit and explicit stereotypes.' *Journal of Media Psychology: Theories, Methods, and Applications* 27, no. 4 (2015): 178–89.

Arendt, Hannah. *The Origins of Totalitarianism*. Harvest, 1973.

Arribas, Gloria Fernández. 'The EU–Turkey Agreement: A controversial attempt at patching up a major problem.' *European Papers – A Journal on Law and Integration* 2016, no. 3 (2016): 1097–104.

Aynsley-Green, Albert, Tim J. Cole, Heaven Crawley, Nick Lessof, L. R. Boag and Rebecca M. M. Wallace. 'Medical, statistical, ethical and human rights considerations in the assessment of age in children and young people subject to immigration control.' *British Medical Bulletin* 102, no. 1 (2012): 17–42.

Azoulay, Ariella. *The Civil Contract of Photography*. Princeton University Press, 2021.
Badiou, Alain. *Ethics: An Essay on the Understanding of Evil*. Verso, 2002.
Bakali, Naved. 'Popular cultural Islamophobia.' In *Islamophobia: Understanding Anti-Muslim Racism through the Lived Experiences of Muslim Youth*, pp. 63–78. Brill, 2016.
Balibar, Étienne. 'Racism revisited: Sources, relevance, and aporias of a modern concept.' *PMLA/Publications of the Modern Language Association of America* 123, no. 5 (2008): 1630–9.
Balibar, Étienne. *We, the People of Europe?: Reflections on Transnational Citizenship*. Princeton University Press, 2009.
Balibar, Étienne, and Immanuel Wallerstein. *Race, Nation, Class: Ambiguous Identities*. Verso, 1991.
Bankier, Miriam E. 'Passe Pas: Rethinking the Passport.' BA thesis. Scripps College, 2020.
Barak, Gregg. 'Crime, criminology and human rights: Towards an understanding of state criminality.' *The Journal of Human Justice* 2, no. 1 (1990): 11–28.
Bareket, Orly, Nurit Shnabel, Dekel Abeles, Sarah Gervais and Shlomit Yuval-Greenberg. 'Evidence for an association between men's spontaneous objectifying gazing behavior and their endorsement of objectifying attitudes toward women.' *Sex Roles* 81, no. 3 (2019): 245–56.
BBC News. 'Trump backs down on migrant family separations policy.' *BBC News*, 21 June 2018, available at: <https://www.bbc.co.uk/news/world-us-canada-44552852>, last accessed 25 September 2023.
Behrmann, Carolin. 'Law, visual studies, and image history.' In *The Oxford Handbook of Law and Humanities*, ed. Simon Stern, Maksymilian Del Mar and Bernadette Meyler, pp. 39–64. Oxford University Press, 2019.
Benhabib, Seyla. 'The generalized and the concrete other: The Kohlberg–Gilligan controversy and feminist theory.' In *Feminism as Critique: Essays on the Politics of Gender in Late Capitalist Societies*, ed. Seyla Benhabib and Drucilla Cornell, pp. 77–95. Polity Press, 1987.
Benhabib, Seyla. *Situating the Self: Gender, Community, and Postmodernism in Contemporary Ethics*. Psychology Press, 1992.
Benhabib, Seyla. 'In defense of universalism – yet again! A response to critics of Situating the Self.' *New German Critique* 62 (1994): 173–89.
Benjamin, Walter. 'Critique of violence' (1921). In *Selected Writings, Volume 1: 1913–1926*, ed. Marcus Bullock and Michale W. Jennings, pp. 236–52. The Belknap Press of Harvard University Press, 1996.
Betz, Hans-Georg. 'The new politics of resentment: Radical right-wing populist parties in Western Europe.' In *The Migration Reader: Exploring Politics and Policies*, ed. Anthony M. Messina and Gallya Lahav, pp. 384–401. Lynne Rienner Publishers, 2006.
Betz, Hans-Georg. 'Mosques, minarets, burqas and other essential threats: The populist right's campaign against Islam in Western Europe.' In *Right-Wing Populism in Europe: Politics and Discourse*, ed. Ruth Wodak, Majid KhosraviNik and Brigitte Mral, pp. 71–88. Bloomsbury, 2013.
Bhabha, Jacqueline. 'Arendt's children: Do today's migrant children have a right to have rights?' *Human Rights Quarterly* 31, no. 2 (2009): 410–51.

Bleiker, Roland, David Campbell, Emma Hutchison and Xzarina Nicholson. 'The visual dehumanisation of refugees.' *Australian Journal of Political Science* 48, no. 4 (2013): 398–416.

Blume, Georg, Marc Brost, Tina Hildebrandt, Alexej Hock, Sybille Klormann, Angela Köckritz, Matthias Krupa, Mariam Lau, Gero von Randow, Merlind Theile, Michael Thumann and Heinrich Wefing. 'The night Germany lost control.' *Zeit Online*, 30 August 2016, available at: <http://www.zeit.de/gesellsch aft/2016-08/refugees-open-border-policy-september-2015-angela-merkel>, last accessed 25 September 2023.

Boffey, Daniel. 'Ursula von der Leyen says EU could punish UK over Brexit breaches.' *The Guardian*, 27 April 2021, available at: <https://www.theguardian.com/world/2021/apr/27/ursula-von-der-leyen-says-eu-could-punish-uk-over-brexit-breaches>, last accessed 25 September 2023.

Bohman, Andrea. 'Articulated antipathies: Political influence on anti-immigrant attitudes.' *International Journal of Comparative Sociology* 52, no. 6 (2011): 457–77.

Bolderson, Helen. 'The ethics of welfare provision for migrants: A case for equal treatment and the repositioning of welfare.' *Journal of Social Policy* 40, no. 2 (2011): 219–35.

Boochani, Behrouz. *No Friend but the Mountains: The True Story of an Illegally Imprisoned Refugee*. Trans. Omid Tofighian. Picador, 2018.

Boomgaarden, Hajo G., and Rens Vliegenthart. 'How news content influences anti-immigration attitudes: Germany, 1993–2005.' *European Journal of Political Research* 48, no. 4 (2009): 516–42.

Brah, Avtar, Mary J. Hickman and Máirtín Mac an Ghaill. 'Thinking identities: Ethnicity, racism and culture.' In *Thinking Identities: Ethnicity, Racism and Culture*, ed. Avtar Brah, Mary J. Hickman and Máirtín Mac an Ghaill, pp. 1–21. Palgrave Macmillan, 1999.

Brown, Jessica Autumn. 'The new "Southern Strategy": Immigration, race, and "welfare dependency" in contemporary US Republican political discourse.' *Geopolitics, History, and International Relations* 8, no. 2 (2016): 22–41.

Buck-Morss, Susan. *Dreamworld and Catastrophe: The Passing of Mass Utopia in East and West*. MIT Press, 2000.

Butler, Judith. *Frames of War: When Is Life Grievable?* Verso, 2009.

Butz, Adam M., and Jason E. Kehrberg. 'Anti-immigrant sentiment and the adoption of state immigration policy.' *Policy Studies Journal* 47, no. 3 (2019): 605–23.

Cade, Jason A. 'All the border's a stage: Humanitarian aid as expressive dissent.' In *Law and the Citizen*, ed. Austin Sarat. Emerald Publishing, 2020.

Cameron, Emilie. 'Indigenous spectrality and the politics of postcolonial ghost stories.' *Cultural Geographies* 15, no. 3 (2008): 383–93.

Canessa, Andrew. 'New indigenous citizenship in Bolivia: Challenging the liberal model of the state and its subjects.' *Latin American and Caribbean Ethnic Studies* 7, no. 2 (2012): 201–21.

Castillo, Pilar. *Passport*. Artwork, 2019, available at: <http://castlepillar.com/passpo rt.html>, last accessed 21 September 2023.

Chouliaraki, Lilie. 'Symbolic bordering: The self-representation of migrants and refugees in digital news.' *Popular Communication* 15, no. 2 (2017): 78–94.

Cockburn, Tom. 'Children and the feminist ethic of care.' *Childhood* 12, no. 1 (2005): 71–89.

Code of Public Local Laws of Baltimore City, art. 24, para. 1.

Commonwealth of Australia v AJL20 [2021] HCA 2, High Court of Australia, 23 June 2021.

Convention on the Law of the Sea (UNCLOS), UN General Assembly, 10 December 1982.

Convention on the Rights of the Child (1989) Treaty no. 27531. *United Nations Treaty Series*, 1577, pp. 3–178.

Convention Relating to the Status of Refugees (Refugee Convention), 28 July 1951, United Nations, Treaty Series, vol. 189. UN General Assembly.

Cornell, Drucilla. 'Toward a modern/postmodern reconstruction of ethics.' *University of Pennsylvania Law Review* 133, no. 2 (1985): 291–380.

Cornell, Drucilla. 'Post-structuralism, the ethical relation, and the law.' *Cardozo Law Review* 9, no. 6 (1987): 1587–628.

Council Decision (EU) 2014/252/EU of 14 April 2014 on the conclusion of the Agreement between the European Union and the Republic of Turkey on the readmission of persons residing without authorization, L 134, 7.5.2014. European Union: Council of the European Union.

Council Decision (EU) 2015/1601 of 22 September 2015 establishing provisional measures in the area of international protection for the benefit of Italy and Greece, L 248/80. European Union: Council of the European Union.

Crawley, Heaven, and Dimitris Skleparis. 'Refugees, migrants, neither, both: Categorical fetishism and the politics of bounding in Europe's "migration crisis".' *Journal of Ethnic and Migration Studies* 44, no. 1 (2018): 48–64.

Creighton, Mathew J., and Amaney A. Jamal. 'An overstated welcome: Brexit and intentionally masked anti-immigrant sentiment in the UK.' *Journal of Ethnic and Migration Studies* 48, no. 5 (2022): 1051–71.

Crossley, Nick. 'The politics of the gaze: Between Foucault and Merleau-Ponty.' *Human Studies* 16, no. 4 (1993): 399–419.

Curtin, Juliet. 'Never say never: Al-Kateb v. Godwin.' *Sydney Law Review* 27 (2005): 355–70.

Curtis, Dennis E., and Judith Resnik. 'Images of justice.' *Yale Law Journal* 96, no. 8 (1986): 1727–72.

Dahlberg, Leif, ed. *Visualizing Law and Authority: Essays on Legal Aesthetics*. Walter de Gruyter, 2012.

Dalsklev, Madeleine, and Jonas Rønningsdalen Kunst. 'The effect of disgust-eliciting media portrayals on outgroup dehumanization and support of deportation in a Norwegian sample.' *International Journal of Intercultural Relations* 47 (2015): 28–40.

Dastyari, Azadeh, and Maria O'Sullivan. 'Not for export: The failure of Australia's extraterritorial processing regime in Papua New Guinea and the decision of the PNG Supreme Court in Namah (2016).' *Monash University Law Review* 42 (2016): 308–38.

Dauvergne, Catherine. *Making People Illegal: What Globalization Means for Migration and Law*. Cambridge University Press, 2008.

Davies, Cemlyn. 'Brexit: EU citizens in the UK "at risk of deportation".' *BBC News*, 17 February 2021, available at: <https://www.bbc.co.uk/news/uk-wales-politics-56092237>, last accessed 25 September 2023.

De Genova, Nicholas. 'Spectacles of migrant "illegality": The scene of exclusion, the obscene of inclusion.' *Ethnic and racial studies* 36, no. 7 (2013): 1180–98.

De Genova, Nicholas. 'Immigration reform and the production of migrant illegality.' In *Constructing Immigrant 'Illegality': Critiques, Experiences, and Responses*, ed. Cecilia Menjívar and Daniel Kanstroom, pp. 37–62. Cambridge University Press, 2014.

De Genova, Nicholas. 'Denizens all: The otherness of citizenship.' In *Citizenship and Its Others*, ed. Bridget Anderson and Vanessa Hughes, pp. 191–202. Palgrave Macmillan, 2015.

De Genova, Nicholas, and Ananya Roy. 'Practices of illegalisation.' *Antipode* 52, no. 2 (2020): 352–64.

Dehm, Sara. 'Outsourcing, responsibility and refugee claim-making in Australia's offshore detention regime.' In *Asylum for Sale: Profit and Protest in the Migration Industry*, ed. Siobhán McGuirk and Adrienne Pine, pp. 47–66. PM Press, 2020.

Dehm, Sara. 'International law at the border: Refugee deaths, the necropolitical state and sovereign accountability.' In *Routledge Handbook of International Law and the Humanities*, ed. Shane Chalmers and Sundhya Pahuja, pp. 341–56. Routledge, 2021.

Deleuze, Gilles, and Félix Guattari. *A Thousand Plateaus: Capitalism and Schizophrenia*. Trans. Brian Massumi. University of Minnesota Press, 1987.

Dennison, James, and Andrew Geddes. 'Brexit and the perils of "Europeanised" migration.' *Journal of European Public Policy* 25, no. 8 (2018): 1137–53.

Derrida, Jacques. 'Force of law: The "mystical foundation of authority".' Trans. Mary Quaintance. In *Deconstruction and the Possibility of Justice*, ed. Drucilla Cornell, Michael Rosenfield and David G. Carlson, pp. 3–68. Routledge, 1992.

Derrida, Jacques. *Of Grammatology*. Johns Hopkins University Press, 1998.

Derrida, Jacques. 'Hostipitality.' *Angelaki: Journal of Theoretical Humanities* 5, no. 3 (2000): 3–18.

Derrida, Jacques. *Specters of Marx: The State of the Debt, the Work of Mourning and the New International*. Routledge, 2012.

Derrida, Jacques, and Anne Dufourmantelle. *Of Hospitality*. Stanford University Press, 2000.

Devetak, Richard. 'In fear of refugees: The politics of border protection in Australia.' *The International Journal of Human Rights* 8, no. 1 (2004): 101–9.

Dewsbury, J.-D. 'The Deleuze-Guattarian assemblage: Plastic habits.' *Area* 43, no. 2 (2011): 148–53.

Diène, Doudou. 'Report of the Special Rapporteur on Contemporary Forms of Racism, Racial Discrimination, Xenophobia and Related Intolerance, Doudou Diène, on the manifestations of defamation of religions and in particular on the serious implications of Islamophobia on the enjoyment of all rights.' A/HRC/6/6. United Nations, 2007, available at: <https://digitallibrary.un.org/record/606485?ln=en>, last accessed 17 October 2023.

Döring, Tobias. 'Turning the colonial gaze: Re-visions of terror in Dabydeen's Turner.' *Third Text* 11, no. 38 (1997): 3–14.

Douzinas, Costas. 'Human rights and postmodern utopia.' *Law and Critique* 11, no. 2 (2000): 219–40.

Douzinas, Costas, and Adam Gearey. *Critical Jurisprudence: The Political Philosophy of Justice*. Hart Publishing, 2005.

Douzinas, Costas, and Lynda Nead. *Law and the Image: The Authority of Art and the Aesthetics of Law*. University of Chicago Press, 1999.

Dowling, Julie A., and Jonathan Xavier Inda, eds. *Governing Immigration through Crime: A Reader*. Stanford University Press, 2013.

Drake, B. Shaw, and Elizabeth Gibson. 'Vanishing protection: Access to asylum at the border.' *City University of New York Law Review* 21, no. 1 (2017): 91–142.

Drywood, Eleanor. 'Challenging concepts of the "child" in asylum and immigration law: The example of the EU.' *Journal of Social Welfare & Family Law* 32, no. 3 (2010): 309–23.

Dunn, Kevin M., Natascha Klocker and Tanya Salabay. 'Contemporary racism and Islamaphobia in Australia: Racializing religion.' *Ethnicities* 7, no. 4 (2007): 564–89.

Eagleton, Terry. 'The ideology of the aesthetic.' *Poetics Today* 9, no. 2 (1988): 327–38.

Eberstein, Anne Sophie. 'Why care matters: Analysing the German response to the European refugee crisis from a global ethics of care perspective.' Lund University Student Papers (2016), available at: <https://lup.lub.lu.se/student-papers/search/publication/8878465>, last accessed 25 September 2023.

El-Enany, Nadine. 'Aylan Kurdi: The human refugee.' *Law and Critique* 27, no. 1 (2016): 13–15.

Elmer, Greg. 'Panopticon–discipline–control.' In *Routledge Handbook of Surveillance Studies*, ed. Kirstie Ball, Kevin D. Haggerty and David Lyon, pp. 21–9. Routledge, 2012.

Engbersen, Godfried, and Joanne Van der Leun. 'The social construction of illegality and criminality.' *European Journal on Criminal Policy and Research* 9, no. 1 (2001): 51–70.

Entman, Robert M. 'Framing bias: Media in the distribution of power.' *Journal of Communication* 57, no. 1 (2007): 163–73.

Ersanilli, Evelyn, and Ruud Koopmans. 'Rewarding integration? Citizenship regulations and the socio-cultural integration of immigrants in the Netherlands, France and Germany.' *Journal of Ethnic and Migration Studies* 36, no. 5 (2010): 773–91.

Esses, Victoria M., Leah K. Hamilton and Danielle Gaucher. 'The global refugee crisis: Empirical evidence and policy implications for improving public attitudes and facilitating refugee resettlement.' *Social Issues and Policy Review* 11, no. 1 (2017): 78–123.

Esses, Victoria M., Scott Veenvliet, Gordon Hodson and Ljiljana Mihic. 'Justice, morality, and the dehumanization of refugees.' *Social Justice Research* 21, no. 1 (2008): 4–25.

Ette, Andreas, and Jürgen Gerdes. 'Against exceptionalism: British interests for selectively Europeanizing its immigration policy.' In *The Europeanization of National Policies and Politics of Immigration: Between Autonomy and the European Union*, ed. Thomas Faist and Andreas Ette, pp. 93–115. Palgrave Macmillan, 2007.

Etxabe, Julen. *The Experience of Tragic Judgment*. Routledge, 2013.

European Commission. Recommendation on a European resettlement scheme, C(2015) 3560. European Commission, 8 June 2015.

European Commission. Recommendation for a voluntary humanitarian admission scheme with Turkey, C(2015) 9490. European Commission, 15 December 2015.

Fackenheim, Emil L. 'The Holocaust and philosophy.' *The Journal of Philosophy* 82, no. 10 (1985): 505–14.

Fangen, Katrine, Kirsten Fossan and Ferdinand Andreas Mohn, eds. *Inclusion and Exclusion of Young Adult Migrants in Europe: Barriers and Bridges*. Routledge, 2016.

Fass, Paula S. 'Children in global migrations.' *Journal of Social History* 38, no. 4 (2005): 937–53.

Favell, Adrian, and Roxana Barbulescu. 'Brexit, "immigration" and anti-discrimination.' In *The Routledge Handbook of the Politics of Brexit*, ed. Patrick Diamond, Peter Nedergaard and Ben Rosamond, pp. 118–33. Routledge, 2018.

Fawzy, Rania Magdi. 'Aestheticizing suffering: Evaluative stance in Pulitzer-winning photos of refugees' crisis in Europe.' *Discourse, Context & Media* 28 (2019): 69–78.

Feather, Norman T. 'Domestic violence, gender, and perceptions of justice.' *Sex Roles* 35, no. 7–8 (1996): 507–19.

Feller, Erika. 'Asylum, migration and refugee protection: Realities, myths and the promise of things to come.' *International Journal of Refugee Law* 18, no. 3–4 (2006): 509–36.

Fetzer, Thiemo, and Shizhuo Wang. 'Measuring the regional economic cost of Brexit: Evidence up to 2019.' Warwick Economic Research Paper 486/2020. CAGE Research Centre, 2020.

Fleay, Caroline, and Lisa Hartley. '"I feel like a beggar": Asylum seekers living in the Australian community without the right to work.' *Journal of International Migration and Integration* 17, no. 4 (2016): 1031–48.

Forsythe, James. 'The EU needs to stop punishing Britain for Brexit.' *The Spectator*, 19 February 2021, available at: <https://www.spectator.co.uk/article/the-eu-needs-to-stop-punishing-britain-for-brexit/>, last accessed 25 September 2023.

Fotou, Maria. 'Ethics of hospitality: Envisaging the stranger in the contemporary world.' PhD dissertation. London School of Economics and Political Science (LSE), 2016.

Foucault, Michel. *Discipline and Punish*. Trans. Alan Sheridan. Gallimard, 1975.

Foucault, Michel. 'The confession of the flesh.' In *Power/Knowledge: Selected Interviews and Other Writings, 1972–1977*, ed. Colin Gordon, pp. 194–27. Pantheon Books, 1977.

Foucault, Michel. *'Society Must Be Defended': Lectures at the Collège de France, 1975–1976*. Trans. David Macey. Ed. Mauro Bertani and Alessandro Fontana. Picador, 2003.

Fox, Peter D. 'International asylum and boat people: The Tampa Affair and Australia's "Pacific Solution".' *Maryland Journal of International Law* 25 (2010): 356–73.

Franko, Katja. *The Crimmigrant Other: Migration and Penal Power*. Routledge, 2019.

Freeman, Michael. 'Why it remains important to take children's rights seriously.' *The International Journal of Children's Rights* 15, no. 1 (2007): 5–23.

Fry, Luke. 'Refugee crisis timeline: How the crisis has grown.' *The Independent*, 15 September 2015, available at: <http://www.independent.co.uk/news/world/europe/refugee-crisis-timeline-how-the-crisis-has-grown/10502690.html>, last accessed 25 September 2023.

Galemba, Rebecca B. 'Illegality and invisibility at margins and borders.' *PoLAR: Political and Legal Anthropology Review* 36, no. 2 (2013): 274–85.

Garoian, Charles. 'The spectre of visual culture and the hauntology of collage.' In Charles R. Garoian and Yvonne M. Gaudelius, *Spectacle Pedagogy: Art, Politics, and Visual Culture*, pp. 99–118. State University of New York Press, 2002.

Geeraert, Jérémy. 'Healthcare reforms and the creation of ex-/included categories of patients – "irregular migrants" and the "undesirable" in the French healthcare system.' *International Migration* 56, no. 2 (2018): 68–81.

Gelber, Katharine. 'A fair queue? Australian public discourse on refugees and immigration.' *Journal of Australian Studies* 27, no. 77 (2003): 23–30.

Gemi, Eda, Iryna Ulasiuk and Anna Triandafyllidou. 'Migrants and media newsmaking practices.' *Journalism Practice* 7, no. 3 (2013): 266–81.

Ghorashi, Halleh, and Ulrike M. Vieten. 'Female narratives of "new" citizens' belonging(s) and identities in Europe: Case studies from the Netherlands and Britain.' *Identities* 19, no. 6 (2012): 725–41.

Giannacopoulos, Maria, and Claire Loughnan. '"Closure" at Manus Island and carceral expansion in the open air prison.' *Globalizations* 17, no. 7 (2020): 1118–35.

Giddens, Thomas. 'Comics, law, and aesthetics: Towards the use of graphic fiction in legal studies.' *Law and Humanities* 6, no. 1 (2012): 85–109.

Gietel-Basten, Stuart. 'Why Brexit? The toxic mix of immigration and austerity.' *Population and Development Review* 42, no. 4 (2016): 673–80.

Gilligan, Carol. *In a Different Voice: Psychological Theory and Women's Development*. Harvard University Press, 1993.

Gittins, Diana. 'The historical construction of childhood.' In *An Introduction to Childhood Studies*, ed. Mary Jane Kehily, pp. 25–38. Open University Press, 2004.

Goldberg, David Theo. *The Racial State*. Blackwell, 2002.

Goodman, Simon, and Susan A. Speer. 'Category use in the construction of asylum seekers.' *Critical Discourse Studies* 4, no. 2 (2007): 165–85.

Goodrich, Peter. 'Maladies of the legal soul: Psychoanalysis and interpretation in law.' *Washington and Lee Law Review* 54 (1997): 1035–74.

Goodrich, Peter. 'The theatre of emblems: On the optical apparatus and the investiture of persons.' *Law, Culture and the Humanities* 8, no. 1 (2012): 47–67.

Goodrich, Peter. *Legal Emblems and the Art of Law: Obiter depicta as the Vision of Governance*. Cambridge University Press, 2014.

Goodwin, Matthew, and Caitlin Milazzo. 'Taking back control? Investigating the role of immigration in the 2016 vote for Brexit.' *The British Journal of Politics and International Relations* 19, no. 3 (2017): 450–64.

Gordon, Eleanor, and Henrik Kjellmo Larsen. '"Sea of blood": The intended and unintended effects of the criminalisation of humanitarian volunteers rescuing migrants in distress at sea.' *Disasters* 46, no. 1 (2022): 3–26.

Gough, Jamie. 'Brexit, xenophobia and left strategy now.' *Capital & Class* 41, no. 2 (2017): 366–72.

Gozdecka, Dorota A. 'A community of paradigm subjects? Rights as corrective tools in culturally contested claims of recognition in Europe.' *Social Identities* 21, no. 4 (2015): 328–44.
Gozdecka, Dorota A. *Rights, Religious Pluralism and the Recognition of Difference: Off the Scales of Justice*. Routledge, 2015.
Gozdecka, Dorota A. '"Barbarians" and "radicals" against the legitimate community? Cultural othering through discourses on legitimacy of human rights.' *No Foundations* 15 (2018): 101–26.
Gozdecka, Dorota. 'Spectropolitics and invisibility of the migrant: On images that make people "illegal".' *Index Journal* 2 (2020): 195–212.
Gozdecka, Dorota A. 'Antigones of contemporary theatre: Capturing problems of today's civil disobedience in a theatre play.' *Law Text Culture* 25 (2021): 204–26.
Gozdecka, Dorota A., and Selen A. Ercan. 'What is post-multiculturalism? Recent trends in legal and political discourse.' In *Europe at the Edge of Pluralism*, ed. Dorota Gozdecka and Magdalena Kmak, pp. 27–42. Intersentia, 2015.
Gozdecka, Dorota, and Sanna Koulu. 'What to do with the other in human rights law? Ethics of alterity versus ethics of care.' In *Subjectivity, Citizenship and Belonging in Law: Identities and Intersections*, ed. Anne Griffiths, Sanna Mustasaari and Anna Mäki-Petajä-Leinonen, pp. 183–202. Routledge, 2016.
Graue, M. Elizabeth, Daniel J. Walsh and Deborah Ceglowski. *Studying Children in Context: Theories, Methods, and Ethics*. SAGE, 1998.
Grewcock, Michael. '"Our lives is in danger": Manus Island and the end of asylum.' *Race & Class* 59, no. 2 (2017): 70–89.
Guild, Elspeth. 'The right to dignity of refugees: A response to Fleur Johns.' *AJIL Unbound* 111 (2017): 193–5.
Gündoğdu, Ayten. *Rightlessness in an Age of Rights: Hannah Arendt and the Contemporary Struggles of Migrants*. Oxford University Press, 2014.
Habermas, Jürgen. 'Struggles for recognition in the democratic constitutional state.' In *The Inclusion of the Other: Studies in Political Theory*, ed. Ciaran P. Cronin and Pablo De Greiff, pp. 203–36. MIT Press, 1998.
Hackett, Lisa J., and Jo Coghlan. 'The history bubble: Negotiating authenticity in historical romance novels.' *M/C Journal* 24, no. 1 (2021).
Hafen, Bruce C., and Jonathan O. Hafen. 'Abandoning children to their autonomy: The United Nations Convention on the Rights of the Child.' *Harvard International Law Journal* 37, no. 2 (1996): 449–91.
Haferlach, Lisa, and Dilek Kurban. 'Lessons learnt from the EU–Turkey refugee agreement in guiding EU migration partnerships with origin and transit countries.' *Global Policy* 8 (2017): 85–93.
Hartmann, Jacques, and Nikolas Feith Tan, 'The Danish law on seizing asylum seekers' assets.' Blog of the *European Journal of International Law*, 27 January 2016, available at: <https://www.ejiltalk.org/the-danish-law-on-seizing-asylum-seekers-assets/>, last accessed 12 May 2021.
Hattenstone, Simon. 'Why was the scheme behind May's "Go Home" vans called Operation Vaken?' *The Guardian*, 26 April 2018, available at: <https://www.theguardian.com/commentisfree/2018/apr/26/theresa-may-go-home-vans-operation-vaken-ukip>, last accessed 21 September 2023.

Hayaert, Valérie. *Lady Justice: An Anatomy of Allegory.* Edinburgh University Press, 2023.
Heath, Anthony F., Catherine Rothon and Elina Kilpi. 'The second generation in Western Europe: Education, unemployment, and occupational attainment.' *Annual Review of Sociology* 34 (2008): 211–35.
Heizmann, Boris. 'Symbolic boundaries, incorporation policies, and anti-immigrant attitudes: What drives exclusionary policy preferences?' *Ethnic and Racial Studies* 39, no. 10 (2016): 1791–811.
Held, Virginia. The ethics of care: Personal, political, and global. Oxford University Press on Demand, 2006.
Hirsch, Francine. 'The Soviets at Nuremberg: International law, propaganda, and the making of the postwar order.' *The American Historical Review* 113, no. 3 (2008): 701–30.
Hirsch, Shirin. 'Racism, "second generation" refugees and the asylum system.' *Identities* 26, no. 1 (2019): 88–106.
Hirvonen, Ari. 'Oikeuden käynti: Antigonen laki ja oikea oikeus.' Doctoral dissertation. University of Helsinki, 2000.
Hobolt, Sara B. 'The Brexit vote: A divided nation, a divided continent.' *Journal of European Public Policy* 23, no. 9 (2016): 1259–77.
Hobsbawm, Eric J. *Nations and Nationalism Since 1780: Programme, Myth, Reality.* Cambridge University Press, 2012.
Hodge, Paul. 'A grievable life? The criminalisation and securing of asylum seeker bodies in the "violent frames" of Australia's Operation Sovereign Borders.' *Geoforum* 58 (2015): 122–31.
Hogan, Jackie, and Kristin Haltinner. 'Floods, invaders, and parasites: Immigration threat narratives and right-wing populism in the USA, UK and Australia.' *Journal of Intercultural Studies* 36, no. 5 (2015): 520–43.
Höijer, Birgitta. 'The discourse of global compassion: The audience and media reporting of human suffering.' *Media, Culture & Society* 26, no. 4 (2004): 513–31.
Honig, Bonnie. *Democracy and the Foreigner.* Princeton University Press, 2001.
Honig, Bonnie. 'Antigone's laments, Creon's grief: Mourning, membership, and the politics of exception.' *Political Theory* 37, no. 1 (2009): 5–43.
Hopkins, Peter E. 'Young people, masculinities, religion and race: New social geographies.' *Progress in Human Geography* 31, no. 2 (2007): 163–77.
Hugo, Graeme. 'From compassion to compliance? Trends in refugee and humanitarian migration in Australia.' *GeoJournal* 56, no. 1 (2002): 27–37.
Hugo, Graeme. 'Australia's state-specific and regional migration scheme: An assessment of its impacts in South Australia.' *Journal of International Migration and Integration/Revue de l'intégration et de la migration internationale* 9, no. 2 (2008): 125–45.
Huijsmans, Roy. 'Child migration and questions of agency.' *Development and Change* 42, no. 5 (2011): 1307–21.
Humphrey, Aaron. 'Emotion and secrecy in Australian asylum-seeker comics: The politics of visual style.' *International Journal of Cultural Studies* 21, no. 5 (2018): 457–85.
Huysmans, Jef. *The Politics of Insecurity: Fear, Migration and Asylum in the EU.* Routledge, 2006.

Ikuenobe, Polycarp. 'Conceptualizing racism and its subtle forms.' *Journal for the Theory of Social Behaviour* 41, no. 2 (2011): 161–81.
Innes, Alexandria J. 'When the threatened become the threat: The construction of asylum seekers in British media narratives.' *International Relations* 24, no. 4 (2010): 456–77.
Jay, Martin. 'Must justice be blind? The challenge of images to the law.' In *Refractions of Violence*, pp. 97–112. Routledge, 2013.
Johnson, Heather L. 'Click to donate: Visual images, constructing victims and imagining the female refugee.' *Third World Quarterly* 32, no. 6 (2011): 1015–37.
Johnson, Richard. 'The institutions didn't stop Trump: They empowered him.' *Political Insight* 11, no. 3 (2020): 4–7.
Jones, Hannah, Yasmin Gunaratnam, Gargi Bhattacharyya and William Davies. *Go Home?: The Politics of Immigration Controversies*. Manchester University Press, 2017.
Jowett, Garth S., and Victoria O'Donnell. *Propaganda & Persuasion*. SAGE, 2018.
Kallis, Aristotle. 'Breaking taboos and "mainstreaming the extreme": The debates on restricting Islamic symbols in contemporary Europe.' In *Right-Wing Populism in Europe: Politics and Discourse*, ed. Ruth Wodak, Majid KhosraviNik and Brigitte Mral, pp. 55–70. Bloomsbury, 2013.
Kallis, Aristotle. 'Far-right "contagion" or a failing "mainstream"? How dangerous ideas cross borders and blur boundaries.' *Democracy and Security* 9, no. 3 (2013): 221–46.
Kampmark, Binoy. 'Undermining NZ: Dutton's refugee ploy.' *Eureka Street* 27, no. 23 (2017): 58–60.
Karakayali, Serhat, and Enrica Rigo. 'Mapping the European space of circulation.' In *The Deportation Regime: Sovereignty, Space, and the Freedom of Movement*, ed. Nicholas De Genova and Nathalie Peutz, pp. 123–44. Duke University Press, 2010.
Kasinitz, Philip, John H. Mollenkopf, Mary C. Waters and Jennifer Holdaway. *Inheriting the City: The Children of Immigrants Come of Age*. Russell Sage Foundation, 2009.
Kassam, Ashifa, 'Spanish aid volunteer abused online for hugging Senegalese migrant.' *The Guardian*, 21 May 2021, available at: <https://www.theguardian.com/world/2021/may/20/spanish-aid-volunteer-luna-reyes-abused-online-for-hugging-african-migrant>, last accessed 26 September 2023.
Kearney, Michael G. *The Prohibition of Propaganda for War in International Law*. Oxford University Press, 2007.
Kelly, Fiona. 'Conceptualising the child through an "ethic of care": Lessons for family law.' *International Journal of Law in Context* 1, no. 4 (2005): 375–96.
Kingsley, Patrick, and Safak Timur, 'Stories of 2015: How Aylan Kurdi's death changed the world.' *The Guardian*, 31 December 2015, available at: <https://www.theguardian.com/world/2015/dec/31/alan-kurdi-death-canada-refugee-policy-syria-boy-beach-turkey-photo>, last accessed 25 September 2023.
Kitzinger, Jenny, and Paula Skidmore. 'Playing safe: Media coverage of child sexual abuse prevention strategies.' *Child Abuse Review* 4, no. 1 (1995): 47–56.
Kmak, Magdalena. 'Between citizen and bogus asylum seeker: Management of migration in the EU through the technology of morality.' *Social Identities* 21, no. 4 (2015): 395–409.

Kronick, Rachel, and Cécile Rousseau. 'Rights, compassion and invisible children: A critical discourse analysis of the parliamentary debates on the mandatory detention of migrant children in Canada.' *Journal of Refugee Studies* 28, no. 4 (2015): 544–69.

Krzyżanowski, Michał. 'Discursive shifts and the normalisation of racism: Imaginaries of immigration, moral panics and the discourse of contemporary right-wing populism.' *Social Semiotics* 30, no. 4 (2020): 503–27.

Kuykendall, Greg. 'Defending those who protect refugees.' In *Proceedings of the ASIL Annual Meeting*, vol. 114, pp. 113–16. Cambridge University Press, 2020.

Kymlicka, Will. 'Multicultural states and intercultural citizens.' *Theory and Research in Education* 1, no. 2 (2003): 147–69.

Langlotz, Andreas, and Danièle Klapproth Muazzin. 'Unveiling the phantom of the "Islamic takeover": A critical, cognitive-linguistic analysis of the discursive perpetuation of an Orientalist.' In *The Expression of Inequality in Interaction: Power, Dominance, and Status*, ed. Hanna Pishwa and Rainer Schulze, pp. 105–41. John Benjamins, 2014.

Larsen, Anna Grøndahl. 'Protection or participation? Editorial evaluation of two news serials concerning irregular migrant children.' *Journalism Practice* 11, no. 7 (2017): 893–908.

Larson, Arthur. 'The present status of propaganda in international law.' *Law and Contemporary Problems* 31 (1966): 439–51.

Lehner, Roman. 'The EU–Turkey-"deal": Legal challenges and pitfalls.' *International Migration* 57, no. 2 (2019): 176–85.

Leiboff, Marett. *Towards a Theatrical Jurisprudence*. Routledge, 2019.

Lentin, Alana, and Gavan Titley. *The Crises of Multiculturalism: Racism in a Neoliberal Age*. Zed Books, 2011.

Lentin, Ronit. 'Ireland: Racial state and crisis racism.' *Ethnic and Racial Studies* 30, no. 4 (2007): 610–27.

Levinas, Emmanuel. *Totality and Infinity: An Essay on Exteriority*. Trans. Alphonso Lingis. Springer Science & Business Media, 1979.

Levinas, Emmanuel. *Otherwise Than Being or Beyond Essence*. Springer Science & Business Media, 1981.

Levinas, Emmanuel. 'The rights of man and the rights of the other.' In *Outside the Subject*, pp. 91–8. Continuum, 2008.

Lopes, Dominic McIver. 'Out of sight, out of mind.' In *Imagination, Philosophy and the Arts*, pp. 215–32. Routledge, 2003.

Lucassen, Geertje, and Marcel Lubbers. 'Who fears what? Explaining far-right-wing preference in Europe by distinguishing perceived cultural and economic ethnic threats.' *Comparative Political Studies* 45, no. 5 (2012): 547–74.

Lupton, Deborah. 'Archetypes of infection: People with HIV/AIDS in the Australian press in the mid 1990s.' *Sociology of Health & Illness* 21, no. 1 (1999): 37–53.

McKay, Fiona H., Samantha L. Thomas and R. Warwick Blood. '"Any one of these boat people could be a terrorist for all we know!" Media representations and public perceptions of "boat people" arrivals in Australia.' *Journalism* 12, no. 5 (2011): 607–26.

Maddern, Jo Frances. 'Spectres of migration and the ghosts of Ellis Island.' *Cultural Geographies* 15, no. 3 (2008): 359–81.

Malkki, Liisa H. 'Refugees and exile: From "refugee studies" to the national order of things.' *Annual Review of Anthropology* 24, no. 1 (1995): 495–523.
Malkki, Liisa H. 'Speechless emissaries: Refugees, humanitarianism, and dehistoricization.' *Cultural Anthropology* 11, no. 3 (1996): 377–404.
Manderson, Desmond. *Songs without Music: Aesthetic Dimensions of Law and Justice*. University of California Press, 2000.
Manderson, Desmond. *Governor Arthur's Proclamation: Images of the Rule of Law*. Routledge, 2011.
Manderson, Desmond. 'Bodies in the water: On reading images more sensibly.' *Law & Literature* 27, no. 2 (2015): 279–93.
Manderson, Desmond. 'The metastases of myth: Legal images as transitional phenomena.' *Law and Critique* 26, no. 3 (2015): 207–23.
Manderson, Desmond. 'Chronotopes in the scopic regime of sovereignty.' *Visual Studies* 32, no. 2 (2017): 167–77.
Manderson, Desmond. 'Blindness visible: Law, time, and Bruegel's justice.' In *Law and the Visual: Representations, Technologies, Critique*, ed. Desmond Manderson, pp. 23–50. University of Toronto Press, 2018.
Manderson, Desmond. 'Here and now: from "aestheticizing politics" to "politicizing art".' In *Sensing the Nation's Law*, pp. 175–90. Springer, 2018.
Marin, Louis. *Portrait of the King*. Springer, 1988.
Mariolle, Tiffany S. 'Combating the harmful effects of gendered racist stereotypes using counter-stereotypical images based in archetypes with African American women.' Doctoral dissertation. Alliant International University, 2019.
Martyn, Georges. 'Inspiring images for judges: Late medieval court room decorations in the Southern Netherlands.' In *The Iconology of Law and Order (Legal and Cosmic)*, ed. Anna Kérchy, Attila Kiss and György Endre Szőnyi, pp. 37–49. Jatepress, 2012.
Masson, Judith. 'Representation of children in England: Protecting children in child protection proceedings.' *Family Law Quarterly* 34, no. 3 (2000): 467–95.
Matthes, Jörg, and Desirée Schmuck. 'The effects of anti-immigrant right-wing populist ads on implicit and explicit attitudes: A moderated mediation model.' *Communication Research* 44, no. 4 (2017): 556–81.
Maurice, Eric. 'EU and Switzerland agree on free movement.' *EU Observer*, 22 December 2016, available at: <https://euobserver.com/justice/136398>, last accessed 25 September 2023.
May, Stephen, Tariq Modood and Judith Squires, eds. *Ethnicity, Nationalism, and Minority Rights*. Cambridge University Press, 2004.
Meier, Kenneth J., Joseph Stewart and Robert E. England. *Race, Class, and Education: The Politics of Second-Generation Discrimination*. University of Wisconsin Press, 1989.
Menjívar, Cecilia, and Daniel Kanstroom, eds. *Constructing Immigrant 'Illegality': Critiques, Experiences, and Responses*. Cambridge University Press, 2014.
Mignanelli, Nicholas. 'Equal protection and the male gaze: Another approach to New Hampshire v. Lilley.' *Journal of Gender, Race & Justice* 22 (2019): 265–90.
Migration Council Australia. 'Rural settlement: Positive stories of migrant and refugee women.' YouTube, 1 December 2020, available at: <https://www.youtube.com/watch?v=AQzlnHqsGH0>, last accessed 21 September 2023.

Milbourne, Paul, and Helen Coulson. 'Migrant labour in the UK's post-Brexit agri-food system: Ambiguities, contradictions and precarities.' *Journal of Rural Studies* 86 (2021): 430–9.

Milic, Thomas. '"For they knew what they did" – What Swiss voters did (not) know about the mass immigration initiative.' *Swiss Political Science Review* 21, no. 1 (2015): 48–62.

Miller, John, 'Swiss high court rules anti-immigration SVP ad broke racism laws.' Reuters, 14 April 2017, available at: <https://www.reuters.com/article/us-swiss-racism-svp-idUSKBN17F1UT>, last accessed 11 August 2021.

Miller, John L., Peter H. Rossi and Jon E. Simpson. 'Perceptions of justice: Race and gender differences in judgments of appropriate prison sentences.' *Law and Society Review* 20, no. 3 (1986): 313–34.

Mirzoeff, Nicholas. 'Ghostwriting: Working out visual culture.' *Journal of Visual Culture* 1, no. 2 (2002): 239–54.

Mitchell, W. J. T. *Picture Theory: Essays on Verbal and Visual Representation.* University of Chicago Press, 1995.

Mitchell, W. J. T. 'Migration, law, and the image: Beyond the veil of ignorance.' In *The Migrant's Time: Rethinking Art History and Diaspora*, ed. Saloni Mathur, pp. 59–77. Sterling and Francine Clark Art Institute/Yale University Press, 2011.

Moeller, Susan D. *Compassion Fatigue: How the Media Sell Disease, Famine, War and Death.* Routledge, 1999.

Moeller, Susan D. 'A hierarchy of innocence: The media's use of children in the telling of international news.' *Harvard International Journal of Press/Politics* 7, no. 1 (2002): 36–56.

Moore, Colin. *Propaganda Prints: A History of Art in the Service of Social and Political Change.* A&C Black, 2010.

Motha, Stewart. *Archiving Sovereignty: Law, History, Violence.* University of Michigan Press, 2018.

Mulcahy, Linda. 'Eyes of the law: A visual turn in socio-legal studies?' *Journal of Law and Society* 44 (2017): 111–28.

Mulvey, Laura. 'Visual pleasure and narrative cinema.' *Screen* 16, no. 3 (1975): 6–18.

Munshi, Sherally. '"You will see my family became so American": Race, citizenship, and the visual archive.' In *Law and the Visual: Representations, Technologies, Critique*, ed. Desmond Manderson, pp. 161–88. University of Toronto Press, 2018.

Murray, David A. B. 'Queer forms: Producing documentation in sexual orientation refugee cases.' *Anthropological Quarterly* 89, no. 2 (2016): 465–84.

Mustasaari, Sanna. 'Best interests of the child in family reunification – a citizenship test disguised?' In *Subjectivity, Citizenship and Belonging in Law: Identities and Intersections*, ed. Anne Griffiths, Sanna Mustasaari and Anna Mäki-Petajä-Leinonen, pp. 135–57. Routledge, 2016.

Mutua, Makau. 'Savages, victims, and saviors: The metaphor of human rights.' *Harvard International Law Journal* 42 (2001): 201–45.

Nail, Thomas. *The Figure of the Migrant.* Stanford University Press, 2015.

Nail, Thomas. 'Migrant images.' In *Moving Images: Mediating Migration as Crisis*, ed. Krista Geneviève Lynes, Tyler Morgenstern and Ian Alan Paul, pp. 147–64. Transcript Verlag, 2020.

Nancy, Jean-Luc. *The ground of the image*. No. 51. Fordham University Press, 2005.
Nedelsky, Jennifer. *Law's Relations: A Relational Theory of Self, Autonomy, and Law*. Oxford University Press, 2011.
Nethery, Amy, and Rosa Holman. 'Secrecy and human rights abuse in Australia's offshore immigration detention centres.' *The International Journal of Human Rights* 20, no. 7 (2016): 1018–38.
Nieuwenhuys, Olga. 'The ethics of children's rights.' *Childhood* 15, no. 1 (2008): 4–11.
O'Dell, Lindsay. 'Representations of the "damaged" child: "Child saving" in a British children's charity ad campaign.' *Children & Society* 22, no. 5 (2008): 383–92.
Outhwaite, William. 'Migration crisis and "Brexit".' In *The Oxford Handbook of Migration Crises*, ed. Cecilia Menjívar, Marie Ruiz and Immanuel Ness, pp. 93–110. Oxford University Press, 2019.
Palmater, Pamela D. *Beyond Blood: Rethinking Indigenous Identity*. UBC Press, 2011.
Papademetriou, Demetrios G., and Annette Heuser. 'Council statement: Migration, public opinion and politics.' In *Migration, Public Opinion and Politics: The Transatlantic Council on Migration*, ed. Bertelsmann Stiftung and Migration Policy Institute. Bertelsmann Stiftung, 2009.
Papadopoulou, Aspasia. 'Smuggling into Europe: Transit migrants in Greece.' *Journal of Refugee Studies* 17, no. 2 (2004): 167–84.
Papailias, Penelope. '(Un)seeing dead refugee bodies: Mourning memes, spectropolitics, and the haunting of Europe.' *Media, Culture & Society* 41, no. 8 (2019): 1048–68.
Penchaszadeh, Ana-Paula, and Senda Sferco. 'Philosophical-political thoughts on the criminalization of solidarity practices towards migrants and refugees today: The case of Carola Rackete (2019).' *Historia y Sociedad* 39 (2020): 213–40.
Perpich, Diane. 'Levinas and the face of the other.' In *The Oxford Handbook of Levinas*, ed. Michael L. Morgan, pp. 243–58. Oxford University Press, 2019.
Peyser, Emily C. '"Pacific Solution"? The sinking right to seek asylum in Australia.' *Washington International Law Journal* 11, no. 2 (2002): 431–60.
Poon, Justine. 'How a body becomes a boat: The asylum seeker in law and images.' *Law & Literature* 30, no. 1 (2018): 105–21.
Pratt, Anna, and Mariana Valverde. 'From deserving victims to "masters of confusion": Redefining refugees in the 1990s.' *Canadian Journal of Sociology/Cahiers canadiens de sociologie* 27, no. 2 (2002): 135–61.
Proctor, Robert N. 'The destruction of "lives not worth living".' In *Deviant Bodies: Critical Perspectives on Difference in Science and Popular Culture*, ed. Jennifer Terry and Jacqueline Urla, pp. 170–96. Indiana University Press, 1995.
Quito, Anne. 'Switzerland's largest political party insists on depicting foreigners as black sheep.' *Quartz*, 16 February 2016, available at: <https://qz.com/617050/switzerlands-largest-political-party-insists-on-depicting-foreigners-as-black-sheep>, last accessed 17 October 2023.
Radziwinowiczówna, Agnieszka. 'Bare life in an immigration jail: Technologies of surveillance in US pre-deportation detention.' *Journal of Ethnic and Migration Studies* 48, no. 8 (2022): 1873–90.
Rancière, Jacques. "Who is the subject of the rights of man?' *The South Atlantic Quarterly* 103, no. 2/3 (2004): 297–310.
Rawls, John. *A Theory of Justice: Revised Edition*. Harvard University Press, 1999.

Reese, Stephen D. 'Prologue – framing public life: A bridging model for media research.' In *Framing Public Life: Perspectives on Media and Our Understanding of the Social World*, ed. Stephen D. Reese, Oscar H. Gandy, Jr. and August E. Grant, pp. 7–31. Routledge, 2011.

Regulation (EU) No 604/2013 of the European Parliament and of the Council of 26 June 2013 establishing the criteria and mechanisms for determining the Member State responsible for examining an application for international protection lodged in one of the Member States by a third-country national or a stateless person (recast), 29 June 2013, OJ L. 180/31–180/59. European Union: Council of the European Union.

Reid, Andrew. 'Buses and breaking point: Freedom of expression and the "Brexit" campaign.' *Ethical Theory and Moral Practice* 22, no. 3 (2019): 623–37.

Renner, Eric. *American Disguise*. Flying Monkey Press, 2007.

Richardson, Alice. 'Sir Redmond Barry and the trial of Ned Kelly: Representing the judge and judgment in nineteenth-century Australia.' In *Judgment in the Victorian Age*, ed. James Gregory, Daniel J. R. Grey and Annika Bautz. Routledge, 2018.

Rimmer, Susan Harris. 'The dangers of character tests under Australian migration laws.' *ISIL Year Book of International Humanitarian and Refugee Law* 8 (2008): 207.

Rolfe, Heather. 'It's all about the flex: Preference, flexibility and power in the employment of EU migrants in low-skilled sectors.' *Social Policy and Society* 16, no. 4 (2017): 623–34.

Romeyn, Esther. 'Anti-Semitism and Islamophobia: Spectropolitics and immigration.' *Theory, Culture & Society* 31, no. 6 (2014): 77–101.

Rorty, Richard. 'Human rights, rationality and sentimentality.' In *Wronging rights? Philosophical Challenges for Human Rights*, ed. Aakash Singh Rathore and Alex Cistelecan, pp. 107–31. Routledge, 2011.

Ross, Sheryl Tuttle. 'Understanding propaganda: The epistemic merit model and its application to art.' *Journal of Aesthetic Education* 36, no. 1 (2002): 16–30.

Rotas, Alex. '"A soft touch": Racism and asylum seekers from a visual culture perspective.' In *Racism Postcolonialism Europe*, ed. Graham Huggan and Ian Law, pp. 77–91. Liverpool University Press, 2009.

Rowe, Elizabeth, and Erin O'Brien. 'Constructions of asylum seekers and refugees in Australian political discourse.' In *Crime, Justice and Social Democracy: Proceedings of the 2nd International Conference, Volume 1*, ed. Kelly Richards and Juan Tauri, pp. 173–81. Crime and Justice Research Centre, Queensland University of Technology, 2013.

Rowe, Elizabeth, and Erin O'Brien. '"Genuine" refugees or illegitimate "boat people": Political constructions of asylum seekers and refugees in the Malaysia Deal debate.' *Australian Journal of Social Issues* 49, no. 2 (2014): 171–93.

Ruddick, Baz. 'Refugee advocates protest outside Brisbane immigration centre to mark nine years of indefinite detention.' *ABC News*, 18 July 2021, available at: <https://www.abc.net.au/news/2021-07-18/qld-protesters-refugee-immigration-detention-bita-anniversary/100302690>, last accessed 11 September 2023.

Rydgren, Jens. 'Immigration sceptics, xenophobes or racists? Radical right-wing voting in six West European countries.' *European Journal of Political Research* 47, no. 6 (2008): 737–65.

Said, Edward. *Orientalism: Western Concepts of the Orient*. Pantheon, 1978.
Sajjad, Tazreena. 'What's in a name? "Refugees", "migrants" and the politics of labelling.' *Race & Class* 60, no. 2 (2018): 40–62.
Saleh-Hanna, Viviane. 'Black feminist hauntology: Rememory the ghosts of abolition?' *Champ pénal/Penal field* 12 (2015), available at: <https://doi.org/10.4000/champpenal.9168>, last accessed 25 September 2023.
Salter, Mark B. 'The global visa regime and the political technologies of the international self: Borders, bodies, biopolitics.' *Alternatives* 31, no. 2 (2006): 167–89.
Saran, Ayesha. 'A commentary on public attitudes on immigration: The United Kingdom in international context.' In *Migration, Public Opinion and Politics: The Transatlantic Council on Migration*, ed. Bertelsmann Stiftung and Migration Policy Institute. Bertelsmann Stiftung, 2009.
Sarı, Elif. 'Lesbian refugees in transit: The making of authenticity and legitimacy in Turkey.' *Journal of Lesbian Studies* 24, no. 2 (2020): 140–58.
Scheel, Stephan, and Vicki Squire. 'Forced migrants as illegal migrants.' In *The Oxford Handbook of Refugee and Forced Migration Studies*, ed. Elena Fiddian-Qasmiyeh, Gil Loescher, Katy Long and Nando Sigona, pp. 188–99. Oxford University Press, 2014.
Schill, Dan. 'The visual image and the political image: A review of visual communication research in the field of political communication.' *Review of Communication* 12, no. 2 (2012): 118–42.
Schindel, Estela. 'Migrants and refugees on the frontiers of Europe: The legitimacy of suffering, bare life, and paradoxical agency.' *Revista de Estudios Sociales* 59 (2017): 16–29.
Schmuck, Desirée, and Jörg Matthes. 'How anti-immigrant right-wing populist advertisements affect young voters: Symbolic threats, economic threats and the moderating role of education.' *Journal of Ethnic and Migration Studies* 41, no. 10 (2015): 1577–99.
Scott, Elizabeth S. 'The legal construction of adolescence.' *Hofstra Law Review* 29, no. 2 (2000): 547–98.
Seglem, Robyn, and Shelbie Witte. 'You gotta see it to believe it: Teaching visual literacy in the English classroom.' *Journal of Adolescent & Adult Literacy* 53, no. 3 (2009): 216–26.
Seidman, Steven A. *Posters, Propaganda, and Persuasion in Election Campaigns around the World and through History*. Peter Lang, 2008.
Sevenhuijsen, Selma. *Citizenship and the Ethics of Care: Feminist Considerations on Justice, Morality and Politics*. Routledge, 2003.
Shachar, Ayelet. *Multicultural Jurisdictions: Cultural Differences and Women's Rights*. Cambridge University Press, 2001.
Sherwin, Richard K. *When Law Goes Pop: The Vanishing Line between Law and Popular Culture*. University of Chicago Press, 2000.
Sherwin, Richard K. 'What authorizes the image? The visual economy of post-secular jurisprudence.' In *Law and the Visual: Representations, Technologies, Critique*, ed. Desmond Manderson, pp. 330–54. University of Toronto Press, 2018.
Simmons, William Paul. *Human Rights Law and the Marginalized Other*. Cambridge University Press, 2011.
Singer, Peter. 'Democracy and disobedience.' *Philosophy* 49, no. 188 (1974): 215–16.

Smith, Daniel. 'What is the body without organs? Machine and organism in Deleuze and Guattari.' *Continental Philosophy Review* 51, no. 1 (2018): 95–110.

Springford, John. 'The cost of Brexit to June 2018.' *Insight*, 30 September 2018, available at <https://www.cer.eu/insights/cost-brexit-june-2018>, last accessed 25 September 2023.

State Religious Affairs Bureau Order (No. 5) Measures on the Management of the Reincarnation of Living Buddhas. Central People's Government of the People's Republic of China.

Steinberg, Saul. *The Passport*. Harper, 1954.

Stewart, Heather, and Rowena Mason. 'Nigel Farage's anti-migrant poster reported to police.' *The Guardian*, 17 June 2016, available at: <https://www.theguardian.com/politics/2016/jun/16/nigel-farage-defends-ukip-breaking-point-poster-queue-of-migrants>, last accessed 25 September 2023.

Stumpf, Juliet. 'The crimmigration crisis: Immigrants, crime, and sovereign power.' *American University Law Review* 56, no. 2 (2006): 367–419.

Stumpf, Juliet. 'The process is the punishment in crimmigration law.' In *The Borders of Punishment: Migration, Citizenship, and Social Exclusion*, ed. Katja Franko Aas and Mary Bosworth, pp. 58–75. Oxford University Press, 2013.

Szörényi, Anna. 'The face of suffering in Afghanistan: Identity, authenticity and technology in the search for the representative refugee.' *Australian Feminist Law Journal* 21, no. 1 (2004): 1–21.

Szörényi, Anna. '"Two dreams in one bedroom": Narrating victimhood and perpetration in Australian refugee history.' *Australian Feminist Studies* 27, no. 73 (2012): 297–306.

Tagg, John. *The Burden of Representation: Essays on Photographies and Histories*. University of Minnesota Press, 1988.

Tagg, John. *The Disciplinary Frame: Photographic Truths and the Capture of Meaning*. University of Minnesota Press, 2009.

Tall, Emmanuelle Kadya. 'On representation and power: Portrait of a vodun leader in present-day Benin.' *Africa: Journal of the International African Institute* 84, no. 2 (2014): 246–68.

Taylor, Charles. *The Politics of Recognition*. Princeton University Press, 1994.

Tester, Keith. *Compassion, Morality and the Media*. Open University Press, 2001.

Ticktin, Miriam. *Casualties of Care: Immigration and the Politics of Humanitarianism in France*. University of California Press, 2011.

Ticktin, Miriam. 'What's wrong with innocence.' Hot Spots, *Fieldsights*, 28 June 2016, available at: <https://culanth.org/fieldsights/whats-wrong-with-innocence>, last accessed 25 September 2023.

Ticktin, Miriam. 'Invasive others: Toward a contaminated world.' *Social Research: An International Quarterly* 84, no. 1 (2017): xxi–xxxiv.

Tiefenbrun, Susan W. 'On civil disobedience, jurisprudence, feminism and the law in the Antigones of Sophocles and Anouilh.' *Law & Literature* 11, no. 1 (1999): 35–51.

Torpey, John. 'The Great War and the birth of the modern passport system.' In *Documenting Individual Identity: The Development of State Practices in the Modern World*, ed. Jane Caplan and John Torpey, pp. 256–70. Princeton University Press, 2001.

Treaty on European Union (TEU), European Union, Consolidated version of 13 December 2007, 2008/C 115/01.
Treaty on the Functioning of the European Union (TFEU), European Union, Consolidated version of 13 December 2007, 2008/C 115/01.
Trump v. Hawaii, No. 17-965, 585 U.S. ___ (2018).
United Nations Relief and Works Agency for Palestine Refugees in the Near East (UNRWA) (UNRWA). *Palestine Refugees in Syria: An Andy Warner Comic*. UNRWA, 2014, available at: <https://www.unrwa.org/sites/default/files/unrwa_comic_web_final_800px.gif>, last accessed 21 September 2023.
United States of America v. Scott Daniel Warren. No. MJ-17-0341-TUC-BGM, 2018.
Universal Declaration of Human Rights (UDHR), UN General Assembly, 10 December 1948, 217 A (III).
UN News. 'Swiss minaret ban discriminates against Muslims, says UN expert.' *UN News*, 30 November 2009, available at: <https://news.un.org/en/story/2009/11/322742-swiss-minaret-ban-discriminates-against-muslims-says-un-expert>, last accessed 11 August 2021.
van Berlo, Patrick. 'Australia's Operation Sovereign Borders: Discourse, power, and policy from a crimmigration perspective.' *Refugee Survey Quarterly* 34, no. 4 (2015): 75–104.
Van Der Valk, Ineke. 'Right-wing parliamentary discourse on immigration in France.' *Discourse & Society* 14, no. 3 (2003): 309–48.
van Rijswijk, Honni. 'From sentimentality to sadism: Visual genres of asylum seeking.' In *Law and the Visual: Representations, Technologies, Critique*, ed. Desmond Manderson, pp. 189–209. University of Toronto Press, 2018.
Virtanen, Simo V., and Leonie Huddy. 'Old-fashioned racism and new forms of racial prejudice.' *The Journal of Politics* 60, no. 2 (1998): 311–32.
Vis, Farida, and Olga Goriunova, eds. *The Iconic Image on Social Media: A Rapid Research Response to the death of Aylan Kurdi*. Visual Social Media Lab, 2015.
Vogl, Anthea. 'Over the borderline: A critical inquiry into the geography of territorial excision and the securitisation of the Australian border.' *University of New South Wales Law Journal* 38, no. 1 (2015): 114–45.
Welch, David. 'Nazi propaganda and the *Volksgemeinschaft*: Constructing a people's community.' *Journal of Contemporary History* 39, no. 2 (2004): 213–38.
Wells, Karen. 'Narratives of liberation and narratives of innocent suffering: The rhetorical uses of images of Iraqi children in the British press.' *Visual Communication* 6, no. 1 (2007): 55–71.
Wendel, Mattias. 'The refugee crisis and the executive: On the limits of administrative discretion in the Common European Asylum System.' *German Law Journal* 17, no. 6 (2016): 1005–32.
Whyte, Sarah, 'New asylum seeker campaign "distasteful" and "embarrassing".' *The Sydney Morning Herald*, 12 February 2014.
Wilkes, Rima, Neil Guppy and Lily Farris. '"No thanks, we're full": Individual characteristics, national context, and changing attitudes toward immigration.' *International Migration Review* 42, no. 2 (2008): 302–29.
Winter, Irene J. 'What/when is a portrait? Royal images of the ancient Near East.' *Proceedings of the American Philosophical Society* 153, no. 3 (2009): 254–70.

Wodak, Ruth. '"Us" and "them": Inclusion and exclusion – discrimination via discourse.' In *Identity, Belonging and Migration*, ed. Gerard Delanty, Ruth Wodak and Paul Jones, pp. 54–77. Liverpool University Press, 2008.
Wolfreys, Julian. *Occasional Deconstructions*. State University of New York Press, 2004.
Woodhouse, Barbara Bennett. 'Hatching the egg: A child-centered perspective on parent's rights.' *Cardozo Law Review* 14, no. 6 (1993): 1747–866.
Wyler, Dina. 'The Swiss minaret ban referendum and Switzerland's international reputation: A vote with an impact.' *Journal of Muslim Minority Affairs* 37, no. 4 (2017): 413–25.
Yew, Elizabeth. 'Medical inspection of immigrants at Ellis Island, 1891–1924.' *Bulletin of the New York Academy of Medicine* 56, no. 5 (1980): 488–510.
Young, Iris Marion. 'Impartiality and the civic public: Some implications of feminist critiques of moral and political theory.' In *Feminism as Critique: Essays on the Politics of Gender in Late Capitalist Societies*, ed. Seyla Benhabib and Drucilla Cornell, pp. 56–76. Polity Press, 1987.
Young, Iris Marion. *Justice and the Politics of Difference*. Princeton University Press, 2011.
Zacharias, Robert. '"And yet": Derrida on Benjamin's divine violence.' *Mosaic: A Journal for the Interdisciplinary Study of Literature* 40, no. 2 (2007): 103–16.
Zagor, Matthew. 'The struggle of autonomy and authenticity: Framing the savage refugee.' *Social Identities* 21, no. 4 (2015): 373–94.
Žižek, Slavoj. *The Sublime Object of Ideology*. Verso, 1989.
Žižek, Slavoj. *Against Human Rights*. Routledge, 2011.
Zug, Marcia. 'Should I stay or should I go: Why immigrant reunification decisions should be based on the best interest of the child.' *BYU Law Review* 4 (2011): 1139–91.

Index

'absolute other' archetype, 89–102
   ongoing barriers to full belonging, 90–2
   'paradigm' control of access to rights, 12–15, 99–102
   race and discrimination dynamic, 92–4
   visual migration-related campaigns, 94–9
Agamben, Giorgio, 85
agency/autonomy, 56–7, 65–6, 125–6
'alien', use of term, 149
Althusser, Louis, 4, 35, 36
'anonymous mass' *see* 'inhuman mass' archetype
Antigonean conflict, 147–9
archetypes of the migrant
   approaches to challenging, 144–5, 152–4
   nature and effect, 23–6, 45–7, 153, 157–8
   see also 'absolute other'; 'bogus' asylum seeker; 'genuine' refugee; 'illegal' migrant; 'inhuman mass'; innocent figure
Arendt, Hannah, 12
Arribas, Gloria, 118
Arthur, Governor George, Proclamation to the Aborigines, 41
assemblage (Deleuze), 109–10
assimilability, 46
autonomy *see* agency/autonomy
Azoulay, Ariella, 44

Barbulescu, Roxana, 116
Betz, Hans-Georg, 96

Bhabha, Jacqueline, 128
boat, arrival by, 60–4, 67–8, 81–4
'bogus' asylum seeker archetype, 53–64, 67–9
   in comic strips and graphic novels, 59–64
   and economic motivations, 54–5, 56
   and moral agency, 56–7
   and personal possessions, 68–9
   synonymity with 'illegality', 55
   and unaccompanied children, 127–9
Bohman, Andrea, 146
Bonegilla Reception Centre, 14–15
Boochani, Behrouz, *No Friend but the Mountains*, 153
Brexit, 54, 79–80, 110–13, 116–18
Bridgerton (television series), 45
Brown, Jessica, 107
Butler, Judith, 25

Castillo, Pilar, 18–19
character tests, 55
charity, refuge as, 57–8
children *see* migrant children
citizen–denizen distinction, 12–13, 45–6, 150
Cockburn, Tom, 126
comic strips, 54, 59–60, 65–6
compassion fatigue, 124–5
'crimmigration', 18
Crossley, Nick, 21
Curtis, Dennis, 40, 41

Dahlberg, Leif, 39
De Genova, Nicholas, 12–13, 25, 57
decolonisation, 21

dehumanisation, 106–20
  absolute others, 95
  fusion of human and non-human, 109–11
  rhetoric and imagery, 107–8, 111–16
  legal outcomes, 116–19
Deleuze, Gilles, 13, 109–10, 115
Derrida, Jacques, 3, 13, 15–16, 45, 59, 76–7
Dewsbury, J.-D., 110
difference-blind approach to rights, 100
discourse, stages of normalisation, 146–7
Douzinas, Costas, 32

Eagleton, Terry, 36
Eberstein, Anne Sophie, 133
economic deprivation, 68–9
economic threat, perceptions of, 54–5, 56, 61–2, 107–8, 128–9
Ellis Island, 13, 14
Entman, Robert, 145
ethical responses, 14, 125–7, 132–4, 147–51
EU–Turkey Agreement, 118–19
'European refugee crisis', 113–16, 118–19, 130–4
evaluation practices, 14–15

Favell, Adrian, 116
Fawzy, Rania, 58
'flood' imagery *see* 'inhuman mass' archetype
Fotou, Maria, 3
Foucault, Michel, 20, 35
frame *see* visual framing
Freeman, Michael, 126

Garoian, Charles, 77
'genuine' refugee archetype, 53–9, 65–9
  and economic deprivation, 68–9
  and passiveness, 56–7, 65–6
  synonymity with 'legality', 55
  and victimhood/suffering, 57–9, 65–6, 127–9
'Go Home' vans (UK), 79–80
Goldberg, David, 92

Goodrich, Peter, 33, 34–5, 37–8, 41–2, 43–4
Gough, Jamie, 117
graphic novels, 54, 59–64
Guattari, Félix, 109
Guild, Elspeth, 108, 116

Habermas, Jürgen, 100
Hafen, Bruce and Jonathan, 126
Haferlach, Lisa, 119
Haltinner, Kristin, 107
hauntology, 76–9
  hauntological imagery, 79–86
Hirsch, Shirin, 91–2
Hogan, Jackie, 107
Höijer, Birgitta, 125
homogenous mass *see* 'inhuman mass' archetype
Honig, Bonnie, 144
host gaze, 20–5, 44, 58–9, 153–4
'hostipitality' (Derrida), 3, 15–16, 59
Humphrey, Aaron, 64

ideological state apparatus (ISA), 35–6
'illegal' migrant archetype, 73–86
  ephemeral nature of, 74–5
  'illegal' as classification, 67–8, 75–6
  spectrality of, 76–9
  spectropolitical imagery, 78–86
  and suspicion of all refugees, 17–19, 55–6
inherited migrant status, 91–2
'inhuman mass' archetype, 106–20
  fusion of human and non-human, 109–11
  rhetoric and imagery, 107–8, 111–16, 149–50
  legal outcomes, 116–19
innocent figure archetype, 124–37
  power of child imagery, 124–7
  images of innocence, 66, 130–4
  more equivocal images, 135–6
  threshold of innocence, 127–9
Islamophobia, 94–8

Johnson, Heather, 108
justice (concept), 39–40, 41–3
Justice (images), 40, 42–3

Kallis, Aristotle, 96
Kmak, Magdalena, 56, 69
Kronock, Rachel, 128–9
Krzyżanowski, Michał, 146, 147
Kurban, Dilek, 119
Kurdi, Aylan, 124, 130–4, 136

Lady Justice, 40, 42–3
Langlotz, Andreas, 95
Larsen, Anna, 124, 129
legal personhood, 43–4
legal profession, 157–8
legal symbolism, 38–9
legal vocabulary, 37–8
Lehner, Roman, 118
Leiser, Clara, 41
Lentin, Ronit, 92, 93
Levinas, Emmanuel, 13, 21
Lupton, Deborah, 46

Maddern, Jo, 78
male gaze, 2–3, 21, 153
Manderson, Desmond, 36, 37, 41, 42, 83
Marin, Louis, 37
Matthes, Jörg, 107, 145
migrant, use of term, 11–12, 17, 19–20
migrant archetypes *see* archetypes of the migrant
migrant children, 124–37
   power of child imagery, 124–7
   images of innocence, 66, 130–4
   more equivocal images, 134–6
   threshold of innocence, 127–9
Migration Council Australia, 153
Mirzoeff, Nicholas, 46, 77
Mitchell, W. J. T., 24, 143
Moeller, Susan, 127
Moore, Colin, 34
Muazzin, Danièle, 95
Mulcahy, Linda, 32–3
Mulvey, Laura, 2–3, 21
Munshi, Sherally, 46

Nail, Thomas, 3, 23–4
National Rural Women's Coalition, 153
Nead, Linda, 32

No More Deaths (humanitarian organisation), 148
NO WAY campaign (Australia), 54, 60–4, 81–4
non-refoulement principle, 118–19

O'Dell, Lindsay, 126–7
Operation Sovereign Borders (Australia), 54, 60–4, 67–8, 81–4
optical apparatus, 35–6, 44–5
orientalising gaze, 21, 58, 61
otherness *see* 'absolute other' archetype
Outhwaite, William, 117

Pacific Solution (Australia), 1, 60, 67–8, 84
Papailias, Penelope, 78
passiveness, 56–7, 65–6
passports, 16, 18–19
Penchaszadeh, Ana-Paula, 149–50
personal possessions, 68–9
photography, power exercised through, 44–5
political communication, 33–4, 46, 54, 79–80, 94–9, 110–13, 116–18, 146–7
Poon, Justine, 83
postcolonial gaze, 21
power, role of the visual, 34–6, 44–5
propaganda, 33–4, 95, 112–13
property rights, 68–9

racial discrimination, 91–2
racialised gaze, 21–2
racialised imagery, 46, 94–8, 111–12, 131
Rackete, Carola, 149–50
referendum campaigns, 54, 79–80, 94–9, 110–13, 116–18
Refugee Convention (1951), 17, 54, 68
refugee, use of term, 17, 19–20, 55
Resnik, Judith, 40, 41
Reyes, Luna, 151
Romeyn, Esther, 78
Roper, Edith, 41
Rousseau, Cécile, 128–9

royal portraits, 37
rule of law, 40–1

Said, Edward, 21
Sajjad, Tazreena, 55
Sartre, Jean-Paul, 21
Scheel, Stephan, 55
Schill, Dan, 46
Schindel, Estela, 58
Schmuck, Desirée, 107, 145
'second' and 'third' generation migrants, 91–2, 93
Sevenhuijsen, Selma, 126
Sferco, Senda, 149–50
Sherwin, Richard, 42–3
Smith, Daniel, 109
social media, 6, 132
sovereign power, 37, 41
spectrality, 76–9
    spectropolitical imagery, 78–86
Squire, Vicki, 55
Steinberg, Saul, *The Passport*, 16
Stumpf, Juliet, 2, 18, 75
suffering, and genuineness, 57–9, 65–6, 127–9
surveillance, 44–5
Swiss People's Party (SVP), 94–8
Swiss referenda, 94–9
Syrian migration to Europe, 113–16, 118–19
Szörényi, Anna, 57–8

Tagg, John, 44–5
Tall, Emmanuelle, 37

Ticktin, Miriam, 55, 110
Tiefenbrun, Susan, 147
Trump, Donald, 2, 134

UK Independence Party (UKIP), 110–13
UN Convention on the Law of the Sea (UNCLOS), 149
UN Human Rights Council, 98
UN Relief and Works Agency for Palestine Refugees in the Near East (UNRWA), 54, 65–6
'undocumented' migrants, 19, 55
US Customs and Border Protection, 80–1, 134–6, 148

van Rijswijk, Honni, 58, 62
victimhood, 57–9, 65–6, 127–9
'visiocracies', 42–3
visual economy, 42–3
visual framing, role and impact, 22, 44–5, 145

Warner, Andy, 65–6
Warren, Scott, 148–9
whiteness, 46, 92, 96–8, 131
Winter, Irene, 37
Wodak, Ruth, 90
Wolfreys, Julian, 77
Woodhouse, Barbara, 126

Zagor, Matthew, 56
Žižek, Slavoj, 36

EU representative:
Easy Access System Europe
Mustamäe tee 50, 10621 Tallinn, Estonia
Gpsr.requests@easproject.com